SUSAN McBANE

A Natural Approach
to Horse Management

Methuen

First published in Great Britain 1992
by Methuen London
an imprint of Reed Consumer Books Ltd
Michelin House, 81 Fulham Road, London SW3 6RB
and Auckland, Melbourne, Singapore and Toronto

A CIP catalogue record for this book
is available from the British Library
ISBN 0 413 62370 X

Typeset by Deltatype Ltd, Ellesmere Port
Printed in Great Britain

(n)636.108 3 m

A Natural Approach
to Horse Management

Contents

This book is dedicated to
ROYAL
who made me realise beyond doubt that
the natural approach to horse management is the best

List of Illustrations

All the photographs were taken by the author, except for 15b for which thanks to Peter Sweet. Diagram 1 was drawn by the author and Diagram 2 is reproduced courtesy of D. J. Murphy from *Horse and Rider*. Thanks are also due to Sam Barr for allowing the photograph on the front jacket to be taken at his Limbury Stud.

I should like to thank the following friends for their generous help with various aspects of this book: Management Consultant Gillian McCarthy, BSc, Janet Eley, BVSc, MRCVS, and Robert Eustace BVSc, MRCVS.

Introduction

The horse is one of the most remarkable animals on earth and one of the most successful. It is highly specialised as a grazing, running animal but adaptable enough to enable it to exist and thrive, in its various types, in widely differing climatic conditions in most parts of the globe. It is a prey animal and as such has a natural aversion to confinement and compulsion; yet it survives, often very well, in artificial housing, permits humans to ride and direct it and subjugates its natural instincts to our wishes, at least superficially.

We owe the horse a huge debt, for without its strength, speed and willingness to cooperate, even please, man would never have been able to develop agriculture effectively, to trade and travel, to expand and settle, to build empires, make history, have fun and fulfil ambitions. We have used the horse for transport, clothing, furniture, weaponry, food and drink; as a status symbol and an ego-booster as well as a friend and companion. Not even the dog has been so useful to us and so crucial to our existence and development in so many different ways as has the horse. Normally, however, we offer the dog a life which is far more natural to it, as part of a pack of which a human is the leader, than is the life we usually offer the horse – and that is the subject of this book.

Plants and animals evolve in such a way as to enable them to function most efficiently in the environment in which they find themselves. Their bodies work within set limits: for instance some bacteria (such as the tetanus bacteria) thrive where there is little or no oxygen, conditions which would kill others. Humans drown in water; fish drown in air. Some plants and animals (such as cacti) have adapted to thrive in hot, dry conditions and die in cold, damp surroundings, and so on. Many organisms are extremely adaptable: for instance, grasses are found almost all over the earth and both humans and horses, in general, can also live in extremes of climate and weather conditions. But within different species individuals may not be so adaptable. Many humans say they hate one particular season of the year; it's either too hot or too cold for them as individuals. Horses and ponies, too, differ widely in type and individual ability to cope with the equally wide variety of climates on earth.

All organisms function most efficiently under the conditions they were best evolved to cope with. They may be able to tolerate changes varying to a certain degree from their optimum environment; outside these limits, however, their efficiency as an organism declines. As far as horses are concerned, this lack of efficiency makes more work and expense for us humans who make use of them, as we try to compensate for the horse's difficulties or lessen their effects on us.

In the world of human employment, it is now no secret that if you put people into an inhospitable environment or working conditions, not only do they not produce their best, or even acceptable, work, but they also take off many more days sick. 'Sick building syndrome' is no longer a flight of fancy, although it isn't the building that is sick, it is the humans who are expected to tolerate the conditions inside it – usually insufficient fresh air and daylight and an unacceptably, sometimes dangerously, high level of electrical wave activity coming from computers, fluorescent lighting, word processors and all the electrical equipment which is a seemingly inescapable part of so many jobs today, not to mention our homes.

We are flesh and blood animals, just like our dogs, horses, other pets and farm animals. If we can suffer from unsuitable working and living conditions, they certainly can. Farm animals have suffered appallingly, and still do, from the grossly unnatural conditions in which most of them are kept, often for their entire lives. Over recent years, some scientific work has been carried out which is showing how deleterious these conditions are on the animals, but little such work has been done relating to horses. One paper I came across, however, by Drs K. Zeeb and A. Rodewald of the Institute of Animal Hygiene in Freiburg, Germany, entitled 'Harm in Saddle Horses due to Shortcomings of Housing and Handling' stated, very generally, that among 172 animals kept, managed and trained conventionally, there were no fewer than 237 instances of illness in two years. Lameness, as might be expected, accounted for 35 per cent of these, respiratory disorders, perhaps surprisingly to many, were not far behind at 29 per cent, digestive disorders made up 14 per cent and miscellaneous others 30 per cent. Work is continuing on their investigations. Stuffy, humid and too-small stables were suffered – at least in some measure – by 140 of the horses, so their poor health and soundness record is not surprising in view of such damaging and artificial surroundings.

But relax! This book is not a plea for all horses to be liberated, freed from all human constraints and given the life nature meant them to live with mile upon mile of open country to roam, grassy plains, hills and valleys, woods, open water and free living and breeding (not to mention early death from injury or sickness and predation). All caring horsemen and women know that domesticated horses are only content and disdainful of humans as long as their living conditions offer everything they need – food, water, shelter, company and space. When things turn rough, food is in short supply, water undrinkable or non-existent, the weather cruel and companionship lacking or unamicable, horses are usually touchingly relieved at the sight of humans bearing food or, even better, coming to catch them up and rescue them! In other words, we have our uses and they know it.

No: what this book is about is examining our normal management methods, assessing the horse's needs as defined by nature and recent research and then seeing if we can't devise better ways of bringing the two closer together to the mutual benefit of horse and human.

1 How the Horse Developed

Evolution: The Making Of Nature's Horse

Ever since man first became interested in the question, estimates as to the age of the earth have made it older and older each time. At present the official age is about 4,600 million years, but even as I write rocks described as 'the most ancient ever discovered' are undergoing various dating techniques which so far seem to be pointing to an age of 5,000 million years. In consequence, the date for life as we accept it first appearing grows later and later. As it is impossible to envisage thousands of millions of years, a convenient way of picturing the earth's history is as a twelve-hour clock. The earliest forms of life, single-cell creatures, seem to have appeared about eight o'clock and man at only five minutes to twelve.

So for many millions of years there was no life on earth, no land, no water and no atmosphere as we know them, just an unimaginable, seething mass of gases and liquid or semi-liquid matter with the potential to form rock when it ultimately cooled, changing its form according to whether it was subjected to temperature change or pressure. The basic chemistry to create life was there, though, and as the earth did very slowly cool and oceans arrived with the creation of water, land in the form of cooled rock formed, initially in one vast continent in the southern hemisphere called (now) Pangea, of which Antarctica is a remnant.

The earth was subject to many changes of temperature, to

physical influences from within itself and without as the inconceivably slow process of evolution carried on. Erosion produced soils by wearing down the rocks and life began in the seas. The atmosphere would have been highly toxic to most of today's life forms and as life forms gradually migrated from the oceans to the land it was not into 'fresh air' as we know it today. In the earth of that time oxygen was a poisonous gas!

Gradually, the vast southern continent broke up and spun away on 'plates' of land, tearing apart, colliding, crumpling up to form mountain ranges and being worn down to form flatter areas. Molten material continued to be added to the changing and developing continents from volcanic activity, earthquakes and general earth movements, and as the continents drifted north, east and west the life forms on them became isolated or were able to migrate to areas previously out of reach.

It is well documented that the first recognisable horse ancestor, *hyracotherium*, formerly called *eohippus*, existed about 50 million years ago. The American continent is usually seen as its 'birthplace' but *hyracotherium* fossils have been discovered in the Old World as well as the New, notably in Germany. Many palaeontologists feel that as the Atlantic, the earth's youngest ocean, was still little more than a swamp during the Eocene, the name given to that time, it would have been quite possible for animal forms to spread across it. The Atlantic is still widening and, in fact, the process of continental drift, as it is called, continues to this day, making its effects felt as America moves slowly westwards, colliding with and rubbing against the Pacific plate, notably at the San Andreas fault in California which is the area which receives the most publicity; the Ring of Fire round the Pacific Ocean provides most of today's volcanic activity, India continues to push northwards throwing the Himalayas up to fresh heights every year and Britain tilts on a diagonal axis with the south-east gradually sinking and the north-west rising measurably each year.

The 'Atlantic Swamp', for want of a better expression, was only one migration route. The Bering land bridge, now the Bering Straits, was another well known one and the island that is now Britain was, of course, joined to the rest of Europe on and off over the ages, the last link across what is now the Strait of Dover having been submerged only 8,000 years ago. Constant land movements, the rising and falling of sea levels and the retreat and encroachment of glaciers during the several ice ages both created and removed migration routes, but they were sufficient for horses and their near relatives to have spread all over the world, more or less, with the exception of Australasia which split off from the vast southerly continent much earlier than other land masses and, to date, contains no direct horse-ancestor fossils.

The fossil record, in fact, is like a vast jigsaw puzzle with millions of pieces missing, huge gaps to be filled and with no guide-picture to tell us what to look for. Piecing it together calls for considerable imagination on the part of the scientists engaged in completing the unknown picture, not to mention self-discipline and restraint to avoid going down blind alleys and putting newly discovered pieces where they don't belong.

It is well known that *hyracotherium* had four toes on its forefeet and three on its hind, like today's tapirs which are relatives of the horse; the toes did not have claws but little hooves. As the earth's climate changed and new forms of vegetation evolved, so did the animals in order to fit them to survive in the changing environment. *Hyracotherium* was a swamp and forest-dwelling animal; there were no grassy plains, which are normally associated with the horse family, at the time it existed. (I often wonder if there might be a few little *hyracotheria* skulking around deep in the Amazon forest waiting to be discovered like prehistoric fish by today's zoologists!) It is likely that its inclinations were those of other forest animals, such as deer, in that it could probably jump (over fallen tree-trunks and so on) quite well. It couldn't have been fast as there was no space to run, but it must have hidden from predators in the undergrowth and thick forest vegetation. This might account for the game of ring-a-ring-o'-roses a horse of mine used to play around a clump of shrubbery in his field whenever I went to catch him, rather than haring off to the furthest corner. Other forest traits, such as browsing rather than grazing, are still to be seen in many of today's horses, of course.

Practically the whole of the earth was tropical forest at this time, and it took a very gradual process over millions of years for the climate to cool, in parts, and prove less hospitable to tropical forest vegetation. Pockets or bands of tropical climate remained, and still do, but spreading north and south of the equator vegetation had to adapt genetically to cooler drier conditions.

Genetics is as fascinating as evolution and just as complex, but we know much more about it. The characteristics or traits possessed by an organism, whether animal or vegetable, are inherited from or through its parents and ancestors by means of groups of chemicals called genes, which can be thought of as hereditary instructions set out each in a certain locus (or position) on a threadlike structure called a chromosome. Chromosomes are composed mainly of that famous substance DNA (deoxyribonucleic acid or 'the stuff of life') plus various proteins, and are present in pairs within the nucleus or control centre of each cell in the body. The domesticated horse, *equus caballus*, has thirty-two pairs of chromosomes. (Przewalski's horse, *equus przewalskii*, has thirty-three pairs and so is usually regarded as a separate species within the *genus equus* or horse family and not an immediate ancestor of the domesticated horse. They can interbreed, however, so are obviously very closely related.)

Each gene is responsible for a particular characteristic. In the horse, genes will determine coat colour, good or bad temperament, jumping ability, speed and so on. As the chromosomes occur in pairs, there are obviously two genes for each trait. During mating, however, the sex chromosomes are passed on singly. The mare's ovum or egg and the stallion's sperm each have thirty-two *single* chromosomes; when the two come together during conception they pair up with each other so that the resulting fertilised egg contains the required sixty-four (thirty-two pairs). The foal will, therefore, have half its genes from its dam and half from its sire.

But what happens if the two genes for the same trait have

different qualities? Do the genes 'fight' with each other to decide which quality the foal will inherit? In fact, some genes are dominant and some recessive (submissive), with others being described as additive or equal in power. Let us take as an example coat colour, which is easy to work with. Two chestnuts mated together will always produce a chestnut, but if you mate a chestnut with a bay you will usually get a bay foal as chestnut, is normally recessive. Other characteristics are not so easy to predict and this is why it is always advisable for breeders to mate together animals which are known to be dominant in the traits they wish the foal to have: if they are trying to breed jumpers it's logical to use horses who have good jumping ability themselves or are known to produce horses of good jumping ability no matter what they are mated with. If, for some reason, this is not possible, at least they should use horses whose very close relatives (brothers or sisters) have jumping ability. If only the dam has good jumping ability and the sire has not, there is a good chance the foal will *not* have such ability unless previous foals from these parents have, because the dam's 'jumping ability' gene may be recessive and be squashed by the sire's dominant gene for non- ability in that area.

As far as evolution is concerned, genes are crucial to survival. We often read, on the subject of how horses adapted to their environment, that as the grassy plains developed so horses developed longer legs for running, and correspondingly longer necks for reaching down to the grass which then became further away, and so on. This gives the wrong impression that it is a foregone conclusion that as an environment changes the flora and fauna, the plants and animals, in it will inevitably change along with it. This is by no means the case. What actually happens is that random genetic mutations (changes) occur which bring into a species different characteristics. At some point during the era of *hyracotherium* a gene must have somehow mutated or changed which, when passed on during mating, caused the offspring to have slightly longer legs than the parents. Other genes must have mutated which gradually introduced larger, harder teeth for grinding up the new, tough vegetation, grass; similarly the head became bigger and longer to accommodate those all-important teeth, the neck grew longer, the heart and lungs bigger and much more efficient, and the number of toes gradually dwindled down to the one we know today. Those strains of *hyracotherium* which by some quirk of fate did *not* undergo genetic mutation carried on producing fox-terrier-sized creatures with small, weak teeth unable to cope with grass, too slow to escape the faster predators (for they, too, adapted to the new scene in the same way), and so on; and with the odds stacked against them, they gradually died out.

This whole process of genetic change, which obviously takes many millions of years, is the reason why some animals flourish in an environment while others become extinct. There have been many horse-types which have not made it to the present day, probably as a result of their being unable to adapt quickly enough or at all to cope with changing conditions, a new predator (early man?) moving into the area or climatic change; if the genetic mutations did not occur at the right time and replicate quickly enough, a species had to discover a niche where the old conditions remained, or it could not survive. 'Adapt or perish' was as true then as it is now. But, in evolution as we are talking about it, it is not a matter of will but of physical chance.

Today's Horse Family

Today, we are left with only three main lines of the horse family, the *genus equus*: the horses, the asses or donkeys, and the zebras. Of the horses, there are domesticated and Przewalski horses – millions of the former, and only a few hundred of the latter living in zoos, safari or wildlife parks with a very few living feral (having been reintroduced) on the Russian steppes, their original home in recent times.

The zebras have three main types with various sub-strains. What is generally referred to as the success story of today's free-living *equidae* is the African plains zebra, of which there are about half a million, mainly in eastern Africa. Then there is the mountain zebra – the Cape and the Hartmann's: only about 300 of the former, all in South Africa and almost certain to become extinct (as did the quagga zebra-type in the same area in the late nineteenth century as a result of being hunted by the Boers), and a few thousand of the Hartmann's. The final zebra type, which is a species apart from the others, is the Grévy's zebra, a tall, elegant animal with large ears and fine stripes and a different social organisation from most *equidae*. There are a few thousand, about 15,000, of these lovely animals, mainly in eastern Africa.

Of the asses or donkeys, there are the Asian (two main types) and the African (two types) with some sub-types. The domesticated donkey (*equus asinus*), of which there are several 'man-made' breeds in the world, is probably directly descended from the African species, having the same number of chromosomes (thirty-one pairs). The Asian wild asses comprise the onager (the biblical wild ass) of the west, numbering a few thousand, and the eastern kulans (several hundred only) and kiangs (about a quarter of a million). The African ones are represented by the Nubian wild ass and the Somali wild ass, both physically striking and elegant animals but especially the latter. Sadly, both species are down to a few hundred in number and owing to the continuing wars in their home area of north-eastern Africa, prospects for their survival do not look good.

If the success of a species is to be judged by its ability to survive and adapt, it has to be said that surely it is the domesticated horse, *equus caballus*, and its feral descendants, which is the most successful rather than the plains zebra, because it has adapted to man's comprehensive interference and subjugation, learned to adapt to a large extent to his ways and wants, to do highly unnatural (and, surely, to it extremely strange and pointless) manoeuvres, to tolerate extreme boredom, not to mention blatant ill-treatment, with great stoicism, and to put up with management methods which are quite opposed to the way nature evolved it to live. No wonder there are millions of them in the world, for it is true that had the horse not been as useful to man as it is, *equus caballus* and its direct antecedents, with their thirty-two pairs of chromosomes, would certainly have gone the same way as their very close relative Przewalski's horse, and been on the verge of extinction, if not actually extinct, by now.

Today's domesticated horse has been developed by man into hundreds of different types and breeds. By the time the horse was first seriously domesticated five to seven thousand years ago, the ancient peoples responsible had, it seems to be generally agreed, four basic natural types with which to work. These had evolved genetically, as described, to suit different environments.

Those having developed in cold climates had thicker skins, longer and thicker coats, rounded barrells which more easily held an inner core of body heat, narrow nostrils and bigger, longer heads to house the bigger air passages needed to warm cold air as it entered the warm body. They had relatively short legs to minimise air movement around them which carried away body heat, and thick, voluminous and often wavy mane and tail hair which helped to hold body-warmed air close to the skin. The actual body coat was often a 'double' coat with long, coarse drainage hairs over shorter, softer insulating hair. Their necks were relatively short, too: 'radiator'-shaped necks lose heat quickly, so the shorter they were the less heat would escape. All these cold-resistant features developed in the course of genetic change and natural selection for features which would help these animals survive in a cold climate. Those so equipped did well, survived and bred, perpetuating their characteristics. Those unable to adapt or survive did not do well, did not breed so profusely and, inevitably, eventually died out or migrated to more suitable areas.

Horses evolving in hot areas, while still possessing the speed qualities and grazing habits of any horse, looked rather different. Their wide, flaring nostrils, thin skin, short coats and sparser, finer mane and tail hair and higher tail carriage were all features facilitating heat loss. Their longer legs encouraged air movement around them to help cool them and they had more, and more active, sweat glands than their northerly cousins. They had shorter, finer heads, longer necks and less rounded bodies.

Ancient man, then, found himself with the four basic types: a northern horse and pony and a southern horse and pony – all, it seems, in the earth's northern hemisphere, and all in the Old World. The fact is well known that horses died out for some still unconfirmed reason in the American continent and were only reintroduced with the Spanish conquistadores; Australasia never had any till English settlers took them there a couple of hundred years ago and Africa seems to have been completely dominated by the zebras and asses rather than the horses.

In addition to the heat- or cold-related characteristics of these early horses, their size has to be explained. It is logical that if keep is good animals will grow larger, both as individuals and as species. Northern-type ponies such as the Shetland found their grazing seasons extremely short and their keep poor, and responded with small size. In areas where the climate was cold but keep better, such as the vast plains and steppes of eastern Europe, Russia and Mongolia, a large animal evolved. The hot-type or southern-type horses evolved in fertile areas, much of which has become desert mainly because of over-intensive and inappropriate farming methods. The Arab horse (so-called), for instance, is almost certain to have initially evolved in and been captured from the old Fertile Crescent (not called that for nothing) and the Tigris/Euphrates river system around ancient Babylonia and Assyria (Mesopotamia), where modern Iraq is now: an area also often called the 'cradle of civilisation'. Smaller southern types, exemplified by today's Caspian, developed in hot but more arid and less hospitable areas, and therefore remained smaller. The 'natural' Arab horse is not large, of course, but his larger cousin, the Turkmene or Turcoman, another southern- or hot-type, is a larger animal and looks very like many of today's rangier Thoroughbreds, which breed it probably helped found.

The horse was doing very nicely for itself and probably regarded man as just another animal with which it had to share the earth, and which seemed pretty innocuous, apart from the odd hunting party. Then man discovered agriculture, and that was really when the horse's problems started in earnest.

Domestication: Enter Man

If we take 50 million years ago as the time when *hyracotherium* was thriving and see which of man's direct ancestors were established then, we find that there were several small primate creatures in two major families, the adapids and the omomyids, rather like small, present-day lemurs, living in the primeval forests. Today's horse family is a grazing, running animal rather than a forest-dwelling browser: the last browsing horse ancestor was *parahippus* from the early Miocene period roughly 24 million years ago, with three toes. Man's ancestors at this period were all still monkeys and very similar creatures, mainly tree-dwelling.

The major breakthrough for the horse family sprang from *parahippus*. This gave rise to the equine *merychippus* in the mid-Miocene, roughly 15 million years ago; this was the first grazing horse with the larger, stronger teeth needed to eat grass, and although it was still three-toed the long legs with fused forearm and second thigh bones enabled it to gallop faster from predators without the danger of the bones twisting and injuring the knee and hock joints. Its escape mechanism, therefore, was well established by this time, and it also actually looked rather like a horse. Around this period man's ancestors, bigger in some cases and very gibbon- or baboon-like, or alternatively ape-like, were still lolloping around on all fours, often ground-dwelling and eating tough vegetation and roots: in other words, none of the qualities associated with man as a predatory omnivore had yet developed, much less his two-legged stance and locomotion.

The first one-toed grazing horse, *pliohippus*, replaced *merychippus* in late Miocene times, say roughly 7 million years ago. What were man's ancestors doing around this time? Unfortunately, the fossil record, that puzzling jigsaw mentioned earlier, is completely blank and offers us no new, higher primates until around 4 or 5 million years ago. Until new evidence is discovered we can only assume that little took place at this period in the way of man's evolution. It is quite possible that, unlike the horse, man did not progress significantly at all for about 10 million years, but it is surely more likely that there were intermediate species of which we have not yet discovered fossils, for the creatures which 'reappeared' in the record 4 or 5 million years ago are noticeably more advanced than the lower primates inhabiting the earth with *merychippus* and the early *pliohippus* creatures.

Now we actually have direct ancestors of man, hominids, man-like creatures showing more of the features associated with modern humans. Many scientists now believe that we split away from the ancestor we share with the chimpanzee only 5 million years ago, and the chimps are today our nearest relatives, not the gorillas as is commonly thought. We know of two main types, *australopithecus* (*pithecus* meaning 'ape' in Greek and *australo* meaning 'southern', not necessarily Australian) and *homo* (human), both of which are the first known specimens to have upright posture, and both originating in Africa. The earliest known australopithecines date from 3.7 million years ago and lived mainly on fruit and nuts. The *homo* types, contemporaries of the australopithecines, are believed to have used tools and maybe weapons. Some were still quite small compared with modern man. One of them, *homo habilis*, used animal products and was ground-dwelling by day but probably spent the night in trees; it is unlikely to have hunted significantly, however. *Homo erectus*, however, a fully upright-walking creature, had a much larger brain (as large as ours but almost certainly not as convoluted and, therefore, not as complex) and was the first of the genus to migrate out of Africa to other parts of the world. He used stone tools and weapons and harnessed fire.

These man-ancestors would have been fully familiar with *pliohippus* and some of them at least probably hunted or scavenged its remains. It was *pliohippus* which gave rise, during the Pleistocene period (1.9 million years ago to 10,000 years ago), to the living genus *equus*. *Homo erectus* was the immediate ancestor of our own species, *homo sapiens* (knowing man), which appeared about half a million years ago and was initially a hunter-gatherer, a lifestyle which still exists in pockets.

This very sketchy run-down of the co-evolution of man and

horse is intended to show just how recent are man's present-day proclivities, structure and mentality compared with those of the horse. The horse was extremely well established as a running, grazing animal as far back as 15 million years ago, but man's hunting activities (for he is now mainly a predator) became significant only 2 or 3 million years ago, and were still not his main way of life. His upright posture is known to have been noticeable about 3 million years ago and many medical experts put this down as the main reason for back problems being so common in humans: we have still not evolved, spinally, to bipedal or two-legged locomotion, yet our forelegs (arms) are now far too short to enable us to go four-legged like gorillas any more. We are at an intermediate stage still: the horse is a long-established and fully developed type, well set in its ways and impervious to any but superficial changes which we may, intentionally or otherwise, make to its instincts, mentality and physical workings.

Early Domestication of the Horse

In this as in many other areas, expert opinion does vary, but it seems that significant domestication and control of horses by man began about 5,000 years ago. However, there are Stone Age rock paintings which seem to show on the heads of Przewalski-type animals lines resembling a headcollar of some kind. Man's early lifestyle was that of a hunter-gatherer, with meat being an exception in his diet rather than the rule. Recent archaeological findings have unearthed in prehistoric human settlements horse bones which have clear marks of animal teeth, probably those of leopards and hyaenas, and this has led to the feeling that early man scavenged on the kills of other an[...] monly store their kills in trees, out of re[...] but not man, and it is quite likely that hu[...] after the leopard had left for a while.

It is also possible that groups of hum[...] other animals, particularly those that [...] cheetahs, off a ground-level kill and acc[...]

his intelligence grew and he developed the cunning to hunt and the imagination and skill to use and make weapons and tools, man's own hunting abilities developed, but as he could never hope to run fast enough to hunt the horse family as would its other predators the wild cats and dogs, he would mainly rely on spears and, later, bows and arrows and similar weapons. Ever an opportunist, he would certainly have taken advantage of any wounded or very young prey.

Many types of early human would be nomadic, following herds they were helpless to stop, picking off the odd animal when needed and also living off various vegetable items wherever they were. It must have occurred to them gradually that it is a lot less hassle to settle than travel and that it would be more convenient to have their own animals around them. They would probably acquire their first animals, of any species, by capturing young or injured ones, as healthy, adult horses would not be worth the tremendous fight which would ensue.

There remained the problem of feeding them, and as agriculture had not developed, man still had to make periodic treks to fresh pastures in order to feed his animals. Having built up herds, however, he would soon realise that the horse could give milk as well as meat, hide, bone and hair, and perhaps it was not long before he thought of resting some heavy item on the back of a well-tamed horse or ass to let it take its weight during a trek or migration. From this it is a short step to developing the horse as a pack animal, very useful particularly in times before the wheel was invented. And if the horse could carry goods, what about living chattels, too, such as a heavily pregnant woman? Historian Anthony Dent has suggested that this was probably, in fact, the first use of horses for riding. Sick or injured humans could also have ridden rather than walked, and it does not take much imagination to rig up some means of harnessing a horse to pull a conveyance for carrying incapacitated humans or goods.

All this probably happened first in the eastern parts of the Old World such as China and Mesopotamia. When horses were first in war it was as chariot horses – riding came later, the ancient Egyptians appearing to have been one of the last important civilisations to cotton on to this.

Cattle, of course, had been used in agriculture, as they still are today, and were in Britain up to the nineteenth century, for pulling heavy loads and for ploughing, that most essential of jobs in an agriculture-based society. Cattle, however, are weaker and slower than horses. Horses plough much deeper than any cattle (and any tractor, come to that) and are faster and more enduring. Once man realised that he could grow food instead of simply having to gather what he could wherever he could find it, human society changed very rapidly in most regions. Exactly how agriculture was discovered will never be known, but it seems likely that early man noticed how some grain thrown away or left on the ground sprouted and grew (rather than sprouting and going 'off' in store). He would already have been thoroughly tuned in to the changing seasons and the growth patterns and seasons of seeding, flowering and so on of all the plants he ate as a matter of necessity. He must have realised that he did not have to accept the plants' chosen places but that he could probably get them to grow where *he* wanted instead. It would obviously have taken a long time for the stage to have been reached where he could grow enough crops to feed himself and his animals, but happen it did, very gradually and sporadically in different parts of the world.

In ancient Mesopotamia, onagers were used in agriculture for some time and efforts were even made to fit them with nose-rings like cattle, on to which fitted basic reins and head-harnesses. Onagers, however, are nothing like so obliging or adaptable as horses, and bite and kick routinely. Horses took over and remain in favour to this day. The use of domesticated horses spread and radiated out westwards and northwards from eastern Asia, but had also occurred in pockets elsewhere. When Julius Caesar landed in Britannia he was met by chariots pulled by ponies. The ancient Greeks, of course, had an advanced horse culture, as did the Medes and Persians, the Chinese, the Mongols and other Asian and eastern European civilisations. Even peoples who seem to have had no real feel for the animal, such as the Romans, used them and horses were traded like any other valuable commodity, given as prestige gifts to potentates and ambassadors, stolen, bartered, auctioned and used, as cattle are in some African tribes today, to measure a man's wealth.

The joint use of the wheel and a harnessed horse served man superbly for several thousand years until fairly recently, within living memory, of course. But the ridden horse is faster than the driven one and civilisations which mastered riding had the upper hand over those which had either no horses or only driven ones. Initially horses were ridden bareback; then simple animal skins would be used to give a rider added comfort and security; means of keeping them on such as a breast-strap and a crupper, and later a girth, were devised and once the stirrup was invented man could ride for longer in greater comfort than ever on more and more complex saddles.

From bitless headstalls, it would be a short step to inventing something like the Indian war bridle – just a simple horsehair rope or rawhide strap passed through the mouth or looped round the lower jaw, with a single rein to the hand. Rigid bits came later and were initially of bone, horn or wood. Some very elaborately decorated early bridles have been discovered which show that the horse was not regarded, even by early man, as simply useful but was also a mark of social status, admired and coveted for its spirit and beauty. Metals came to be used – iron, copper, brass and later bronze and steel: today, of course, developments in materials continue to progress from nickel alloys and stainless steel to the new plastics, not to mention the familiar rubber and vulcanite.

Breed Development

Man would have appreciated how well suited to his particular area were the horses and ponies naturally found in it. As trade in horses developed, it would become noticeable fairly quickly that horses unused to a certain environment did not thrive as well as the native inhabitants and needed special care. Man would buy certain horses and ponies for their different qualities, and by mating the newcomers with the natives would try to produce stock with the best qualities of both; but he also had to take the disadvantages, too. Inventive as always, however, he developed his own regional and sometimes national breeds which not only would withstand the local climate but possessed the qualities of use he required in his animals.

Today there are hundreds of different breeds of horse and pony devised by man for his own purposes but still showing all the characteristics of their wild ancestors. A breed as such is an artificial state of being developed by man and as all breeds are created by mating different types of animal there is actually no such thing as a genetically pure breed: even Arab and Caspian horses, which are of all domesticated horses the nearest to their wild ancestors, must have come about by natural (and obviously indiscriminate) mating by whatever *equidae* were in a given area, and so are not pure in the accepted sense. However, when a breed authority decides to close the stud book and admit no more stock other than that from already registered parents, the breed then, particularly after many generations of such 'closed' breeding, acquires a sort of purity, or rather exclusivity.

The Effects of Domestication on the Horse

Because of the mixing of genes of wild stocks and the spread of tamed horses from area to area, people to people, interbreeding, at first indiscriminate, had by the time the great civilisations around the Mediterranean had become established (and possibly before) produced a veritable hotch-potch of mongrel equines which had reached the point of no return; it is quite likely that many truly wild horse sub-types had already become extinct by then. Have you ever noticed when watching wildlife pro-grammes or reading about natural history that individuals of a species are all more or less identical in ap_____ This i____ only because in-herd, family breeding, ____ takes place, obviously produced individua____ but because, with truly wild species, a____ creatures evolve to suit their environmen____ especially over the long period of time____ evolution, all be more or less identical, e____ flaging colour schemes. All starlings look the same, all badgers look the same, all Arabian oryx look the same, all African elephants look the same, all zebras of a given sub-species look the same and all Przewalski horses look the same.

But all individuals of *equus caballus*, the domesticated horse and pony, definitely do not look the same, with a *very* few exceptions such as the true Exmoor pony. All Hanoverians do not look the same, all Morgans do not look the same, all Thoroughbreds do not look the same. Even with ancient breeds acclaimed by their enthusiasts as 'the purest in the world' there is variety: all Arabians do not look the same and neither do all Caspians. If we cannot expect specific breeds to consist of identical individuals, and they are all the same zoological species, we certainly cannot expect the species encompassing them, *equus caballus*, to produce identical individuals either.

The different wild stocks had differing characteristics from region to region arising as a result of the species adapting to that particular niche. When these were all indiscriminately mixed, characteristics from previous generations would appear at random and breeders, as they grasped in a primitive but practical way the facts of heredity, would select individuals with preferred traits and try to produce foals with those traits. Attempts to mix radically different stocks, say hot-bloods with cold-bloods, would produce foals which might not mature in an alien environment and even if they did would not really thrive without extra and special care. In comparatively recent times, attempts to introduce Arab blood into Welsh Mountain ponies and Dartmoor ponies in the United Kingdom with a view to 'improving' the native stocks resulted in practice in lessening the breeds' famous hardiness with disastrous results. And today, non-pure-bred natives turned out on Exmoor and Dartmoor, for example, never thrive as well as the natives. We do not learn our lessons, it seems. And these are only national examples.

Domestication has produced widely varying types, breeds and individuals, then, almost none of which really breeds true which, breeders say, is part of the excitement of breeding).

agriculture developed and man used his horses more and

more, it was realised that the horse's natural food – grass, or dried grass in winter when man got that far – was insufficient to keep it in good and strong enough condition to work hard. Evidence exists of early civilisations feeding grain to horses, although who was the first to do so is not really known. Man must have realised, then, that horses with access to grain did better. Over a period of time, it would also have become obvious that horses which had forebears from a region where keep was good became stunted when removed to more arid areas or regions where excessive cold made great demands on their energy requirements. Feeding an artificial but generous diet of grain, for example, would enable those horses, as a breed group, to grow once again to their former height and degree of development, features genetically determined in their original, home area. The parents would remain stunted but their offspring would have the genes to reach certain development standards, given the food to do it. It would also, therefore, be realised that animals had to be well fed and managed *from birth* if they were to develop into healthy specimens: development lost in the early years is not made up later.

As man became static and settled, sporadically throughout the world, so the horse's natural nomadic habits were curbed; but his desire to roam, which is instinctive and still strongly felt, was not. Management systems still vary from country to country, but initial methods of keeping horses together consisted of fencing them into enclosures or tethering the lead animal, usually a matriarchal mare, so that the others stayed near. Mounted herdsmen would be used in some societies, and still are, and gradually stabling systems developed – the most artificial system of all. I should like to think that early civilisations realised that the more naturally horses were kept the better they thrived, but experience down the ages has shown this not to be so, and in view of the many, many people around the world who regard stabling as the obvious way to keep horses, it seems that this is another lesson which has yet to sink in.

As well as having considerable repercussions on the appearance and growth rates of the horse, domestication has had other far-reaching effects. It is true that, given reasonable care, domesticated horses do live longer than free-living ones. They are fed and watered, protected against and treated for disease and injury (although also more exposed to them in other ways) and are usually sheltered from the weather; but most of the effects of domestication on the horse have been bad, not good.

Infestation with internal parasites is not a problem with genuinely free-living horses, although external ones do accept their hospitality. Unless a wild population, or a feral one with generous grazing grounds, were cut off and prevented from moving on to fresh pastures when necessary, as happens in Britain's New Forest, there would be no build-up of worms; natural grazing systems, with many other species and types of animal, not least cattle, would kill off many parasites dangerous to horses. In domestication, particularly in countries where small or overstocked grazing areas are the norm (depending on the owners' circumstances), parasites build up very quickly and cause serious health problems. This necessitates the administration of drugs to control infestation levels from an early age if irreversible damage is not to be done to a youngster's blood vessels and internal organs which can shorten its life and lessen its usefulness to man.

One of the most unpleasant and, to many horses, distressing disadvantages of domestication has undoubtedly been the restriction of movement imposed: horses were meant to have unrestricted access to exercise and their minds and bodies function best when they do, but most domesticated horses, except breeding stock (depending on how they are kept and with the exclusion of most stallions who are largely housed), domesticated horses and ponies are kept very short of exercise and many are given too much work (which is not the same thing as exercise). This all increases stress on the horse and is the cause of many physical and psychological disorders.

Domesticated horses are also kept on an artificial and erratic diet which often does not follow the natural pattern of eating the same type of food for about two-thirds of the time. Free-living horses eat for about sixteen hours a day, and walk gently around while doing so. Horses in paddocks may emulate this behaviour to a large extent but much depends on the horse's state of mind and the size of the paddock. If a horse is turned out on poor pasture with no company it may well stand by the gate or elsewhere much of the time, moping. Stabled horses, of course, are completely at the mercy of their attendants' imposed routines which often leave the horse for many hours out of the twenty-four with no food available – a completely unnatural state which causes considerable hunger (in itself an unnatural condition for the horse), digestive disruption resulting in colic and, in an effort to relieve the physical discomfort and mental anxiety caused by hunger and lack of occupation, such vices as wood- or tail-chewing, rug-tearing and probably crib- biting and wind-sucking.

Lack of time-consuming, gentle exercise such as free-living horses take can result in bodily systems often working below par. When the horse is completely stabled it may find that after a comparatively short warming-up period, demanding work is expected, followed, it is hoped, by another shortish cooling-down period. All of this is completely unnatural, and purely the result of artificial housing systems resulting from domestication.

Lack of natural social contact with other horses can also over-stress many horses and ponies. Herd life is the rule rather than the exception in the world of the wild or feral equine and horses deprived of equine company can become frightened. A herd provides moral support and a sense of security which the lone horse cannot experience. People often express the opinion that their horses 'seem fine' or are 'quite all right' alone or with sporadic human company (hardly a substitute!), or with a donkey, cow, sheep or goat for company. I can only say that after over forty years of associating with horses I have only ever come across two animals who *genuinely* preferred their own company to that of others of their kind. My experience is that horses and ponies kept alone, when finally given the company of other horses and ponies (*not* donkeys which, although *equidae*, are not perceived as such by 'real' horses and ponies), show very plainly how happy they are to have some real friends at last. They usually thrive better physically and take on a new air of contentment and belonging, as if this new situation is what is right for them – which, of course, it is.

From the disease point of view, domestication has brought other ills. Laminitis (fever in the feet/founder) is definitely a condition of domestication caused by, among other things, incorrect feeding, concussion, badly maintained feet, unsuitable shoeing, physical stress, blood disorders or drugs used to combat some other disorder. Horses with laminitis and/or turned-up toes are simply not seen in natural conditions. Navicular disease is a condition still undergoing research but here again it is felt to be a result of inappropriate management, work, shoeing, trimming and bad foot conformation. Horses prone to this sort of disorder would not thrive in the wild and the condition would therefore never take hold in a free-living, free-breeding population.

Colic is another fairly common complaint caused by stress and inappropriate feeding and is probably uncommon in the wild. Even herds moving from one grazing area to another, and therefore giving themselves a sudden change in food, will eat along the way and so accustom themselves to the new food gradually as the old grasses recede along the way and the new ones become more common as the new grazing grounds are reached.

There are many injuries suffered by domesticated horses which would not occur in the wild, but falls, fights, rough going and so on probably account for a corresponding number in feral animals. Such things as girth galls, saddle and bit injuries and so on are purely domestic injuries, but wild animals can inflict serious injuries on each other, of course, and sprains and bad knocks can occur in falls or when galloping over rough ground.

Exposure to the weather is something else which many domesticated horses suffer. Most owners overlook a horse's need for shelter from extremes of weather and climate, seeming to think they are impervious to them. In the wild, however, herds are free to seek whatever shelter they can find in their areas and, in a truly natural and wild world, if they found an area inhospitable they would migrate elsewhere, as many species of bird and animal do, including zebras and their wildebeeste grazing companions. Wild animals, of course, are subject to wide-ranging climatic conditions such as extended drought, storms, excessive rains, winds and so on, but generally they are adapted to the regions they inhabit and are equipped by instinct and experience to seek out areas offering protection. Domestic animals frequently have nothing but a straggly hedge or a man-made fence to huddle behind, neither of which offers any shelter at all, and suffer considerably as a result.

Even though this seems such a black picture, well-managed horses in domesticity can have a much better life than wild ones. I do like to wonder, though, whether, if you put all the options on the table and asked the horse which life he wanted to choose, he would not return to the herd. I tend to think he would follow the call of the wild and take his chances. The horse, of course, cannot be presented with such an option or make such a decision. Few human animals, however, would be willing to give up all the advantages of their modern lifestyle, most of which (medical knowledge, dentistry, electricity and other modern fuels, and so on) have evolved only over the last hundred years or so, and return to life in a cave, a teepee or a mud hut and a life expectancy less than half of what we have now.

Today's Horse: The Product of Evolution and Domestication

The horse which has come down to us today may look much more varied in size, type and colour than its wild ancestors, but in reality it has hardly changed at all underneath the veneer. It is still by nature a highly specialised runr grazer programmed to eat for about sixte exercise gently while doing so. Because fundamental nature is one of nervousnes very perceptive and alert. It has an except prey animal, has a reasoning process rathe man who is mainly a hunter. This has led

ve no reasoning power at all. Its sleep habits are
animal: cat-napping rather than enjoying 'a good
and needing about half the total amount of sleep
rmally needs the company of its own kind if it is to
us ample personal space; and, finally, it is nothing
like as immune to extremes of weather as we tend to think.

It is not generally suited to being stabled, to having its exercise
restricted or to performing frequent or extended stressful work,
to living alone, to producing foals in midwinter, to eating a lot of
food at one go followed by hours with no food at all, to having its
personal space invaded, to being sat upon and being made to
carry or pull weight, to the frequent jumping of high, wide
obstacles, to wearing restrictive metal shoes or to suppressing its
instincts for self-preservation and 'behaving itself', or to many
other less significant things. All these we expect it to do and are
often surprised when it doesn't, or won't, so used are we to
submissive, well trained, well behaved, cooperative animals in
general. So how does the horse cope with these quite extraordinary demands? Simply by means of being extraordinarily
adaptable, a quality which has enabled it to survive so well, plus
having, by sheer good fortune from our point of view, an
unaccountable willingness to cooperate and be led or guided,
and even, in many individuals, an apparent desire actually to
please and to try.

In the process of breeding horses to meet his own requirements, man has deliberately bred out, by avoiding breeding
from animals with unwanted traits, the horse's naturally aloof
temperament, its readiness to bite and kick and its tendency to
be very easily upset and prone to fight for its freedom when tied
down or cornered. Of course, many horses may still do this but
generally horses are very much more docile even before breaking
in than their feral and wild counterparts.

It seems that domestication is also reducing the horse's
natural intelligence and the 'streetwise' quality possessed by all
wild creatures. Studies on the skulls of domesticated horses and
zewalski horses having died some time ago show the latter to
larger brains, and when they were compared with

Przewalskis who have died in captivity this smaller size is also shown in the latter. It seems extraordinary to think that this change is happening so quickly, however, and until more work is done on this it will remain no more than an idea or theory. Some experts feel that once a captive population of any animal has lost wild survival techniques and qualities they are lost for ever, but experience with feral herds shows that in many cases they are quite capable of thriving and reverting to wild tactics.

Perhaps this reversion depends on chance matings and the passing on of genes of which we humans are not aware. For example, although the breeding of Przewalski horses is carefully controlled to prevent too much inbreeding, and many of them are left alone as much as is practicable so that they do not become 'humanised', we must remember that they are not living anything like a truly wild life in a zoo, safari or wildlife park. The traits they would possess and show in the wild to enable them to survive in their environment are probably not shown in captivity. Perhaps, therefore, we are unknowingly breeding them out of this now quite small gene pool because we cannot select for them when arranging matings. Perhaps we shall only know the truth when these stocks or their descendants are returned to a natural environment. So far, those Przewalskis which *have* been reinstated in their original homelands are doing very well indeed, which is an encouraging sign.

By selecting matings to pass on the traits he wants and eliminate those he does not, man is obviously producing his version of what he wants the horse to be, and there can be little doubt that, despite its basic instincts still being very near the surface, the modern domesticated horse, although often physically much more imposing than his wild forebears, must psychologically and temperamentally be but a pale shadow of them. Normally, it is only in the world of racing, where horses are bred for speed alone, that temperament is taken to be of little importance. Indeed, in that sphere of the horse world it is usually felt that you often have to put up with a bit of 'temper' (meaning *bad* temper or hot-headedness) if you want a top-class racehorse. Nevertheless there have been many top racehorses who have been sweet-natured; but it has been a matter of chance rather than judgement in selecting mates.

A Canadian study on the differences of the digestive tracts of feral and domesticated horses found the latter had shorter intestines than their free-living cousins, and put this down to a gradual adaptation caused by the lower-roughage diet of domestication: domesticated horses in the study were on conventional concentrate feeds three times a day with hay night and morning, which is common practice, despite its unsuitability, in many countries where horses are habitually kept stabled. The study took place over a number of years, apparently, and every time a horse died its carcass was used in the study. As hay and coarse grass are digested lower down the digestive tract, it was felt by the researcher that, as the domesticated horses were not consuming the amount of roughage they would if free, the intestine did not need to be so long and so had very gradually shortened slightly but significantly. Their stomachs, however, were slightly larger than those of the feral mustangs studied because, it was felt, of the concentrate portion of their diet. This is interesting; but again it seems remarkable that such a change should occur within a few generations, as all the feral horses used were descended from horses which were fully domesticated early last century.

Selecting mates for certain characteristics must obviously apply to a horse's action and physical attributes, as nearly all horses today are required to be athletes and to perform much more extravagant feats than wild ones (although an interesting study a few years ago clocked a Somali wild ass, with a Land Rover, galloping at spurts of 40 mph in the desert and maintaining an average speed over three miles of more than 30 mph, which is as good as a good racehorse, a highly bred and artificially maintained Thoroughbred). Jumping ability is obviously selected when arranging matings, and so is action in the dressage horse. Today's successful dressage horses are mainly continental European-bred warmbloods, noted for their elastic swinging strides and their cadence. Hock action, too, is particularly looked for by knowledgeable horsepeople, including judges in the sports of showing and dressage.

A British study comparing the hocks of two domestic horses with those of one Grévy's zebra and one Przewalski horse (all dead) found that the horses had what are termed significantly 'bistable' hocks whereas the zebra and the Przewalski horse did not. The hocks were all mounted on a dynamic testing machine, flexed and extended and measurements taken of the angle of the joint and the force placed on it by the machine. The hock has a natural balanced resting position. If the hocks in the study were flexed or extended a little way from that position they would spring back to it, but if moved a little further they reached a point of no return and came to rest either fully flexed or fully extended, as the case was. This movement is controlled in the hock by means of ligaments which bind the hock together and are at their shortest when the joint is at the end of its range of movement, whether flexed or extended. The ligaments 'flip' the joint from one extreme to the other.

The study found that although the four animals all had bistable hocks, the zebra and the Przewalski had hocks which were very much *less* bistable than the horses' and the researchers concluded that this could well be because domesticated horses are partly bred for elegant movement and this 'snapping' movement of noticeably bistable hocks looked more exact and incisive, more elegant to the human eye, and so had been artificially selected for by man when planning matings. This is only one example of how man is manipulating the domesticated horse, but an interesting one. In breeding for a specific type of action, he presumably does not realise that he is, in fact, changing the actual working of the horse's physique.

Domesticated breeds of dog, of course, are very much more varied and far removed from their direct wild ancestor, the grey wolf, than are horses from their direct wild ancestors. It is tragic that in the dog world there have been produced freaks of living flesh that could not possibly make a living in the wild and many which can only survive in domesticity because of the help given by the veterinary profession. So many need various operations to make their bodies function acceptably or even to live a reasonably comfortable life. Horses have not fared as badly, probably because most of them need to work or produce working animals. In the dog world, working animals are in the minority and the – to me – weird tastes of its showing fraternity are allowed to produce whatever travesties of dog-flesh the whim of the time decrees is fashionable, regardless of the consequences for the dogs themselves who have to suffer the distressing, uncomfortable and sometimes painful results.

There were international comments some years ago about heavy horses mostly bred for show developing nasty temperaments, and more recently it has been noticed that Arabians are being produced in increasing numbers with excessively flat backs on which you could easily stand a tea tray! Some animals show little difference between the withers, the back and the quarters, and this damaging conformation is often accompanied by a greatly over-exaggerated *mitbah* (the curve of the throat) with the result that the horse's nose is (naturally for it) stuck out and up to a far greater degree than is practical for the horse or acceptable to the rider (if any), who has the probably impossible task of trying to get the animal to go in some sort of semblance of a feasible working outline with the hind legs underneath, not left behind in the last county, and the head and neck fairly long and low for initial schooling (although not in the equally exaggerated 'grazing position', as it has been called), and the front of the face being gradually encouraged to approach the vertical for more advanced schooling, accompanied by a higher but smoothly rounded neck carriage. Horses schooled to stand squat, as I call it, with their hind legs out behind them in an unnatural and uncomfortable stance, and their noses in the 'browsing' position have, over the months and years, developed their muscles, tendons and ligaments to enable them to try to cope with it. It stands to reason that when, if ever, they are backed and ridden, they are not merely starting from scratch on a relatively undeveloped physique, they have also to undo the deleterious effects of a previously mastered position which is diametrically opposed to the position they will, or should, be asked to assume when ridden. This is making life uncomfortable and more difficult for them and for their trainers.

The classical aim of asking a horse to go with his hindquarters lowered and legs 'underneath' him, and his head and neck initially long and low, though not too much so, has been proved over the centuries, as truly correct, classical equitation has been developed and refined, to be the easiest and most comfortable position for the horse carrying weight to adopt. In this position he is working *with* his own physique and centre of gravity, not against it. If you watch any horse at liberty moving through his paces and cavorting around, you will see that this is what he does naturally when unencumbered by weight on his back. He *does* at times throw out his nose and does not go with his nose approaching the vertical, other than when doing standing starts or other movements requiring greater effort such as sharp turns and so on. He certainly does have his hind legs well under him and does not stand with them back and straight. The extra effort he must make when ridden is counteracted by a correct head carriage which, when accompanied by energetic use of the hind legs and quarters, gradually lowered and used more underneath the horse as schooling progresses, makes life altogether easier for him.

Showing fashions are, of course, purely a feature of domestication and this is one particularly unfortunate trend which, it seems, is becoming internationally established. Having tried to trace the origins of the head-up-legs-out stance, I find that it went over to America from Europe with various generations of settlers from different countries, took hold there but died out in Britain. Now, however, because it has taken hold in the American Arab world as well as with Saddlebreds, Morgans etc., the fashion has spread back to the European show rings in the Arab horse world and has jumped back across the English Channel. It is now fully established in British Arab showing and, incredibly, is starting to infiltrate, of all things, warmblood showing on the continent and is just starting to show signs of infecting British warmblood breed showing, too.

I say 'of all things' because warmbloods are produced above

all for hard, stressful *work*, even if they do not all make the top levels of competition. There are some extremely knowledgeable people involved in breeding, producing, presenting and riding warmbloods and I hope against hope that this ugly and counterproductive fashion can be nipped in the bud before it becomes normal practice in this and other show rings, perhaps by judges refusing to judge or grade animals not stood up and presented in a natural way so that their conformation and type can be plainly assessed. This is one refinement of domestication which I should definitely love to see scrapped.

Breeds and Types Today

Every country had its own breeds, whether classed as native or 'manufactured'. Most countries have indigenous pony breeds and many of these have attained worldwide recognition and significance, such as the Icelandic pony, the Norwegian Fjord pony, the Haflinger, the various British mountain and moorland ponies, and so on. Indigenous breeds such as these are normally naturally suited to their countries of origin and were intended to live largely out exposed to the elements and to work either as pack animals or doing light farm work which, again, necessitated long hours out in all weathers.

Agriculture has also been the lot of many horse breeds and types, too. Heavy horses, like many breeds of carriage horse, nearly became extinct when motorised tractors and other farm vehicles became widespread, but pockets remained in various countries, not only the less developed ones, where horses continued to be used, and today their advantages are once again being realised. Some countries use them for other purposes, too. A few local councils use them for short-distance delivery and parks maintenance, and breweries, of course, have long seen their value as publicity media as well as a more economical method of short-haul deliveries than motorised drays. Worldwide, probably the most famous heavy horse breeds are the French Percheron and the English Shire, plus the Scottish Clydesdale, these breeds having been freely exported all over the world to be bred pure in their new countries or crossed with other breeds and types.

But when it comes to fame, surely there is no more famous horse than the British racehorse – the Thoroughbred. Based on various oriental breeds, particularly the Arab and, I feel, the Turcoman or Turkmene, it was originally produced entirely for the sport of flat racing and bred solely for speed. It has a history of not much more than 200 years but its achievements in the field of racing and competition have been phenomenal. Crossed with various indigenous British animals (and, who really knows, some imported ones, too?), it is an excellent example of a highly unnatural breed which, given appropriate care, thrives in a completely unsuitable environment. It is a thin-skinned horse of hot-blooded origins quite unsuited to the relatively cold, damp and windy British climate. Surely there can be no horse breed or type of any significance in the world of ridden sport and even that of carriage driving without an infusion of Thoroughbred somewhere in its formation, and the breed is still used to refine, 'breed up' and change according to whim and public demand many competition breeds today.

Many warmbloods are heavily infused with Thoroughbred blood and even the superb Irish Draught horse, an all-purpose, mainly agricultural horse of stocky but not heavy build, with clean legs and often oozing quality and character, may have Thoroughbred in its pedigree. The Thoroughbred and Irish Draught crossed and with further crosses of Thoroughbred make some of the best competition horses in the world, particularly where speed, courage, endurance, jumping ability and the possession of a 'fifth leg' are called for. Horses of this breeding excel particularly at cross-country work such as eventing, hunter trials and, of course, hunting proper.

The Irish Draught itself is an example of a breed of horse eminently suited to its environment, as is the British Cleveland Bay from Yorkshire with its east winds and generally tough climate. Originally a pack horse, the Cleveland Bay, enjoying a resurgence after a decline, is mainly now in demand for breeding carriage horses for the sport of four-in-hand carriage driving.

The metier of the domesticated horse today is without doubt mainly as a sports horse, either for competition or for pleasure riding. Just about all countries with any equestrian interest have their own breeds and most have imported the Thoroughbred and Arab, the latter really being the tap-root of most breeds and a superb riding horse in its own right, as well as making a driving horse with panache and elegance, although few seem to be seen in harness. The breed is currently hampered by an increasing segment of its enthusiasts who are masking its true attributes by inappropriate presentation and now, more seriously, by breeding conformation faults into the breed, as already discussed. A good Arab which is also a good horse is hard to beat as a general riding horse with endurance riding as a speciality. I cannot understand why so many people think they are useless: if they were, they would not have been used for thousands of years for the most demanding work imaginable, military campaigning, or used almost exclusively, until their own offspring, the Thoroughbred, came along to share the honours, of improving just about every breed and type of horse and pony in the world.

2 Conformation and Movement

Action is Everything

The horse in natural conditions, as we have seen, is largely a creature of movement, living most of its life on the hoof round the clock, lying down comparatively rarely. Its body fits it for this lifestyle and it is no effort to the horse. Indeed, horses forced to be inactive or, even worse, to lie down, suffer certain mental distress and physical harm, particularly if these impositions are prolonged. If a horse, for example, is required to lie on its side for an operation, problems can start developing in the lung on the 'ground' side as it is squashed by the horse's considerable weight. Naturally forming fluid cannot be cleared from it as it would be by movement and circulation, and respiratory distress and stress on the heart can follow. Horses do not normally sleep of their own accord lying flat out for more than half an hour at a time, usually less. When we stable horses, we confine them to an area of about 12ft square and think nothing of it, yet this is not normal behaviour for a horse at liberty. If we spotted a horse in a field standing in the same 12ft-square area for twenty-two hours out of twenty-four we would surely think there was something drastically wrong with it, but we force the horse to do exactly that in what we regard as a normal regime for a stabled horse.

Basic Conformation

The Skeleton and its Muscles

The framework of the horse's body is the skeleton, which consists of bones, many of which articulate upon each other and others of which, such as those in the skull, are fused together. Joints such as those in the spine and legs are protected at their ends by cartilage (gristle) and a lubricating fluid in the joints (called synovial fluid) bound in a sealed unit by special tissue. The skeleton is 'lashed' into shape and supported by ligaments which are strong bands, cords or sheets of fibrous tissue and which largely prevent the bones from collapsing in a heap. A particularly important ligament, for instance, is the *ligamentum nuchae*, which goes from poll to withers and supports the head with very little effort from the horse. The ligaments of the legs are obviously important in maintaining the positions of the bones and those of the spine in keeping the column of vertebrae in position, and so on. Ligaments attach to bones at various points or run freely between them.

The ligaments are helped in their supportive role by the muscles, and the tendons which grow from the muscles. Together, muscles, tendons and ligaments support and move the skeleton. Muscles can work only by contracting or shortening: they cannot and do not *actively* lengthen and stretch. A muscle will be attached to, say, two bones by means of its tendons, long or short fibrous cords, very slightly elastic. When the muscle contracts it obviously exerts a pull on the tendons which causes the bones to move. For example, the muscles behind the forearm will contract and the associated tendons attached to various parts of the lower leg are pulled accordingly, bringing the bones of the leg with them, so flexing or bending the leg. Then, to straighten out the leg again, the muscles at the front of the forearm contract, pulling on their tendons attached around the front of the lower part of the leg, and this straightens out the leg again.

Muscles also have a 'balance' system between them, maintaining a certain tone which prevents joints being over-flexed or over-straightened, as it were. A muscle, however, can only return to its normal, uncontracted size and shape by relaxing and being pulled back again by its opposing number.

The skeleton not only gives the body its shape but also protects certain vital organs within the ribcage, such as the heart and lungs. Tough tissue known as connective tissue separates and links various different parts of the horse and the skin covers and protects almost the whole horse.

Bone

Anyone who has suffered a broken bone will know without doubt that bone is not an insensitive, dead substance, rigid and unfeeling. It consists of a hard, fibrous substance composed partly of phosphate and partly of carbonate of lime. In young animals the softer fibrous tissue predominates, while as the horse ages the lime salts increase in proportion; so a young animal's bones are more resistant and malleable in some ways than an older horse's bones. However, brittleness also increases with age, making the bones of an old horse more prone to fracturing without apparent cause. It should be remembered that an average riding horse weighs about half a ton: his very weight puts a stress on his bones even before taking into account the sometimes extreme athletic effort, and resultant stress, we ask of our horses. The simple act of getting up can break an old horse's back while youngsters, particularly, for example, two-year-old racehorses, are particularly prone to concussion injuries as their softer bone is less able to withstand jarring. Obviously, the safest time for a horse to work is his mid-life period when the skeleton is fully mature and the bone hard and strong without being either comparatively soft or brittle.

Bones are covered by a protective membrane called the periosteum (peri = around, osteum = bone) the inner surface of which constantly produces new bone enabling the main bone to grow in thickness. This is partly a natural growth and 'repair' process and partly a natural reaction to stress on the bone, more bone being produced as the body senses it is needed to stand up to pressure. This remodelling process, as it is known, is one of the often overlooked factors in getting a horse fit: it is not only the heart, lungs and muscles which need to be gently and gradually stressed but the bone, too, and bone takes longer to respond to stress than softer tissue – another good reason not to rush a fitness programme.

Working horses when they are too young puts unreasonable stress on their bones, not only their leg bones, and predisposes them to back problems, splints, bone spavins, sore shins (common in young racehorses where their cannons sustain tiny fractures or the concussion stresses the periosteum, causing inflammation) and other bone disorders.

It is important to understand how long the horse's skeleton can take to mature in order to work with nature and not against it when putting horses to work. The wastage of young horses in the flat racing industry is phenomenal simply because they are over-stressed before they are ready for work.

The so-called dense bone of which the long bones, such as the leg bones, are made has at the ends growth plates, specialised cells which produce bone to lengthen these bones. As the horse matures, the plates harden into bone, and the growth plates are said to have closed. This expression is used because, when X-rayed, the hard bone in the legs shows up as white on the X-ray and the immature, less dense growth plate appears darker or 'open'. Although the growth plates may appear to have 'closed' or matured some time during the youngster's third year (as a two-year-old plus) – a period during which some racing yards fairly regularly have their two-year-olds X-rayed while others don't bother at all – the bone will not have reached its fully mature state and bone injuries can regularly occur in young animals up to four or even five years of age.

A horse can be said to mature roughly from the ground up, so while the legs may be able to withstand fairly hard work in the three-year-old racehorse (at which age the Classics are run), the spine does not mature until five or even six years of age. As it is the spine which takes much of the stress in jumping (more than is generally realised, I feel), surely this is an excellent case for stopping the increasingly prevalent practice of 'popping' (i.e.

jumping) youngsters (sometimes even yearlings) over fences to detect as early as possible whether or not they have any inherent jumping ability, so that they can be marketed early as potential jumpers. It is not only the legs which suffer but particularly the spine in the lumbar area, roughly from the end of the ribcage to the protruding wings of the pelvis, commonly but incorrectly called the hip (the hip joint being deeper and lower inside the hindquarters).

Bone is not solid. The long leg bones, for instance, are like closed-ended tubes, the centre of which is filled with fatty yellow marrow. Shorter and more irregularly shaped bones contain the important, blood-forming red marrow and are more open in structure, not as dense as the long bones. Different types of bone have, therefore, different structures, different purposes, different strengths and different rates of maturing. Bone is a very complex substance well able to do its various jobs when, like any bodily substance, it does not undergo unreasonable stress and has the support of a good, well balanced diet. It changes throughout life, and changes in diet and management accordingly can help prolong its useful life, and, therefore, that of the horse.

Muscle

We tend to think of only one type of muscle, the one with which we are most practically concerned – the type which provides the movement and power and which we try to condition when getting a horse fit; but there are, in fact, three main types of muscle. The type with which we are most familiar is called voluntary muscle because it is under the control of the will to a large extent, and is the type which forms the meat of food animals. There is also involuntary muscle which is found, for example, in the walls of the stomach, the intestines, the walls of blood vessels, the uterus, the bladder and so on. This is not under the control of the will. The third is also involuntary but is the highly specialised cardiac (heart) muscle. The first two types of muscle consist of bundles of little fibres served by nerves and interspersed by blood capillaries (thread-like blood vessels). It is the contraction of the fibres which shortens the muscle and causes it to 'work'. The fibres are smaller in involuntary muscle than in voluntary muscle. Cardiac muscle, however, has its fibres in a mesh-work formation rather than in bundles and is easily identifiable, to the knowledgeable, under the microscope.

Each voluntary muscle has an 'origin' to a static part of the skeleton to which it is attached and, at its other end, an insertion or attachment to the bone it moves. Muscles such as those in the forearm and thigh have their insertion a long way from the fleshy 'belly' of muscle, this being made possible by a length of modified muscle tissue, tendon, which is also made up of fibres.

Muscles work by means of a nerve impulse reaching them from some part of the brain or spinal column (which runs down the backbone inside the hollow vertebrae), either as a reflex, instinctive reaction such as the horse rapidly using his muscles to keep his balance over a rough patch of ground, whirling away from something startling or recoiling like lightning from something painful such as a thorny bush, or as the result of free will, such as the horse deciding to walk over to the water trough or to obey a request from his rider. The impulse passes down the fibres of a motor nerve (which initiates movement, as opposed to the sensory nerves which sense stimuli and pass the information to the brain) to the muscle where complicated chemical reactions occur involving the use of energy, and the end result is that the muscle moves.

Energy production is a very complex process in the body but it is obvious that without energy there is no movement, voluntary or involuntary. The horse gets his raw materials for energy (which is involved in every life process and is constantly being used up as long as the horse lives) from his food. This is digested and broken down into its various components and carried to the parts of the body which need it (in this case the muscles) by the bloodstream. The nutrients are absorbed from the intestines into blood carried in capillaries in the intestine walls, processed by the liver and carried by the blood to their destination. In the muscles, the energy is used or 'burnt' up (for which process oxygen is also needed, again carried to the muscles by the blood which has picked it up in the lungs) and in the process, waste toxic substances are formed in the muscles. If the muscles become overloaded with these toxins – usually because the work is too hard or too prolonged for the horse's state of fitness and the bloodstream is unable to remove them quickly enough – the horse starts feeling fatigued, even exhausted. His natural reaction would be to rest, obviously, but if we force the horse to continue muscle damage can occur because the chemical state of the muscle is not conducive to work: the muscle does not have enough energy or oxygen to function and is also hampered by the presence of too many waste products. The muscles may even cramp up painfully, when the horse has no choice but to stop, or even collapse from exhaustion.

As will be seen in Chapter 11, muscle can, obviously, be made 'fitter' by conditioning so that the horse can stand more and more work before fatigue sets in. After severe exertion, however, even in very fit horses, a long enough period of rest and relaxation (roughly three weeks, depending on the work) will be needed for muscle to recuperate to the extent when it can once more undergo severe work.

The horse is, by nature, a highly specialised running animal and can run for quite long periods and distances away from predators without tiring. His strong points are rapid acceleration from a standing start (up to a full-speed gallop in a very few seconds: 0–35 mph in about five seconds as one researcher put it) and cantering continually for miles, if necessary, although in nature a few hundred yards usually suffices to escape being killed. One reason he has inbuilt stamina is because he has no muscle tissue below the knee and hock: it is muscle tissue which brings on the feeling of exhaustion or simple fatigue and the horse's muscles are arranged so that he can move quite fast for longish distances with the most economical operation of his muscles, working his long legs with their single-digit hooves from a relatively long distance away. It is not only his forearm and thigh muscles which are involved in movement, of course; those of the whole body are used to assist and support the actual leg muscles.

The legs are also quite light compared to his body weight (which, for instance, humans' are not) and the part of his leg which has to move most and furthest, the hoof, is very light, so necessitating as little muscular effort as possible to move it.

Because the body and its movement are ruled by basic physics, a good, balanced physical structure is needed. The basic elements of good conformation are well known and discussed in detail in two excellent books – *The Right Horse* by Janet Macdonald and *The Less-Than-Perfect Horse* by Jane Thelwall – to which readers are referred. Very basically, any horse, to move well and with the least effort to and stress upon himself, must be balanced and in proportion within himself and must move 'straight', which means his legs should not be 'bent' or 'crooked' and should move in the same plane, the hind legs following the path of their respective forelegs without deviating. A horse which does not move straight (a) uses up excess energy in excess movement and (b) risks over-stressing various parts of the leg or body by suffering excessive, uneven forces or stresses caused by irregular impact when the foot hits the ground. Also, of course, horses with crooked legs tend often to hit themselves and bring themselves down, something which is fatal in the wild when being pursued by a predator and just as fatal, when it frequently occurs, in domestication, for no horse will find a ready market if he can't stay on his own four feet: in our society that usually means he ends up sooner rather than later in a pet food tin, so the end result is the same: premature death.

Good, proportionate conformation is not something devised by man. It is an essential mechanism evolved in nature for survival, but man at some point recognised that what we now call well made horses used themselves better than others, could work harder for man without coming down with injuries and so forth, and, when kept naturally, were better at escaping predators.

Action

Let's look at a simplified version of what happens to the horse in action during a single stride.

The stride is initiated by a hind leg. The muscles of the hip are the most important muscles of propulsion and the hindquarters are the 'engine' of the horse, providing the thrust forward and upwards. The pelvis is an important attachment for muscles of propulsion and it should be long and deep to provide adequate space and attachment area for the necessary muscles.

The hind leg is picked up and flexed to clear it from the ground, brought through the air and impacted with the ground as it straightens. On impact, it flexes again slightly and then straightens out to give the thrust against the ground which moves the body forward. The force travels partly down into the ground but largely up the leg, lessening as it is absorbed by the leg and particularly the joints. At the hip joint the force is transferred through the pelvis to the spine, travelling along the spine.

The spine itself flexes slightly up and down during each stride and the pelvis or loin area also flexes slightly back and forth as the leg goes forward and back.

As the hind leg hits the ground at the hoof and pushes the horse forward, the foreleg is itself being flexed and carried forwards. It straightens to its fullest extent at its most forward point and then, staying straight, it is brought slightly back before it impacts with the ground. The foreleg does not flex again slightly on receiving weight as does the hind leg. Its job is not to propel the horse forward but to support the weight of the body and the force coming into the forehand along the spine. It remains rigid at the knee like the spoke of a wheel, while the fetlock and foot joints do give under the weight to help absorb the concussion. The fore hoof hits the ground and receives the force of the impact which travels up the leg and is largely absorbed in the forehand, and also by the foot and fetlock joints and the elbow.

There is no shoulder joint as in humans. The shoulder in the horse is bound to the ribcage by means of ligaments, muscles/tendons and connective tissue in an arrangement called the 'thoracic sling'. This is a great shock absorber for a part of the horse which normally carries two-thirds of the horse's weight, a weight increased by force and speed. An ordinary joint would be significantly stressed by this level of weight and force. A basic law of physics is 'force = mass (weight) × acceleration (speed)': this means that the heavier and faster the horse (and his tack and rider) the greater the force borne by his body, the greater the stress on his forelegs during motion and the greater the propulsive power needed from the hindquarters and legs. The propulsive power, however, is greatest during starting off, particularly at a standing start into a fast speed, during jumping (especially over a high obstacle at a slow speed) and during pushing into the collar when getting a heavy load going (or, of course, drawing a load uphill).

Horses have four natural gaits – walk, trot, canter and gallop – and some breeds, notably the Standardbred, naturally pace as well. The pace is a trot-type gait, being a two-time gait, but instead of moving its legs in the familiar diagonal pairs, the horse moves both legs on one side forward together. Horses who race in harness trot or pace: pacers are slightly faster than trotters because in pacing the body is suspended 'flying' through the air for slightly longer than in the trot gait. The ground has a natural braking effect on the horse; whenever a hoof hits the ground the interruption slows down the gait, so the longer a horse can spend in the air the less interruption there is to his movement and the faster he goes. However, pacing *is* more stressful to the horse. Other induced gaits are rarely natural, although there are a few exceptions. Even so, horses with a natural propensity for a particular gait usually have to be schooled and the gait refined for it to be produced at its best.

There are two factors which influence the efficiency of the horse's action, apart from his basic conformation, and they are the state of the going or ground and the slight elastic recoil which assists his movement without using extra energy.

Ground Conditions

When the hoof hits the ground, some of the force goes into the ground and the ground is displaced before springing back. If the ground is soft the spring-back will not help the horse as by the time it occurs the hoof will already have left the ground again for the next stride. If the ground is hard, the spring-back will take place before the hoof leaves the ground and jar the hoof. The ideal surface is one where the spring-back finishes at the moment the hoof leaves the ground, giving the horse maximum forward thrust.

Soft ground may permit the hoof to sink in and avoid some jar, but the muscles then have to pull harder to get the hoof out of the ground and into the air again. In muddy, holding going, it is plain that fast work or sudden movements can easily cause injured tendons and muscles. On hard ground, however, whether baked earth or prepared roads and highways, the main danger is concussion.

Few horsemen and women will deny that the ideal surface for horses is springy, old turf, but this sort of going with its matrix or mat of interwoven grass roots below the surface is rare indeed. Even Britain's top class racecourses are periodically reseeded and receive various treatments which interfere with the root-mat, even though they are not actually ploughed up.

An American professor, George Pratt, some years ago tested various British racetracks and concluded that the courses which produced the fastest race times were not the hardest, as popularly believed, but those of ideal going, as described above, because of the spring-back.

All-weather tracks are still being developed and it is generally felt, at the time of writing, that the ideal surface has not yet been produced. The current main problems are kick-back of the material, which is inhaled by horses following and which subsequently causes significant respiratory problems, and instability of the material, which reduces horses' confidence and, therefore, speed and can actually cause falls, particularly on bends. (As regards kick-back, tests are going on at a research establishment in Ireland where horses are put on a treadmill up to racing speeds and endoscopically examined while they are galloping. The fibre-optic endoscope [fibrescope or simply scope] is inserted up one nostril and can give a view of the respiratory system while the horse is actually working – and the kick-back material previously inhaled can actually be seen in the throat and further down.)

A particularly good surface coming more and more into use seems to be 75 per cent hardwood chips, 25 per cent softwood chips with a surface covering of shredded rubber. This is in use at Kildangan Stud in Ireland and in Newmarket and various other centres, and is found to give good spring-back with insignificant dust levels and greatly reduced kick-back.

Racehorse trainers and others not infrequently make trips to the nearest suitable beach when training conditions at home are unsuitable because of ground that is baked, frozen or water-logged, and although sand can certainly be better than those conditions, I wonder how many people realise what completely dead going it provides. Having lived and ridden by the sea most of my life I can confirm that work on a beach is hard work and can be very tiring. Soft, loose, dry sand is, of course, useless but beaches continually washed and packed down by the sea, particularly those which develop a raised crown or dome along them, can become as hard as concrete when dried out. Horses can and do split pasterns and develop various concussion disorders from doing fast work on a ringing-hard beach while their riders sit on top blissfully unaware of the stress and danger.

If the horse's hooves do not make an imprint three-quarters of an inch deep, the beach is too hard for cantering. If you can hear a ringing sound when your horse canters or gallops, slow down, as this, too, indicates a hard beach. The safest place, from a 'give' point of view, to do fast work is at the edge of the sea as the tide is going *out*: here the sand will be soaked and not hard, yet not so soft as to be dangerous. However, don't expect any helpful spring-back from any kind of beach because there isn't any. The going can also be very inconsistent.

Elastic recoil

The slight elasticity of the tendons not only helps to absorb some of the force of the stride, particularly on hard ground, but also acts as an energy storage system to help the horse's next stride get going again. As he puts his feet on the ground, he puts weight on the foot, the joints flex (apart from the knee) and as the weight starts to be lifted from the foot the tendons, which have been slightly stretched by the force and weight on them, naturally recoil, throwing the horse back up into the air. These auxiliary biological springs conserve the energy of the body bouncing up and down.

This effect also works within the ribbons and sheets of tendon tissue in the horse's back. The spine, as mentioned, flexes gently up and down slightly during action. As the back bends slightly the tendon tissue is stretched, then recoils and springs back again, helping keep the hind legs swinging backwards and forwards and providing another energy-saving mechanism.

Natural Cruising Speed

The horse is lucky in having four gaits to choose from to get it around. The walk, trot and canter are, of course, very different from one another but the gallop is very similar to the canter. Some years ago, two American researchers, Drs D. Hoyt and R. Taylor of Harvard University Museum of Comparative Zoology, concluded that a horse consumes no more energy when he gallops a mile in four minutes than if he walks that distance in fifteen minutes, because he automatically moves from one gait to another when it becomes energy-economical to do so. Apparently, through oxygen-sampling techniques used on horses on a treadmill, they found it was as uncomfortable and wasteful of energy to make a horse go too slowly within a gait as too fast.

The work showed that if, through training and the horse's cooperative and willing nature, a horse remained in the wrong gait for his speed, his energy consumption increased greatly. For example, a horse which normally walked at slightly below 3 mph used up one and a half times more energy if it was asked to trot at that speed. In each gait, the horse has an optimal speed at which energy consumption is minimal: the researchers found, surprisingly, that this minimal amount was the same for each of the three main gaits. Therefore, provided a horse changes gait, up or down, at the optimal speed, he can keep his energy consumption at the same minimum level whatever gait he is in. To prove the point, the researchers also managed to measure the horses' speeds and gaits when they were running freely in paddocks, and came up with the same finding.

Other researchers have done similar work on wildebeest, gazelles and zebras and found that they all operate at a restricted range of speeds within each gait when trekking to different watering holes and grazing grounds – although how they managed to do this on the wildebeests' Great Trek up and down Africa twice a year (accompanied by zebras) makes the mind boggle!

As a matter of interest, work was also done on a very different animal, the kangaroo, and also the springhare, both of which hop very fast and very powerfully. In the kangaroo, it was found that the higher the speed, the greater the elastic recoil in its tendons, the more (relative) energy is saved and the more efficient the gait becomes. However, as kangaroos do not hop everywhere at top speed (about 40 mph) there is perhaps a missing piece of the jigsaw to fit into place.

This natural cruising speed of the horse is something well known, even if not fully appreciated in some cases, by endurance riders, who know that if a horse can be permitted to go along at his own speed and choosing his own gaits, he will complete his journey much less tired than a horse whose gaits have to be regulated constantly by his rider, either because he is going too fast for the competition he is entered in, or too slowly.

Those interested in the techniques of equitation, whether for competitive dressage or not, are also well aware of just how tiring to a horse flat work, as it is called, can be, with its lengthening and shortening of stride above and below the horse's natural length of stride. Although the object is to retain the *rhythm* of the stride, the actual speed (in terms of ground coverage per minute, say) obviously varies according to the length of the stride. At any gait, if the horse is asked to perform outside his normal stride length (and therefore speed) and rhythm, he is going to be using up more energy than he would if left to himself because he is not, as we have seen, operating at his individual minimum-energy consumption level, and this accounts for the tiring and often stressful nature of schooling work as opposed to, say, hacking when the horse may be allowed to go along at more natural speeds with fewer demands from his rider.

Without embarking on a discussion of different seats and techniques or schools of equitation, it should perhaps be mentioned that the way a person rides also has a significant effect on the horse's gait and energy consumption and, therefore, on how efficiently he can move. A horse has constantly to adjust his balance with every stride even when free: when ridden this adjustment is magnified by the weight, placement on his back and posture of the rider, not to mention the nature of the rider's aids. Unfortunately, the current practice of equitation/dressage (as opposed to its theory as laid down in the FEI rules) is not one which favours energy-saving in either horse or rider in many western countries, particularly the UK, Ireland, North America, Belgium, the Netherlands, Sweden, Denmark and, particularly, Germany, where the most common system favours riding more by means of hand and leg than by weight, back and seat as practised in the more classical, Latin or Romantic schools and cultures.

Most methods advocate that the rider should sit as nearly as possible over the horse's centre of gravity which, for practical purposes, means sitting with the seatbones just behind the withers (and using a saddle which at least does not force one out of this position, and preferably which positively makes it easy to do so), although the widespread American Saddle Seat popular in the central and eastern states of the USA actually advocates that the rider sit *out* of balance with the horse and behind his centre of gravity to show off the forehand and elevated gaits encouraged in this form of equitation.

Sitting *in* balance over the centre of gravity obviously makes life much easier for the horse and allows him not only to use his body naturally with the least effort but also to obey his rider's wishes more easily and to do so with the least stress on his body. Purposely sitting out of balance with the horse certainly makes life more difficult, unpleasant and stressful for him, interferes with the correct and natural use of his body and places weight specifically where it is most difficult for the horse to carry it, almost on the loins.

Of course, no part of the horse was *meant* to carry weight. The backbone is constructed by nature in a very slightly domed shape, not apparent from the outside, which is a very strong structure from which to sling weight underneath, mainly the heavy and voluminous intestinal tract. However, given time to mature and build up gradually in strength and fitness, the horse can certainly carry *correctly placed* weight easily, up to about one-sixth of his own weight being considered not an unreasonable burden, depending on the task in hand. Carrying the same amount of weight *out* of balance, however, would put the horse under unreasonable stress.

Even when the rider is sitting as nearly as possible over the centre of gravity, the way he uses his body and weight once there also has a bearing on the horse's gaits and how he can use his body. The old requirement of a quiet, still seat with the rider striving in a relaxed, controlled way to stay with his horse, rather than too much movement of shoulders, arms, legs and sometimes seemingly rather wild use of the rider's body-weight, does have a lot to recommend it and happily seems to be making something of a comeback among some of the newer generation of competitive dressage riders from whom so many young riders seem to take their cue.

To end this section, I'd like to offer two examples of how much difference correct weight placement can make to the horse's movement. If you pick up a shovel of something heavy and try to carry it with one hand, you will find it very much easier if you hold it in balance near the blade of the shovel than if you try to carry it by the end of the handle. If you fill a backpack with a heavy load, it's much easier to carry it near your own centre of gravity on your shoulder area than strapped round your waist. If you then tried running a mile with it in both positions, both firmly and then loosely strapped on, you would also probably realise how much easier for the horse a firm, quiet seat is, with the rider moving around as little as possible, compared with a rider who is all over the place and using the saddle as somewhere to come back to rather than somewhere to operate from!

Whilst riding may not be a 'natural' pursuit at all, there is no doubt that by obeying nature's rules of gravity and balance the whole process is easier and more enjoyable for both horse and rider, is much less stressful and therefore favours a longer, happier working life for the horse/human partnership.

The Hoof

The single-digit foot such as only the horse family possesses is the ultimate specialisation for speed in the animal world. True, there are faster animals who have two or more toes to their feet, but few who can go on for as long as the horse family who combine fair speed with tremendous endurance.

The horse's ancestors had varying numbers of toes to their feet, tiny hooves which ultimately reduced to the one with which we are familiar and which is the equivalent of the tip of our middle finger. The splint bones on either side and just behind the cannon bones below knee and hock are, it is believed, the remains of two other toes and their related bones; some also believe that the chestnuts on the insides of the legs and the horny little ergots under the fetlocks are the remains of others, although there is no skeletal evidence to support these views. When horses, usually young ones, 'throw a splint' a painful, hot swelling occurs which is a typical inflammatory reaction to concussion or a blow (the causes of splints) which usually hardens into a bony lump, extra bone having been thrown out by the periosteum to help heal the injury. Sometimes, though, splints can be reabsorbed spontaneously and just disappear.

The hoof can and does cause a good deal of trouble in the domesticated horse and it has been said that of all cases of genuine lameness 70 per cent are in the lower leg and most of those in the hoof.

The hoof is a miracle of 'bio-engineering'. It is very small when you consider that at times (in canter and gallop and when landing from a jump) one hoof is responsible for bearing the weight of the whole horse.

The main bone of the foot, the one which gives it its shape, is the pedal bone. Above this is the short pastern bone and fitted into the joint, just behind the two, is the little navicular bone. The long pastern bone comes next and its joint with the lower end of the cannon bone forms the fetlock, which has the two little sesamoid bones to each side of and just behind it.

The foot contains vital sensitive structures such as ligaments, tendon, the sensitive tissue (sensitive laminae) lining the outside of the pedal bone, nerves and blood vessels. Attached to the side/rear wings of the pedal bone are two plates of cartilage called the lateral cartilages, which are instrumental in absorbing concussion and preserving the elasticity of the foot, for the foot is not a solid, rigid block, unmoving and unfeeling.

The horny part we see from the outside when the foot is on the ground is the hoof wall which, for convenience, we divide (although there are no joints or dividing lines) into the toe (front), quarters (sides) and heels (back, although the horn does not go all the way round the foot at the back, where there are fleshy bulbs forming the actual heels). Inside the wall are horny leaves resembling the leaves on the underside of a mushroom, called the insensitive laminae, running from top to bottom, which interlock with the already mentioned sensitive laminae on the pedal bone. The laminae have protruding from them little secondary laminae, so the bond is extremely strong and is really the only thing which keeps the foot together.

The spongy ridge we can feel immediately above the wall is the coronet, from which the hoof grows downwards in tubules of horn, a modified, toughened skin substance. There is a varnish-like layer of thin horn, the periople, which grows down the outside of the wall from just above the coronary band and which helps prevent undue evaporation of essential moisture from the horn, so helping maintain the tough nature of the wall. Brittle feet are usually more in need of moisture than oil. The periople can help prevent the absorption of too much moisture into the foot during very wet conditions, although most moisture is taken up from the bottom of the wall, the surface which bears the weight of the horse on the ground, seeping up within the horn of the wall. (An old Irish remedy for brittle feet is to remove the horse's shoes and to stand him during the day on a squelching wet bed of soggy peat; it works very well, provided the horse gets a decent dry bed to lie on at night.)

The underside of the foot is, of course, far from flat. The bearing surface of the wall has running inside it a white area of horn which identifies the bonding point between insensitive and sensitive laminae inside the foot and beyond which nails must not be driven otherwise the sensitive structures inside the foot will be injured and the horse lamed. The outer quarter inch or so of sole, inside the white line, may bear weight, but the remainder rises in a slight dome shape, particularly in the hind feet. Horses with flat feet for reasons of conformation, disease or perhaps old age are very sensitive to rough going, small pebbles on the road and so on.

Running from the bulbs of the heels is the indiarubber-like frog, tough elastic horn which is an important aid, but not the only one, in the blood-pumping mechanism and, therefore, the blood circulation of the foot. It has a central groove, the cleft of frog, and grooves at the sides, the lacunae, bounded by the bars of the heels, horny ridges where the wall of the foot turns inwards on the underneath of the foot. Sometimes this area is called the buttress of the heels. This uneven surface helps greatly with grip on the ground; many wild and feral horses are surprisingly footsure on all sorts of going.

Above the sole and frog inside the foot are, respectively, the sensitive sole and frog; the back part of the foot, inside the heels, as it were, is taken up by a fibrous/fatty, spongy material, more or less insensitive, called the plantar or digital cushion.

The function of the foot, the stresses and forces placed on it and the blood circulation within it have been the subject of intensive research for some time and our knowledge of the foot, its normal functioning and its disorders is improving all the time and also changing somewhat.

When weight is placed on the foot (something which happens

all the time, even as the horse moves around his stable, except when he is lying down, of course), the plantar cushion is compressed on to the frog and out against the lateral cartilages and the foot expands slightly at the heels. This action is vital to foot health as it enables the jar to be dissipated throughout the foot and partially out through the hoof wall. There is also slight movement at the white line which is composed of softer horn than either the wall or the sole. This squashing effect alternately closes and opens the capillaries in the foot, pumping the used blood back up the leg via the veins and allowing room for fresh blood to take its place via the arteries down the leg. Veins have little valves along their length so that the used blood cannot flow back down the veins but is sent on its way.

The domed sole of the foot can well bear this weight from above and on softish ground, where the frog is in contact with the ground, there is direct further pressure on it to assist the process. However, the old idea of frog pressure is now seen to be only partially correct. It is the whole squashing and expansion of the foot which is most important in keeping the foot functioning and healthy. It used to be said that in a recently shod foot the frog must touch the ground, but this is simply not possible on a hard surface such as hard earth, concrete or a tarmac road. Indeed, domestic working horses carrying weight on sometimes rough traffic-bearing roads would soon have their comparatively soft frogs worn away if this were actually the case.

Shoeing Processes

There are two main ways to shoe a horse – hot and cold. In hot shoeing the shoe is pressed lightly against the foot to burn the freshly trimmed horn so that the farrier can see where the metal touches and where it doesn't. An even contact (in the normal foot) is essential to bear and distribute the forces evenly, and when the metal is red-hot it is easier for the farrier to shape the metal to get a perfect fit. In cold shoeing, little can be done to alter the fit but despite this many horses (including racehorses) are successfully shod cold and once a good farrier gets to know a horse's feet he can make shoes to fit him beforehand with the guidance of an old set.

An in-between method which allows excellent results and is ideal for horses who dislike being shod hot, for whatever reason, is to shape the shoe hot, cool it down before trying it on the hoof, then reheat it to make any alterations, and so on. I have had this method used for years and can recommend it with complete confidence.

Although hot shoeing, and the above variation, may produce the best fit, there is a disadvantage to pressing hot metal against the horn in that it dries out and inevitably slightly weakens the horn, also shrinking it slightly. Then, after the horse is shod and, in normal use, the hooves get wet the horn expands again, with the obvious result that the shoe is then slightly too small. In my experience, too, many farriers burn the horn far too much, creating the clouds of smoke which all good books on farriery tell us is a sign of poor workmanship! It is a pleasure to watch a really good farrier at work, just touching the shoe to the foot to singe it rather than pressing it on to 'make a bed' for the shoe (in reality burning the horn down to fit the shoe). In Britain, at last, the supply of good farriers is gradually improving although the profession itself freely admits it has a long way to go.

Whatever method is used, it is important to make the shoe to fit the foot and not vice versa. The horse is a very heavy animal and needs as much foot as possible, correctly trimmed, balanced and, when appropriate, shod so as to help him not only bear his weight on his feet but move fast and nimbly. The ills of such vices as dumping and generally cutting the foot about to fit an unsuitable shoe are well known, as are those of careless trimming: they result in misdirected forces on the foot causing unnatural stresses, too little hoof in some parts to bear the stress, too-tight nailing which prevents adequate expansion of the foot with long-term deleterious effects on blood circulation and foot integrity and, a fault which seems to be quite common these days, the encouragement of a long toe/low heels foot conformation by shoeing short at the heels, leaving the heels unsupported. They eventually 'sink' or collapse down and inwards and, with the toe also being left too long when trimming, the back part of the foot is over-compressed as the horse walks more on his heels, encouraging navicular disease and laminitis. The problem is compounded by compression of the coronet as the over-long toe breaks over and sends too-strong pressure up the wall at the toe, pressing on the horn-forming coronet.

If this goes on for long enough (weeks or months) the horse will suffer from mechanical, traumatic laminitis as the wall is forced away from the pedal bone and starts to crack below the injured coronet. Extra stress is also placed on the tendons and ligaments and fairly soon the horse is crippled. Fortunately, this practice has received a good deal of publicity recently and as seminars and research continue it is hoped that it will cease, unless in cases where there is a clinical reason for its temporary use.

Hooves for Horses

Obviously, not all types of horse and pony have identical hooves. It is an evolutionary trait that animals developing in marshy areas have lower, flatter and generally bigger feet than those from hard, dry regions. Shire horses, and other heavies, have 'soup-plate' feet enabling them to work and live on wetter land than Arabs and other oriental types better suited to hard, dry earth. Some oriental breeds have very small, tough, almost atrophied frogs which seem to serve little purpose whereas horses with coarser blood have comparatively large frogs for the size of their feet.

Oriental breeds and their descendants and crosses also usually have higher, possibly narrower feet in relation to body size than their cold-blood cousins; for example, the Turkmene horses I have seen seem to have almost contracted, boxy feet in comparison to a typical English hunter of the same height. Yet this type of foot is ideal for their environment of rough, stony, hard, sandy earth.

Some years ago there was consternation in the Quarter Horse world as show fashion dictated that these chunky, well muscled horses should have small, dainty feet for appearance's sake. It was not long before all sorts of foot problems, normally of the concussion kind, began to show themselves in such stock and the trend is now reversing towards sensible feet which enable the breed to work hard, as many of them do, including racing, without undue ill effects, at least those encouraged by too-small feet.

Going Barefoot

In a natural lifestyle horses and their relatives do not, of course, need shoes. Early civilisations realised that although wild horses and domesticated and semi-domesticated ones could make very long treks and live largely on the hoof, when it came to the extra wear and tear on the hoof caused by carrying and pulling weight the horn needed protection. Early shoes were simply animal skins tied round the pastern, which wore out very quickly. The Romans used cured leather shoes with hardened leather sole pads which laced up the leg; and so things developed. It was the Romans, too, who first seem to have used metal, clip-on 'hipposandals', but it was the Celtic Gauls who first nailed on iron shoes recognisable as forerunners of our modern horseshoes.

Some earlier shoes covered the whole of the foot, Arab shoes having a hole for the sand to run out. Those which left the frog exposed sometimes have nail holes right back to the heels but others have them only in the front half so it seems to have been appreciated somewhat patchily that the back half of the foot needs to expand. One thing which is noticeable in most early shoes, including those in common use only a few hundred years ago, is a web wider than we are used to.

Despite the protection offered by nailed-on metal shoes, they do, of course, have disadvantages. Even the most carefully applied shoe cannot help but partially restrict foot expansion. Burning on dries out and shrinks and weakens the horn, and nail holes break and weaken it. If the horn is strong and tough with an adequate moisture content it can withstand these effects, obviously, as evidenced by the very many shod horses who live long, productive lives.

A master farrier once said to me that the best shoe is no shoe: with that in mind, just how realistic and feasible is the idea of working horses without shoes?

First, as mentioned, horn quality needs to be good, supported by an adequate, balanced diet, with ample biotin, calcium, methionine and methylsulfonylmethane (MSM) to promote growth and health of skin, hair and horn, and good and balanced foot conformation. The horse should have virtually perfect action so that no part of a hoof is over-stressed, which can cause uneven production of horn to counteract the wear and force and gradually deform the feet. In nature, a horse with notably poor action and conformation is unable to live as effective a life, despite natural compensations, and would not thrive, usually succumbing to predation before long, but in domesticity we put things right with expert trimming and shoeing, enabling the horse to survive and work. Finally, the horse should habitually work on softish going or, minimally, on *smooth* hard going. Gritted tarmac and ridged concrete, for example, chip and wear horn more quickly than smooth tarmac and smooth concrete. Also, the former surfaces can cause the horse discomfort as his frog will be in contact with the ground if he is shoeless and he may soon go lame.

If you do wish to try your horse barefoot, a few months' preparation would probably help him. Most horses are given at least one, or more, periods a year as a holiday in the field with their shoes off. Horses whose work is seasonal often have several months off like this, but even year-round family horses should have a break, after which it will be noticeable that the feet have expanded and may be a full size larger than before after several weeks or months of natural function.

The nature of the horse's work should also be taken into consideration. There are circumstances where, because the work is fast and the weight carried quite considerable (compounded by speed and jumping), a natural, shoeless foot might, in fact, over-expand and be subject to internal injury such as tearing of the sensitive structures and bruising, and the horn may split under the stress. Also, it should be remembered that good though the horse's antislipping foot formation is under normal circumstances, work in mud barefoot under a rider or drawing a comparatively heavy vehicle may cause the horse to slip and slide around which, in itself, causes muscle and tendon injury as the horse uses these structures to counteract the slipping and keep his balance. You cannot fit studs to a shoeless foot!

The first thing to do is assess the horse's diet with the help of a scientifically qualified expert such as a veterinary surgeon or equine nutritionist. He or she will assess the whole diet for balance of nutrients, including vitamins and minerals, paying particular attention to your requirement of optimal hoof quality. Horn is produced at the coronet; once it has formed nothing you feed has any effect on it, and few hoof dressings actually sink in and improve its condition. The nutrients are carried to the coronet in the blood and as it can take from nine months to a year for a complete new hoof to grow down to the toe (the longest part of the hoof), you should think in terms of this length of time if your horse's diet and/or hoof quality has previously been lacking.

Once the horn seems up to standard at ground level, have a discussion with your farrier and tell him what you intend to do. You will still need his services to keep an expert eye on the feet and to trim them, if only to balance them up in the event of uneven action or smooth off any little chips. He will probably remove your horse's present shoes and simply smooth off the feet round the bottom edge of the wall to discourage chipping. The extra horn left on, which would have been removed prior to new shoes going on, will help counteract wear and give the horse some extra protection as he gets used to the new feel. His body will sense that harder horn is going to be needed and gradually, over the weeks and months, this will be produced as a natural response to stress.

Like a fitness programme, take it easy at first if you are working on hard going. Half an hour three times a week may do initially until you see how your horse adapts. If he seems *very* footsore keep to soft going for a while, but remember that, all the foregoing considerations taken into account, he probably will adapt in time and may well prefer going *au naturel*. Working and living unshod may, in fact, be prescribed after certain foot disorders to let the foot get back to nature and give things a chance to take care of themselves under expert supervision.

A product which seems to be ideal for horses working barefoot and those having problems with shoes is Hoof Bond.* It is a non-toxic polymer resin liquid, applied to the sole, bearing surface and wall up to a quarter of an inch below the coronet which, the marketing company claims, forms a molecular bond, greatly strengthening and also protecting the areas treated and flexing with the hoof. It was developed from the technique used to bond insulating tiles to spacecraft and users report excellent results on horses who either cannot keep shoes on, have naturally poor-quality horn, have foot problems during and following diseases and other disorders of the foot or are required to go barefoot when either working or resting. For horses working barefoot it sounds like a godsend; apparently, too, it helps greatly with those needing shoes but who constantly spread or throw them due to poor horn quality, action or difficult working conditions. Racehorses, endurance horses, cow ponies, jumpers and family hacks and ponies alike seem to benefit.

The product is applied every few weeks, depending on your horse, and the simple sponge application is finished off by exposure for a few seconds to an ultra-violet light or strong sunlight. The marketing company can also supply a small hand-held light. Expert supervision of the feet, and trimming when required, will still be needed from your farrier.

Shoe Alternatives

Many owners would love to be able to 'do' their horses' feet themselves. Farriery is a very skilled craft and there is much more to it than rasping down the feet, knowing how to shape metal (horseshoes these days being normally made of mild steel)

*Full details of the product can be obtained from Hoof Bond Inc., PO Box 368, Route Old 132, Hyannis, Massachusetts 02601, USA, who will also be able to tell readers in other countries how to obtain the product. British readers should contact Hoof Bond UK, The Gables, Wyken Road, Stanton, Bury St Edmunds, Suffolk, IP31 2DJ, telephone (0359) 51065.

and, critically, how to nail it on to a living creature without harming him. The whole anatomy and physiology of the legs and, to a large extent, body conformation and function have to be studied and understood, together with disease processes, balance, action, the effects of weight on the back and on the feet and much, much more. However, the desire to avoid the expense and process of having one's horses shod remains as far as many owners are concerned.

Rubber horseshoes have been tried: as early as the 1920s rubber shoes were tried on horses working on metalled roads but they caused joint problems, slipping in the wet and instability of the shoe itself. Plastic horseshoes followed and serious attempts to use them have been going on for twenty to thirty years but they are almost impossible to alter, once made, to achieve the exact fit needed, and some still do not wear well enough. Earlier designs still had (and have) to be nailed on, but modern development in glues have produced stick-on shoes which permit forces in the foot which are much closer to those experienced by a shoeless foot than those in a foot wearing a nailed-on, metal shoe, which must be good. Some users say that the shoes do not stay on well enough, others say they do, and some claim that their horses' performances (in various disciplines) have been transformed.

Another variant is the plastic, or metal, shoe which sticks not only to the bearing surface of the hoof but also by means of 'fingers' of plastic which extend up from the shoe and are glued to the wall of the hoof. All variants are currently being tested in the laboratory and in the field and it seems that it will not be long before a real breakthrough occurs which will bring some kind of synthetic shoe which does not have to be nailed on into quite general use. The main problem at present is their cost: they are presently between 50 and 75 per cent more expensive than a new set of nailed-on, metal shoes, and their wearing qualities are not usually as good. There is no doubt, however, that even in their present forms, non-metal and/or stick-on shoes are very useful in many cases, such as for surgical or medical use or for horses who, usually because of poor horn and a thin wall, cannot keep conventional shoes on.

Shoe-boots which have a shoe and covered sole/frog area on a boot which clamps or otherwise fastens on to the hoof around the coronet area have also been available for some time and, again, they do have their uses, although most users would not claim that they replace conventional shoes. They are ideal as a temporary measure when a horse casts a shoe or for keeping on a hoof dressing as they come in various sizes and really can be applied by the 'ordinary' owner. Wear is saved on these as they are removed when the horse is not working.

There is no doubt that any measure which enables the horse's foot to function more nearly as nature intended must benefit foot health in the long term, particularly if it can protect the foot, as required, at the same time. If such a shoe emerges, it will be the first *major* breakthrough in farriery for about 2,000 years!

A Better All-purpose Shoe

The horseshoe with which most of the horse world is familiar now is largely based on the English hunter shoe, as it not only protects the hoof but is specifically designed for the type of athletic performance most riding horses are bred and used for today. It does, however, bear only on the very outer rim of the hoof – the bearing surface of the wall, with some coverage of the white line.

Some farriers and vets are in favour of a shoe with a wider web which covers not only the white line but that inner quarter-inch or so of sole which naturally bears weight in an unshod foot. This would cause no problems to the foot and would spread the load of the horse's weight over a slightly larger (and more natural) area, thus decreasing the total force and stress any one part of the foot has to bear. Given a load of a set amount, it is much easier to bear it if it is spread than if it is concentrated: if you hold an apple in the palm of your flat hand there is no pain whatsoever, but if you applied the weight of that apple to a needle poised on the palm of your hand it would certainly hurt.

In addition to this wider web (and wider-webbed shoes are already commonly available on the continent of Europe), some experts would like the shoe to be shallower, bringing the frog more into use. It is felt that this would not mean the shoe wears out sooner because, as described, the load and therefore the wear is spread and so has less effect. There is nothing to stop any horse owner asking his or her farrier to fit such shoes, but most farriers prefer to alter ready-made shoes of a set pattern, and there is no doubt some would not want to be bothered as they would have to be specially made. The shoe could still be concaved out and fullered like a normal shoe and this would retain the comparative lightness and performance qualities of the hunter-type shoe.

Pads and Studs

The relief of concussion is something which has interested farriers, vets and owners for years, and hoof pads of various types have been used with varying degrees of success. Opinions also vary as to their usefulness and, indeed, benefit.

Pads can either be fitted over the entire under-foot area or made simply to be fitted between shoe and horn. With the type that cover the sole and frog, too, there are often 'fillings' which are packed into the foot first to prevent dirt and moisture getting in and setting up discomfort, softened horn and infection. Some materials, such as polyurethane, are absorbent and actually hold moisture, which can create the above problems. Pads of any type are held by some experts to favour premature loosening of the shoe as they do, obviously, 'give' in use (otherwise they would be no good), and encourage slight movement of the shoe on the foot which gradually loosens the best nailed-on and fitted shoe.

Some brands of pad have been marketed without any real testing of their ability actually to absorb the concussion they claim to lessen, but others are properly tested and do have published results of tests which appear to prove their purpose. It is always a good plan to ask the manufacturers of any pads you may be thinking of using if they can supply such information, and, in any case, discuss the matter with your vet and/or farrier – who may, of course, have suggested pads in the first place.

Studs are another bone of contention and often not understood in relation to the harm they can do the horse's feet and legs. True, they do greatly help a horse keep his feet and prevent slipping in the various conditions for which the different designs are intended, which is obviously a good thing, but if left in the shoes when the horse is *not* working in those conditions they seriously upset the foot balance and can cause actual injury. The principles of foot balance are shown in the accompanying diagrams and captions, but basically, anything which throws the balance out of true can cause excess force and stress on the part of the hoof (and the leg above it) which hits the ground first.

left:
From the side, the angle formed by the toe of the wall and the long pastern bone should be about 45° in the forefeet and about 50° in the hind feet. The important point is that there should seem to be a straight line (allowing for the coronet) running unbroken up the front of the toe and long pastern bone.

right:
From the front, the ends of the coronet should appear to be equal heights from the ground surface. The same applies when looking at the foot from the back, the heels being of even height.

Imagine a situation where the horse has a sizeable stud in, say, the outside heel only (a common practice) of each hind shoe. The hoof is trimmed in a balanced way as befits that particular horse and then a stud is put in. When the foot is put on the ground (apart from the fact that the horse must feel as though he is standing on a pebble all the time) the structures immediately surrounding and above the stud are obviously compressed more than normal, and this compression runs all the way up the leg. His weight also falls over away from the stud on to the stud-less heel, which then receives weight in an uneven way, with a slight stretching effect on the tissues and bone on that side of the foot and leg.

If the studs are put in both heels, this is slightly better, but the weight is then thrown forward to the toe which also unbalances the foot.

Of course, studs are needed in certain circumstances, and if, for example, they are used in mud the unbalancing effect will not be felt much, but if the horse is subsequently kept standing around on hard ground, particularly if ridden and worked with the stud(s) still in, quite a lot of harm could be done. It is when the horse is working that the most force is placed on his feet and legs and the effects of the studs are felt most – and potentially, obviously, the most harm can be done if the studs used are larger than necessary or not right for the prevailing conditions. Hard ground can cause most problems from a stud point of view as the extra bulk of the stud does not sink far into the ground; and there is a case for at least putting studs in both heels, which is a little less damaging to the balance of the foot and leg than having a stud on one heel only, but many riders would undestandably be afraid of the horse inflicting considerable injury on himself from an inside-heel stud.

Studs should be used with great discretion and after discussion with a good farrier, put in as near to the competition/work time as possible and always removed immediately after work. Certainly do not hack or travel your horse to his venue wearing his studs.

For general use and for animals doing road-work, little stud or frost nails can be used: these will effectively help stop the horse slipping without needing to use studs proper. They are simply ordinary horseshoe nails with a little blob of hardened metal on the head or ground surface and are put in the normal nail holes nearest each heel. They retain hoof balance and prevent slipping as well, although it should be remembered that a *slight* slide as the horse puts his hoof down is natural and desirable as an aid to absorbing jar.

Young horses first put to roadwork frequently slip and slide a good deal and may lose confidence without the aid of stud nails, although they adapt in time. If the nails are used in every nail hole during icy conditions they do have the effect of shortening the horse's stride temporarily.

Corrective Trimming

Corrective trimming is used, as its name implies, to correct conformational faults in foot and leg and also faults in the horse's action. It is a complex subject, like everything to do with farriery, and requires a comprehensive understanding of the structure and function of the foot and leg.

The best time to start corrective trimming is when the horse is a foal, before the age of six months, for this is the time when it is most likely to be significantly effective as the bones are softer and more easily influenced by changes in foot balance. Foals may be born with congenital or hereditary deformities which look really serious and even life-threatening at first; but, as the foal matures, and perhaps with corrective trimming alone, or maybe combined with leg braces, surgery or surgical shoes, apparent miracles can be worked. As the animal ages, it is much more difficult to put things right. The foot can be trimmed, certainly, but altering the weight and forces on an established conformation too suddenly can put great unaccustomed stress on the foot and leg which may cause not only pain but also damage to structures used to operating in a particular way. Little by little is normally the rule with corrective trimming.

In a case where, due to poor farriery, unsuitable shoes and bad trimming, the feet and legs have been thrown 'out of true' for that individual, in other words, his naturally good conformation has been compromised by poor workmanship, corrective trimming can gradually restore him to his previous state and relieve the discomfort and even pain he may have been going through meanwhile. But where a horse has a congenital deformity which has not been corrected during extreme youth, corrective trimming cannot be expected to work miracles, particularly if unaccompanied by any other treatment.

The aim should not be to try to make all horses and ponies conform to an ideal if this would cause them distress of any kind. Animals with a naturally non-ideal foot conformation and balance who have, perhaps over the years, learned to compensate for it, or whose bodies have produced natural compensations, may be better left alone or simply kept from further deviation from an ideal foot shape. The three questions owners should ask themselves are: (1) is the horse prone to hitting himself because of his conformation/action? (2) does his defect cause lameness or is he normally sound? and (3) is the defect causing over-stress, pain or injury elsewhere in his body? These should be considered and discussed with the farrier.

It takes skill, judgement and experience, in most cases, to decide whether a defect of foot or limb conformation or of action is something the horse was born with, has developed due to the stress of work or has actually been induced by faulty farriery, which can bring about all sorts of disorders and deformities. Laminitis of a traumatic or mechanical kind is one, as already described, as are navicular disease, pedal osteitis (although some vets deny this condition even exists!), stress on tendons and ligaments and, indeed, any condition which is caused by over-stress or unnatural (to the individual) forces on the foot and leg. The good farrier will make any alterations very gradually, particularly in the mature horse (unless, to his experienced eye, a substantial alteration in foot shape would be immediately beneficial) to give the bones and soft tissues alike a chance to adapt to the new forces and way of functioning.

It is very well worth while discussing with a competent farrier all aspects of your horse's feet and legs. A good craftsman will welcome this and be pleased that you are interested in his work and opinion as well as your horse's comfort and way of going, particularly if you show you do know something about it and are keen to learn more.

It is not that difficult to learn to trim and balance your horse's feet yourself (see Diagram 1 and Plates 10–14). I know several owners who have been doing this for some time and whose horses work quite happily.

3 Circulatory Systems: Liquid Transport

Not all of a creature's working parts are as vital as each other. A horse can live, for example, without an eye but not without his liver. The blood and its means of circulation, the blood vessels comprising arteries, veins and capillaries, are fairly familiar to most of us, and the lymphatic system, although perhaps less familiar, is at least known to exist; but perhaps the full extent of their work and importance to the horse are not well appreciated. Blood is obviously essential to life: it is a liquid organ without which the horse would quickly die, and the lymphatic system plays an important supporting role in nutrition and, particularly, fighting infection and trauma.

The Blood

Without its pump, the heart, blood would be of no use to the horse. The heart has branching from it various arteries and veins which themselves branch into smaller and smaller branches and ultimately into a matrix of threadlike vessels (the capillaries). The whole system is continuous and the blood circulates round and round extremely rapidly. The heart has its own mini circulatory system to ensure its own supply of food. It is a muscle and needs food, oxygen and the removal of waste products just like any other muscle.

The purposes of blood are to carry nutrients from the digestive system and oxygen from the lungs to wherever in the body they are needed and to carry away waste products and carbon dioxide gas. The normal waste products are excreted by the lungs, kidneys and gut and in the sweat. Carbon dioxide is breathed out with every breath, the kidneys excrete waste products in the urine, having filtered them from the blood, and the droppings passed out at the rectum consist of toxins and unnecessary nutrients and fibre, for not everything the horse eats is used by the body for the production of tissue or energy.

The blood also carries the body's chemical messengers, hormones, from the endocrine glands which produce them to wherever they are needed, and helps maintain a correct water and chemical balance in the tissues. As it carries heat it also helps to regulate the body temperature: when heat needs to be lost, those blood vessels near the body surface dilate to let through more blood so more heat radiates to the outside through the skin, but when heat needs to be conserved, those vessels constrict, reducing the amount of blood near the outside world and so reducing heat loss.

Blood and lymph both have a vital role to play in overcoming disease caused by bacteria, viruses or fungi and in repairing mechanical damage and injuries such as sprains or wounds. Special cells 'take out' antigens (germs), and defence cells (antibodies) are produced and left circulating in the blood for varying lengths of time to fight off a future attack of disease. Blood is capable of plugging and sealing off wounds by its ability to clot so that healing can take place under a protective scab which is shed when the skin beneath is ready to take over its protective function.

Components

Blood is largely fluid, its plasma portion, a straw-coloured liquid, forming about 66 per cent of the blood volume, with the rest made up of specialised cells of three main types – red blood cells, white blood cells and platelets. Plasma contains three specific proteins, including its vital clotting agent fibrinogen, plus the nutrients and waste products which it transports.

Red blood cells are responsible for carrying oxygen which is absorbed, in the lungs, into the red pigment they carry called haemoglobin. In the body tissues, the haemoglobin gives up its oxygen and takes in carbon dioxide instead, which is later exchanged for oxygen in the lungs again, in a process logically called 'gaseous exchange', oxygen and carbon dioxide both being gases.

White blood cells are of five main types and between them engulf or in other ways put out of action germs and allergy-producing substances and stimulate the production of anti-bodies.

Platelets are concerned with internal clotting to help plug breaks in injured or diseased blood vessels.

Blood will also contain various substances such as enzymes (complex organic chemical compounds) which, according to their nature and amount, can aid veterinary surgeons in the diagnosis of illness and injury, such as muscle damage.

Circulation

Blood is pumped round the body by the heart, a powerful muscle in the chest, slightly on the left side, from which branch major arteries and veins. The heart consists of four chambers, the two top ones being called the right and left atria and the two bottom ones the right and left ventricles. The circulation is kept on course, always in the same direction, by valves, one at the outlet of each chamber, and along the larger veins.

Blood is forced from the top chambers to the bottom ones by the contraction of the muscular heart walls at the top of the heart, making the chambers smaller and so forcing the blood down to the ventricles, which then themselves contract to send blood out along the blood vessels.

Blood in the right side of the heart is pumped to the lungs where it picks up oxygen and releases carbon dioxide. Blood high in oxygen (oxygenated blood) is bright red, whereas blood low in oxygen (deoxygenated blood) is a darker, more purple colour. The blood returns from the lungs to the heart, the left side this time, and is pumped from the left atrium down into the left ventricle and then, with considerable force or pressure, on round the body delivering its oxygen to where it is needed via the capillary network. It then returns via the veins to the right atrium of the heart to begin the journey again.

Blood from various parts of the digestive system travels a more circuitous route, emptying into the liver, the body's 'food factory', where it gives up much of the nutrient content it has absorbed from the stomach and gut; it then joins with blood coming from the hind end of the body before returning to the right atrium of the heart. Once the nutrients have been broken down into usable forms by the liver, they are carried by blood once more, in the general circulation, to wherever they are needed.

The Lymphatic System

Lymph is a colourless fluid similar to blood plasma but containing less protein. It derives from the blood as fluid seeps from the capillaries into the spaces between tissue cells and passes into the thin-walled lymph vessels. Lymph circulates slowly round the body in a branching system of these vessels purely by means of being massaged by body structures, particularly muscles, as the lymphatic system has no heart to help this process.

Lymph carries nutrients to various parts of the body which have no blood supply, such as bone cartilage and the cornea, the clear front part of the eye, and nourishes the body cells which are bathed in it. It also picks up waste products and returns them to the bloodstream for disposal.

It also carries lymphocytes, white 'defensive' cells made in the bone marrow, important in fighting disease. At various points along the lymph vessels are nodes (glands) where large cells engulf intruding disease cells and also send a warning message to the lymphocytes to manufacture antibodies.

Heart Defects

Some years ago, veterinary surgeons changed their declarations of soundness or otherwise when examining horses for purchase by a client. Whereas previously a vet would declare a horse 'sound' or 'unsound', nowadays more leeway is available as vets describe the horse's state of health, mention any defects they may find and state what sort of work the horse could be fit for. As far as the heart is concerned, not all defects significantly affect a horse's capacity to work.

A heart murmur is an irregularity of blood flow through the valves which may not be closing properly, allowing blood to flow through when it should not or 'leak' back into the chamber from which it has just been pumped. Murmurs are often significant and the heart often increases in size to compensate for any possible poor performance so that the horse still receives an acceptable service from his heart.

'Dropped beats' are also quite common in resting horses. The heart 'knows' how much blood is needed to be pumped through at any one time and may well be able to afford to miss a beat and extend its resting period between beats with no ill effects on the horse. Owners who habitually take their horse's pulse/heart rates may have noticed this in a relaxed horse and should not be alarmed. Once the horse perks up a bit and becomes more alert to his surroundings or begins work the dropped beats cease.

Irregular rhythm of the heart, resulting in rapid, weak beats, is more serious as insufficient blood is pumped through to cater for the horse's needs and this can certainly affect his health and performance. The condition can sometimes be treated with medication but it is unlikely that such a horse would be advisable for hard work.

The heart can become permanently weakened as a sequel to some respiratory disease such as influenza or strangles, and broken-winded horses frequently end up with an over-stressed heart because the heart will respond to the lack of oxygen generally available because of the poor condition of the lungs by working harder. Over the years, this takes its toll.

Although heart attacks and 'furred up' arteries such as occur in humans are not known in the horse because of his healthy vegetarian diet, damage to the blood vessels can be caused by migrating parasite larvae. The vessel walls become thin and 'balloon' out, and can burst at any moment without warning, causing immediate collapse and sudden death. However, like humans and other animals, horses with aneurysms, as these defects are called, *can* live for years.

Anaemia

Anaemia is a symptom or sign of a disorder and not a disease itself, but it is a condition which is bandied about by owners as though it were something fairly common, easy to treat and nothing to worry about. The literal translation of the word is 'no blood' but we take it to mean a deficiency of haemoglobin (the iron- and oxygen-carrying component of blood) or of red cells which themselves contain haemoglobin.

There are various reasons why a horse or pony might be anaemic and the underlying reason for the condition should be determined by a veterinary surgeon. From the point of view of natural management, horses kept stabled on hard feed and/or working hard can suffer from anaemia due to their management and workload. The hard-working horse will use up more red blood cells to 'service' his body's requirements and the cells can use up vitamin B12 and also iron more quickly than they can be replaced, so a supplement of these two nutrients may have to be given. Horses on artificial diets with insufficient addition of green feed or opportunity to graze may go short of folic acid which is found in such natural feed. Folic acid is important in the production of white and red blood cells, so deficiency can cause anaemia. It is wise to allow horses to graze all year round or at least to feed hydroponically grown grass and/or supplement the diet with dried grass cubes or cobs, lucerne (alfalfa) or, if you can be sure of a safe supply in sealed vacuum packs, of silage. Hayage products should also contain adequate amounts, but check the analysis panel on the bag. Your veterinary surgeon or a nutritionist will be able to advise about supplementation and suitable feeds.

Filled Legs

Many owners have had to adopt a resigned, stuck-with-it attitude to filled legs in horses. Some animals seem to have them constantly whereas others on identical management regimes never get them. The legs are puffy from the hock (or knee) downwards and this disappears with exercise, only to recur when the horse has been standing again for a few hours.

Filled legs are due to the poor circulation and congestion of lymph in the extremities, usually the hind legs, because of insufficient exercise and simple freedom to move around for that individual. Horses in too-small loose boxes which more or less compel them to stand still most of the time are candidates for filled legs, as are those on too many concentrates, or limited work and turn-out.

As described, lymph is circulated around the body by the movement of tissues next to the lymph vessels, particularly the muscles. There are no muscles in the lower legs, so this, plus insufficient movement, results in some animals in congestion of the fluid and puffy legs. As the causes are obvious, so is the treatment. Bandaging the legs to keep down the puffiness is not addressing the root of the problem.

Lymphangitis

This is an altogether more serious problem, not to be confused with the above condition. It is caused by a fungal or bacterial infection and is more common in under-exercised, over-fed horses in good condition. The leg (or legs) becomes very swollen, hot, hard and painful, particularly from the hock (or knee) downwards, the horse runs a high temperature, is often off his feed and lame, and is obviously ill and uncomfortable. The lymph vessels may be able to be felt as hard, cord-like structures, and the nodes as lumps, within the swelling. The cause may be external, an infected cut, say, or a systemic infection (one present in the body) and it could be that the more highly toxic state of the blood in horses on a high-concentrate diet and insufficient exercise simply exacerbates the problem and gives the lymphatic system too much to do. Apart from keeping the horse generally healthy so that his immune system can more easily fight infection and probably deal with it before the owner or handler even knows it is present, it is obvious that more appropriate management for the horse in the form of a more natural, digestible diet and more exercise and freedom to move around greatly helps prevent this condition.

Lymphangitis is extremely unpleasant for the horse, particularly in a bad case where fluid can ooze out of the skin and ulcers form. Veterinary treatment should always be sought for the condition. It is not enough simply to 'mash the horse down' for a few days – a useless, counterproductive and outdated practice anyway (see Chapter 5) – as medication in the form of pain killers, antibiotics and diuretics (to help drainage and removal of excess fluid) will almost certainly be needed, according to the vet's judgement of the case.

Natural Advantages of the Horse's Circulatory System

The horse, as already mentioned, is one of nature's most efficient running animals, his strength being reasonable speed with stamina. For strenuous and continuous work an animal needs an extremely effective supply of oxygen, in particular, and of nutrients which are used to provide energy and 'burnt' or oxidised in the muscles. Both oxygen and nutrients are carried to the parts where they are needed by the bloodstream. There are some features of the horse's circulatory system, in particular, which specifically equip him for this sort of performance.

The first is the heart's *stroke volume*. This is the amount or volume of blood which is pumped by the heart with each beat or stroke. The object of training is to supply the muscles and other working parts with as much blood (and, therefore, oxygen and nutrients, and the waste-removal facility) as possible for as little effort as possible, the heart being most effective when it beats slowly but with a high throughput for each stroke. The horse is capable of greatly increasing the amount of blood pumped by the heart in response to the demands of exercise or work, and also as fitness increases the heart needs to beat less fast at a given workload than earlier in a fitness programme.

The *heart* or *pulse rate* can also be increased very much more, relatively, than in, say, the human athlete. In a healthy, resting horse the heart rate will be about thirty-two to forty beats per minute. In a resting, fit equine athlete the rate may reduce to twenty-five beats per minute but can be increased to between 240 and 250 beats per minute at peak work, a relative increase which would kill a human.

Another feature is the *packed cell volume* of the horse's blood. When blood is spun in a centrifuge, the cells pack in a layer at the bottom of the test tube, the top part of the tube's contents being the plasma. The volume of the blood cells (the packed cell volume, PCV or haematocrit) is usually 40 to 50 per cent of the total blood volume, but the speed and stamina of the horse is largely due to the fact that he can increase his PCV during work to 60 or 70 per cent, so the blood contains a higher percentage of oxygen-carrying cells to fuel the production of energy. The horse is able to store red cells in his spleen, from which they are discharged into the circulation when needed during work.

The combination of these features means the horse can produce a greatly improved effective blood flow to the muscles and sustain its effects far above the capabilities of most other animals, providing oxygen and nutrients and removing the waste products of metabolism, which increase during work, so maintaining an inner environment conducive to speed and stamina.

Blood Doping

A few years ago there was much publicity in the media about human athletes giving themselves artificial transfusions of their own blood to increase the number of red blood cells circulating in the bloodstream and, therefore, the amount of essential oxygen available to enable extra energy to be burnt in the muscles. It was not long before some people tried to apply the saame principle to equine athletes, presumably not appreciating the fact that the horse's body does not function in the same way as a human's and that the process not only does not help the horse to perform better but can actually endanger its health.

The general principle behind the practice is that as each red cell carries a set amount of oxygen, increasing the number of cells in circulation will also increase the oxygen. To overcome the problem of matching blood groups, the human or equine athlete's own blood is removed some weeks before an important event, stored at a constant temperature (which can itself cause problems) and replaced or transfused back into the body just before the event, ostensibly increasing the oxygen-carrying capacity of the blood.

In humans this has the desired effect. The horse, however, stores red blood cells in his spleen, which contracts and pushes more cells out into the bloodstream as the muscles demand according to work and oxygen use. The oxygen-carrying capacity of the blood can be increased by over 50 per cent in this way, quite naturally. As there are more cells in the blood, the PCV is increased, making the blood thicker. Thickening it even more by means of artificial transfusions is not only needless but can be counterproductive by making the blood more viscous and that much more difficult to pump around the body, putting more stress on the heart.

4 Respiration: A Breath of Fresh Air

As one of nature's most athletic animals, the horse places far greater stress on his respiratory system than many other species. It is an extremely effective one, ideally suited to his natural life and with few drawbacks; two rather significant ones, however, are that he cannot normally breathe through his mouth, which deprives him of an alternative or additional intake/outlet facility, and that his rate of breathing in canter and gallop is tied into his gait – he must breathe in rhythm with his stride pattern (this subject is dealt with in Chapter 11).

Structure and Function of the Respiratory System

The respiratory system begins, rather obviously, at the nostrils. The air passages pass up through the head and throat directly down the windpipe or trachea which branches into right and left; these branches (bronchi) enter the lungs and there subdivide into smaller and smaller air passages called bronchioles. On the end of each bronchiole is an air sac (rather like a hollow bunch of grapes) called an alveolus, and this is where the critical business of gaseous exchange takes places.

The system is lined with sensitive mucous membrane and is liberally supplied with blood. As air is taken in at the nostrils the blood warms it and the mucous membrane, which secretes mucus, cleans out much of the debris which may come with it, such as dust particles. The sensitive airways are supplied with tiny hair-like projections (cilia) which have a wave-like action towards the 'great outdoors' and which move foreign particles along and out of the system. Particles coming from the lungs and trachea end up mainly in the throat and are usually swallowed, but in cases where the 'traffic flow' is heavy, such as in infection or allergy, some mucus and its foreign bodies come down the nose. In this way much matter which would cause problems is disposed of.

It is interesting to note that in current research using racehorses and other equine athletes trained to work at fast, working speeds on treadmills, veterinary and research workers have been able actually to see significant amounts of dust and debris in the lungs of horses worked on artificial surfaces such as all-weather racing tracks (where kick-back of material is still a problem), outdoor maneges and indoor schools. The better surfaces, where a real effort to reduce dust is made, obviously produce fewer problems, but horses coughing after work on some tracks is still a problem.

The breathing apparatus works, mechanically, rather like a bellows. The lungs are protected by the ribcage and separated from the abdominal contents by a dome-shaped sheet of muscle called the diaphragm. Between the ribs are muscles (the intercostal muscles) which contract, lifting the chest up and out and sucking in air: the diaphragm also contracts and flattens somewhat with the same effect. Oxygen-rich air rushes into the alveoli, the walls of which are only one cell thick; the de-oxygenated blood in the capillaries takes up oxygen and gives out carbon dioxide. As the muscles relax, the chest cavity becomes smaller again and the air, now heavy in carbon dioxide, is pushed out, and so it goes on. Lung tissue is elastic and, having been stretched somewhat during inspiration, reverts to its former state with no actual work during expiration.

As mentioned in Chapter 3, this taking-in of oxygen and getting rid of the waste product carbon dioxide is essential to the production of energy and the maintenance of life. The horse's natural head carriage, with the nose stretched out in front during fast paces, ensures an almost straight airway so as to inhibit the flow of air as little as possible. The horse is also, by nature, a creature of the great outdoors where he has ready access to clean, oxygen-rich air. In this way, he functions superbly and zoologists who have spent much time observing horses in their natural state, living ferally in America, France and South Africa, and in semi-domesticated herds in eastern Europe and other regions, all report that the horses enjoy excellent respiratory health. Not so their domesticated, largely stabled cousins, among whom respiratory disease and allergic conditions are increasing year by year.

Head Carriage

Most horsemen and women appreciate the need to give horses doing fast work a reasonable amount of freedom of the head. Horses *can* travel fast with their heads at the vertical, as anyone who has ever been run away with will know, but their breathing is more laboured and inefficient than if they were allowed to travel with the head and neck in a more natural position, more approaching the horizontal. Racehorses, of course, are the extreme example of this stretched-out carriage: in their job maximum efficiency is paramount.

It is often said that dressage movements and attitudes are simply those performed in nature by the horse, adapted by man for display and for obedience training purposes. We aim to get the horse to perform them on request, and we certainly ask him to perform them for longer periods than he would in nature. But the head carriage asked for in collection, with the front of the face just in front of the vertical, or actually vertical, is certainly not an attitude adopted by the horse at liberty for more than a very few seconds at a time.

It is claimed that this head carriage is part of the overall balance needed by the horse to be able to perform these movements easily and efficiently under the unnatural weight of a rider. It is certainly true, though, that many high-level competitive dressage horses look and sound as though they are in a certain amount of distress through being asked to maintain this collected posture of head and neck for much longer than they would at liberty. It is also true that it is quite possible to get a horse to go from the back end, with lowered hindquarters, engaged hind legs and relaxed, rounded back in the way we are taught represents the highest physical efficiency for dressage movements, *without* his neck being raised and flexed at the poll and with his face vertical or nearly so. I have seen several displays of high school work on completely long and loose reins, and two with the horse wearing no bridle, and in each case the horses went in the way described with the difference that, although they did naturally raise their necks somewhat in accordance with the lowered quarters, their faces were not vertical or even nearly so, and there was no doubt they looked much more comfortable and their breathing was not an effort to them.

With the head carried in a 'collected' attitude and the windpipe more or less constricted at the throat, airflow cannot but be hampered; and although dressage movements are not performed at speed they can be strenuous, and it would seem reasonable to allow the horse to breathe more freely. Of course, this would doubtless result in the horse being marked down for not being 'on the bit', not 'accepting the bit' or being 'un-collected'; the development of this argument falls outside the scope of this book, but if the object of schooling, dressage and high school work is to get the horse to perform easily and willingly under a rider the movements he would perform of his own free will at liberty, in other words movements he is naturally capable of performing anyway, *and in a natural attitude* which is what is always claimed, where could be the objection in allowing a horse greater freedom of head and neck and easier and more efficient breathing? Acceptance of the bit is only a means to an end: if the horse is going as required without the bit or without the often-seen constraint and rather dominating contact exerted through it, that particular means has simply been sidestepped but the end result has been achieved just the same, and that is what is important. The means should never replace the end result as the goal to be aimed at.

Air Quality

No matter how efficient the horse's respiratory system, it can only use the air available in the horse's immediate environment. In countries and regimes where horses are largely stabled, such as in many western countries and in management systems devised for working and performance horses, that air quality is often bad enough, given the normally very poor ventilation of stables, but air quality over the whole planet is deteriorating all the time due to the effects of general pollution. Veterinary surgeons in many countries report increasing incidences of allergic conditions and respiratory disease, even in horses kept outdoors in some areas.

General air quality is very hard for individuals to do anything about. Of course, the real answer is to avoid polluting the environmental air by enforcing much stricter controls on industrial emissions internationally and making compulsory within a very few years the fitting of three-way catalytic converters to all cars (and possibly banning from use those which cannot be adapted to their use). Unleaded petrol is only one tiny factor in reducing pollution, most of which comes from the use of motor transport and industrial emissions. Cutting down our use of cars can certainly be done with a little planning and common sense, and there must be numerous circumstances in which horse owners can turn their horses to driving as well as riding! The car has, after all, only been used widely for personal transport for about fifty years but the horse has been so used for thousands.

Even moving to the country is not the whole answer to this problem in the immediate future, although it would help, because pollution spreads readily and has even been seen by scientists hanging in a frightening pall over both north and south poles. In Britain, the area with the best air quality is consistently the Highlands of Scotland and even here the well known indicator of clean air, the stag-antler alga, is harder to find than formerly.

We have no choice but to accept, nowadays, that 'fresh air' is not so fresh as it used to be. This alone presents a permanent challenge to our horses' respiratory systems, an unwanted handicap. They are starting off at a disadvantage. The problems we add to the situation in the form of stable airspace polluted by dust, stable mites and their excreta, fungi, moulds and spores associated with them, decaying organic matter of all kinds from bedding to the horse's own skin and hair, and ammonia fumes from urine-soaked bedding and also droppings, all compound the challenge to the physical resources of an animal designed to run on pre-Industrial-Revolution-type air! (Our problems really started when man learned to control fire but escalated beyond all imagination with the advent of industrialisation.)

We hear a lot about the protective ozone layer of the earth gradually disintegrating due to pollution and we tend, therefore, to think of ozone as a beneficial gas, but its presence near the ground can be extremely harmful. Whereas in recent winters smog has once again been a lethal problem in cities and industrialised areas due to anti-cyclonic weather conditions trapping sulphurous air pollution near the ground (such smogs occur particularly often in eastern Europe with its less stringent pollution legislation), the problem in summer is the increasing one of vehicle exhaust emissions, which in the presence of sunlight undergo conversion to nitric acid gas, sulphuric acid and ozone, a pollutant cocktail which can be lethal to mammals, birds and other forms of life.

It seems that horses out in such conditions are more at risk than those indoors because the ammonia given off by urine has a neutralising effect on the sulphuric acid (and other acid pollutants), so lessening its effects. I hesitate to mention this in case it encourages some horse keepers to clean out stables less often! But it seems to be an accepted scientific fact now and if such conditions are prevailing in cities and industrialised regions there seems to be a case for not mucking out quite as thoroughly as usual. However, as ammonia itself is an irritant to the delicate mucous membranes, those in charge of horses would have to learn where to draw a very fine line.

In the UK in recent years, horses have also been showing

increasingly the symptoms of hay fever in humans and the problem has been traced to the increasing acreage put down to oilseed rape, the pollen of which seems to be particularly prone to triggering off symptoms similar to those of chronic obstructive pulmonary disease (COPD). At times when the crop is giving off pollen it is advisable to keep susceptible horses in indoor accommodation of some sort, upwind of nearby crops if at all possible, or at least with ventilation outlets on the sides of the building nearest to the wind-borne pollen firmly shut, and other, opposite ones created.

Allergy and Disease

Whenever an allergen or pathogen (an object or substance which causes an allergic or disease condition) enters the horse's system his natural defences come into play. The blood and lymph 'fight off' and 'neutralise' dangerous intruders. Special blood cells detect and immobilise or kill off intruders. And other substances are produced which help this process.

Allergy

As far as respiratory allergy is concerned, most horse owners know this as 'broken wind' or 'heaves', or as emphysema or, more recently, as COPD (chronic obstructive pulmonary disease) or SAD (small airway disease). When an allergy-causing substance is inhaled, say spores from hay or straw, the body over-reacts, in certain horses, and specialised cells called mast cells produce an organic compound called histamine, too much of which causes swelling and increased irritability of the delicate mucous membranes lining the lung and throat tissues and the nasal passages.

Horses with the allergic reaction which eventually leads to broken wind suffer swelling and irritation which actually reduces the space available in the tiny air spaces and passages in the lungs. The body's natural reaction to irritation is to produce mucus and the very presence of mucus again takes up space which should be occupied by air. So the horse's breathing capacity is reduced already on two fronts in this condition.

Veterinary treatment can include the administration of antihistamines and other medications (bronchodilators) which dilate or expand the air passages, loosen mucus so it can be coughed up and swallowed or enabled to run out down the nostrils (mucolytics), reduce the production of mucus and generally reduce the inflammation. A substance called sodium cromoglycate can be given by inhaler to stabilise the mast cells and prevent them over-producing histamine.

If the allergic reaction is not dealt with the lung tissue can be damaged: it loses its elasticity and effectiveness and the familiar condition broken wind results. When a healthy horse breathes, the intercostal muscles (those between the ribs) raise and separate the ribs which sucks air into the enlarged chest cavity when it inhales, but they simply relax and let the natural elasticity of the lungs returning to an unstretched state push the air out. In broken-winded horses, however, an extra muscular effort is needed by the abdominal muscles to push against the lungs and force out the used air, heavy with carbon dioxide and water vapour (and other products). This 'double expiration' can be noticed in such a horse and, over time, the abdominal muscles develop in response to use, like all muscles, and produce the characteristic diagonal line along the flank seen in chronically broken-winded horses.

Disease

Even if the horse is not actually broken-winded, and even if his reactions to allergens are not noticeable, many experts believe that constant challenge to the mucous membranes is bound to irritate them slightly and this puts them into a slightly weakened state ideal for invasion by disease-causing bacteria and viruses. Even a healthy respiratory tract can be invaded by germs, of course, but a weakened one, and especially that of a broken-winded horse, is even more susceptible to their attacks.

Actual bacterial or viral disease is counteracted by the body's natural immune system (see Chapter 7) and, again, can leave the respiratory system in a permanently weakened state even if treatment is given, particularly if insufficient time is allowed for convalescence after the disease has been overcome. The period taken for the lung tissue to recover is at least three weeks and a figure of six weeks is given by some authorities.

Vaccination is available for various diseases in different countries. In Britain, we have no licensed vaccine against strangles, for example, although it is available in other countries. Here, we normally vaccinate against influenza and sometimes against rhinopneumonitis. Vaccination greatly boosts the horse's defences against disease but, in the face of a heavy challenge, for instance the horse going into an area rife with disease or faced with a particularly virulent strain of bacteria or virus, the horse can still become infected, albeit less seriously than an unvaccinated horse. Of course, if a strain of a disease is present against which the horse is not vaccinated, he will succumb just as badly as an unvaccinated horse because he is, in fact, *un*vaccinated against that particular strain.

Horses have been physically ruined by respiratory disease and allergy and, as mentioned, these problems are on the increase, due, many believe, to poor air quality worldwide and inappropriate housing systems prevalent in many equestrian countries. There are also natural factors involved, such as mutated (altered) viruses and bacteria producing races of 'super-bugs' against which the horses' immune systems are not so effective, although natural evolution would, in time, put this right as new immunities are built up in the face of new challenges.

Housing Systems and Ventilation

One of the major mistakes we tend to make in housing horses is to put them in individual cells we call stables where they have much less space to move around than is natural, much less airspace, much changed air quality, no real physical contact with other horses and all in all a much lower quality of life than in those countries or establishments where horses are kept in a

1a. The Przewalski horse is the last wild relative of the domestic horse but it seems doubtful that there are any truly wild ones left, most of those now living wild having been reintroduced to former habitats. The Przewalski's natural home is Mongolia and surrounding regions and the physical characteristics of the species show how well it is adapted by nature to a bleak, very cold environment – tough skin, dense mane and tail hair (with upright rather than flowing mane), thick coat hair compared with oriental-type animals, hard, large feet, short, thick neck and large head with slit-like nostrils.

1b. An ideal way of accommodating horses under cover. This covered yard has Yorkshire boarding from horses' head height upwards. The alternate boards provide shelter from wind, rain and sun but allow ample fresh air in and permit stale air to pass out easily. The doors at the far end of the covered yard can be left open so that the horses can come in and out as they wish. Outside is a exercise area (fenced in) with a gate, which again can be left open or closed, as desired, leading to grazing. There is water provided in the covered area and outside, and the horses can be fed indoors or out, as appropriate. Horses kept in such conditions are calm, settled, amenable to each other and to humans, less subject to stress (provided their companions are carefully selected) and lead a much more natural and suitable life than that experienced in individual stables – or cells, as described by one leading veterinary surgeon. Contrary to popular opinion, this method of housing horses is also suitable for fit competition horses as well as working animals leading a less demanding life, breeding stock or resting animals. Provided they are not overcrowded, horses do not bicker and kick, so the fact that they are shod is incidental. Turnout rugs can be worn by clipped horses in cold weather and the method saves a great deal of time, money and labour.

2a. Exercising horses in company on long hacks is the most natural way of giving them activity and mental occupation as it simulates life and migrations in the herd. Domesticated horses and ponies often form friendships with other types of animal (including humans, of course) and although dogs, in natural conditions, prey on horses, these two friendly ones are part of this horse's social family and form company on a hack even though there are no other horses around. In cases where a horse has taken a dislike to dogs, or to a particular dog, it is obviously stressful for him to be frequently in its company and this association should not be forced with a view to his 'just having to get used to it' from the point of view of discipline. Getting used to something does not decrease the stress of the resulting situation (just like two incompatible humans living or working together), so there is no point in forcing it.

2b. Although many people doubt whether or not horses actually come to love their owners and handlers in the way that dogs do, there is no doubt that they regard them as pals and members of their inner social circle. In a herd of horses out at grass, it is not uncommon for them to come running up to a human who may be present should trouble arise, such as marauding dogs. Timid horses may also go to a human for protection if being bullied by another dominant horse just as a foal may run behind its dam.

3. This is a useful and easy way of obtaining a little more control and restraint than is possible with a difficult horse wearing an ordinary headcollar. Simply wrap the leadrope, which is clipped to the back dee in the ordinary way, round the muzzle like this and hold it snugly, but not tightly enough to hamper breathing significantly, below the lower jaw. Interfering with the breathing can easily panic some horses and defeat the object of more control.

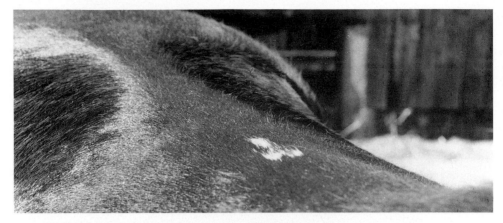

4a. This old saddle sore has been sufficiently serious to cause the hair follicles to become damaged and the hair to grow back white (the principle used in security freeze-marking horses) but not to cease growing altogether. It is worthwhile checking under such scars to see whether or not there is a permanently thickened patch of skin and flesh which could cause problems with saddle fitting, although this is more likely to happen where the patch is bare rather than white.

4b. Horses meeting each other for the first time usually weigh each other up visually from a distance at first and may sniff the air to see if any information can be gained by smell, before taking the risk of approaching. The next step is to approach warily, maybe with a certain amount of stamping and squealing, and to arch the neck and sniff each other's nostrils, exchanging breath and personal smells, in a side-on way, like this. There may then be further stamping and squealing. Friendly horses communicating with each other by nostril when they are both side by side and facing the same way but strangers never do.

5a. The best land for horses is well-drained loamy or sandy land. Clay land, like this, although impossible to avoid in some areas, is not at all good. In summer it bakes hard and cracks and in winter it becomes a stiff or liquid-holding quagmire which loosens or sucks off shoes and greatly increases the risk of mud fever. Over the years it can be improved by the addition of much organic material (such as old stable manure) and sand to improve drainage. In well-used areas such as gateways, shelter entrances and around troughs, it is probably best to dig it out and lay sand over rubble for a long-term cure.

5b. Although horses and their relatives are creatures of the open spaces, they do need shelter and, to them, anything is better than nothing as this pony demonstrates. a full day, or even a few hours, out in hot sun with no significant shelter can be most distressing to horses, who can certainly suffer from heat stroke even if their temperatures are not being raised for them by having to work. It is not unreasonable to suppose that they have the same symptoms as humans when they have been out in the sun too long, such as fatigue, depression and headaches.

6a. Rolling is an important personal and social activity for all members of the horse family. It is believed that horses roll to help clean the skin, as the dust provides an unfavourable environment for parasites. Rolling in mud which then dries on provides a solid protection against wind, too, and mud and dust have a drying effect on the coat and skin, so help remove excess grease. On a family/herd level, rolling, usually in specially selected patches, helps to coat each individual herd member with the herd or family smell. This strengthens the bonding between them and eases identification between members and outsiders, a process during which horses depend very much on smell. Horses obviously greatly enjoy rolling and every opportunity should be provided for them to do so. They get forehand first . . .

6b. . . . then flop the quarters down.

7a. They may do one side first,
writing and wriggling about in ecstasy . . .

7b. . . . and kicking their legs in the air as well as
rubbing their heads on the ground or in the mud.

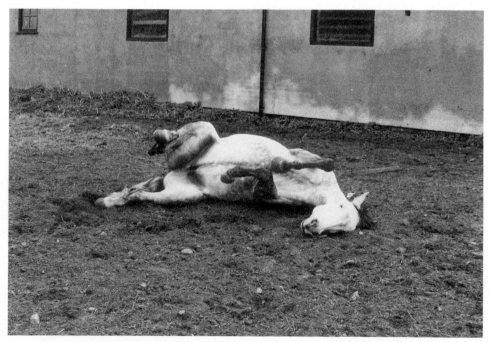

8a. It is said to be a sign of a good, well-conformed horse if the animal can roll right over and do the other side without getting up, although both fat horses and those with high withers may have trouble doing this. Often, a horse will get up and get down on the other side to give it equal treatment.

8b. Always watch rolling horses to make sure they shake after getting up. Failure to do so can mean that the horse is rolling due to pain of some sort, usually abdominal, rather than for other reasons.

manner appropriate to *them*, and not aimed primarily at the convenience of the humans associated with them.

Horses have been segregated for human convenience since the earliest civilisations flourished. Standing stalls have been dug out in Babylonia and Assyria, before that in Sumeria (in the same region), in ancient Egypt and more recently in ancient Greece and Rome, so the idea is not new, presumably because humans, like horses, have not changed in all that time. We still want our own way! Anything for an easy life, we think. In individual stables, horses are easily available, can be kept clean so reducing work, can have their diets controlled so as to help make them stronger and fitter for our purposes, and can be kept 'safe' from the physical attentions (bites and kicks) of other horses, which may possibly put them out of action (work) and render them permanently or temporarily useless to us. Stabled horses are also sheltered, we say, conveniently overlooking the fact that shelter can be more easily and cheaply provided in ways more acceptable to the horses; and we have in the past provided, and sometimes still do provide, elaborate, ornate stables, luxurious to our eyes, designed by some of the top architects and designers of yesteryear and today, to the honour and glory of the horse, not caring or, to be generous, not realising that the horses concerned would be much happier out in the fields and pastures which often surround those equine palaces.

This chapter is concerned with respiration, and from this point of view conventional stables are anathema to horses. Quite simply, most of them offer such inadequate ventilation and air quality as to warrant a health warning being emblazoned on each box. 'Beware all ye who enter here' would be quite suitable, or the more current 'living in a stable can seriously damage your health'.

The simplest way to test the ventilation in a stable is to use your own body and particularly your nose. Complicated formulae are given concerning air flow and cubic metres of airspace per animal, and if you can work them out they are reasonable (although one I managed to decipher seemed quite inadequate) but the easiest thing to do is this.

Spend some time out in the open air and then enter your horse's stable. Breathe in normally and pay attention to the feel, smell and temperature of the air. Does it seem warmer than the air outside? Does it have *any* discernible odour at all which was not present outside? And does it seem (subjective, this) 'thicker' than the air outside? If the answer to any one of those questions is 'yes' you've got a problem, and so has your horse. But all is not lost! There are several simple, cheap ways of vastly improving the ventilation in your horse's box.

You may feel that even if the air in your horse's box is not of outdoor quality it can't be that important because your horse shows none of the usual symptoms of respiratory distress – no coughing, no rather high at-rest respiratory rate, no runny nose, no poor exercise tolerance or work ability. However, there is much to be said for the school of thought which believes that even if this is the case, the fact that his air quality is lower than it could be means that at a sub-clinical (barely noticeable) level his body is having to use up valuable energy resources in fighting off whatever challenge there is, energy he could use for work, well-being, body functioning and so on, and he is, therefore, constantly working at a disadvantage and health-wise is always just a little below par. Improved ventilation and the other management techniques mentioned in this book would significantly help overcome this and ensure that, as far as practically possible, your horse is not starting off with an unwanted handicap.

Let's take the size of the stable first. It is generally considered that a loose box (called box stalls in the USA) should be not less than 12ft square (about 3.5m square) for a 16 hand high horse as regards floorspace. This is just about enough to ensure that he can turn round, lie down, sleep flat out, roll and get up again in reasonable safety and comfort. A little extra size would not go amiss. In height, many prefabricated loose boxes on sale in the UK offer a height of only 7ft 6in or 8ft (about 2.3m) to the eaves of a ridge-roofed box (double planed). Even from a safety point of view this is insufficient (should a horse feel like standing on his hind legs, his head can reach a height of 10ft 6in or about

3.2m), but from the point of view of airspace and ventilation it is extremely poor.

If the usual ventilation features of an open window and top door on the same side of the stable are all that is made available, then this will simply not provide anything like enough air change to maintain a healthy atmosphere inside the box. In any case, if the window is, unavoidably, at horse's head height and, as is usually recommended, is of the inward-opening Sheringham type, this means that if the wind is blowing into the openings the horse will be in a permanent draught and the box will not be big enough for him to get out of its way. The solution of many owners to this is to shut the window, making the ventilation problem even worse, and sometimes even to shut the top door as well.

With a safe and reasonable height of 10ft 6in (3.2m) to the eaves, there is the possibility of having the window well above the normal head height of a horse so he can get out of the way of a draught from the door should he wish to, and there will never be any need to shut either the window or the door.

But this is only part of the story. There are many times when it is actually desirable to create a cross-draught in a stable, such as on close, muggy days, very hot, airless days or in any conditions when the ventilation leaves something to be desired. Very few ready-made boxes offer this facility, perhaps because so much of the established and accepted literature on horse management stipulates that a cross-draught must be avoided at all costs! Yes, if the ventilation points are level with some part of the horse. Otherwise, a cross-draught *above* horse's head height is exactly what you want much of the time.

A suitable facility for this can be created by having a window on the opposite wall of the box to the door, or, more cheaply, by having louvres there or just by removing an odd plank or a few bricks, or whatever, so that air can both escape and be renewed continuously. Windows in the walls are not necessary, in practice. Roof windows are more efficient in every way and are safer. There is no possibility at all of the horse breaking them and there is then no need for a protruding guard inside the stable, again dangerously sited at horse's head height, to protect the horse from the inward-opening Sheringham window!

But perhaps the most important ventilation feature for any box is a ridge roof ventilator. Warm air rises, as we all know, and with an open ridge (all or part-way down the ridge) with a protective cowl over the opening, the air can freely rise and escape instead of being imprisoned in the box. As it escapes, fresh air is automatically 'sucked' into the box through lower ventilation points, keeping the atmosphere much healthier.

Boxes should really have effective ventilation points on all four sides of the box, but the minimum requirement, in my view, is a sizeable ridge roof ventilator and, for an ordinary loose box, an ever-open top door. These together are much more effective than the usual door and window coupling. For rows of boxes, or those where, for some reason, it is extremely difficult to alter the ventilation, consideration should be given to providing electrically operated air extraction units (domestic kitchen-type suction fans are suitable), permanently set to take stale air out, one at each end of a row of boxes and, for rows of six boxes or more, in one of the middle boxes, too, on the side opposite the door. Although their slight hum (and modern ones are very quiet) may be a little irritating, they don't need to be on all the time, but are a definite boon where ventilation is a problem.

Large stable complexes such as American barn-type stabling can, perhaps surprisingly, cause even more problems than loose boxes opening to the outdoors because stale air tends to pool in the boxes and there is often no outlet at all in these buildings, apart from the double doors at one or both ends of the building. Such housing systems are slowly being replaced in some yards in the UK and Ireland because of the easy spread of disease in them and the fact that their poorer ventilation actually encourages the spread and breeding of bacteria and viruses, unless elaborate steps are taken to seal off the barn into smaller units. Equally elaborate ventilation and air-conditioning systems, electrically operated, are often necessary to maintain a healthy atmosphere.

Conditions in such stabling complexes can be improved by

allowing each box inside them a top door to the outside (like a conventional outdoor loose box) and even, as in the better-designed buildings, a separate outdoor entrance for each horse. The top doors on both sides of the building can then be left open unless extremely severe weather prevents this. The whole building can be given a continuous ridge roof ventilator, or several can be installed at intervals down the roof. Leaving both sets of double doors open does help, but the air coming in does not, in practice, reach the actual stables, tending rather to blow down the central aisle. Matters can be improved slightly by installing wire grid doors or standing the horses in their stables with an American-type webbing barrier across each entrance, or a simple bar, rope or chain, as appropriate, although this is not fully adequate. Other ventilation devices such as louvres and windows can, of course, be installed with advantage.

As so many farm buildings are converted to horse accommodation, these ventilation devices should be considered and installed during building or conversion wherever possible as it is easier at this stage to do than later when the building is in use and finished.

When stables are of the single-pitch roof type, ventilation can become even more critical than with ridge-roof boxes. The lowest part of the roof should be at least 10ft 6in (3.2m) high for safety anyway, and at the back of the box. This means that, if there is no other outlet, stale air can at least rise and roll up the inside of the roof and leave via the door and window, although there should really be some opening just under the roof at the highest point to ensure efficient removal. In a high enough stable, it's a good plan to have an opening along the top of the wall opposite the door (which is usually the lowest one) to enable a cross-draught to be created when required.

The use of ionisers in offices and homes to create a 'fresh air' feel and help asthma sufferers has led to their being marketed to horse owners, and they do seem to have a beneficial effect on air quality in stables. They work by emitting negatively electrically charged ions (atoms) which attract the positively charged dust particles floating (maybe invisibly, maybe not) in the air. The effect is to attract the dust to the surfaces of the stable (ledges etc.), clearing the air and filling it with negatively charged ions which make the air feel fresh and invigorating.

As part of good hygiene is regularly to vacuum, pressure hose or steam clean the stable anyway, you will find this activity even more important because of the action of the ioniser and it will probably bring home to you just how much dust can float around in the stable.

It is always a good idea to site stables in as dust-free an area as possible, because even if plain, ordinary dust has no disease- or allergy-inducing effect, it can act as a simple physical irritant to the respiratory tract and also the eyes. Stables sited round a surfaced exercise ring which gives off dust whenever a horse sets foot in it should be avoided at all costs, especially those ranged around an indoor arena of any kind. Maybe you don't notice the dust, but you only have to check the ledges, seats and floors around the arena to reassure yourself that it does fly around – and into your horse's lungs. Watering or, as is done in some cases, oiling the surfacing material may help damp down the dust somewhat, but this is nowhere near as effective as avoiding stabling your horse near it altogether.

Other aspects of accommodation and air quality are covered in Chapters 5, 7 and 12.

5 Feeding and Nutrition: The Way to a Horse's Heart

The Horse's Natural Diet

It is fairly certain that the thing which most preoccupies horses' minds is food. When a horse snatches a bite of something which looks and smells delicious when he is supposed to be working it usually elicits a reprimand from his rider or handler, yet he is only doing what he has been programmed by nature and evolution to do – eat most of the time. Like us, the horse has twenty-four hours in a day but, unlike us, he spends in natural conditions about sixteen hours of that time grazing and browsing. The acquisition and chewing of food is extremely important to both his physical well-being and his mental contentment, a fact often overlooked by those managing horses in domesticated environments.

As a herbivore, the horse needs a very frequent intake of his natural food: grass, leaves and herbs. Carnivores, on the other hand, can get all of their nutrient requirements in one large meal per day, or, if a large carnivore such as a lion, in one meal only every two, three or more days. Provided they can catch enough animals, they have no problem. Animals' bodies are made of proteins, fats, carbohydrates, minerals and vitamins, which are all present in skin, flesh, bone and other body tissues. In the wild, most parts of the animal are eaten by a carnivore. They only stop eating when they have gorged themselves, and scavengers then take over, such as certain birds and insects. (Most carnivores also are not averse to scavenging or stealing someone else's kill.) Carnivores do not have to worry about finding different foods to provide a balanced diet: they will only suffer a vitamin-deficient diet, for example, if they eat vitamin-deficient meat.

The whole food chain depends on vegetable, plant, life. No animal can make its own energy. Only plants can do that, by trapping the sun's energy in the form of light and warmth and using it to build their own bodies from nitrogen, carbon dioxide and water, plus the nutrients which are in the soil where the plants grow. Different soils produce different plants according to their content and what certain plants need to flourish. In the end, all animals – including humans – depend on plants for power, energy and the means of life.

Herbivores have to be very choosy about their diets because plants are chemically very different from animals. In addition, carnivores, for example dogs, have much less sensitive digestive systems (mouldy old bones or rotten meat seem to be particularly attractive to dogs, for example, and to do them little harm, whereas a horse would hardly ever even eat mouldy food unless exceptionally hungry, and maybe not even then).

Herbivores also have another problem. Because plants are mostly cellulose (a fibrous substance, much of which is not actually digestible but provides an important mechanical function in absorbing water, bulking out the ration and stimulating the intestinal movements which move the food along the intestinal tract), with little protein and energy and, according to the time of year and weather conditions, a lot of water, they have to consume an awful lot of food to obtain the required levels of feed value. However, horses are what are called generalist grazers and browsers: they eat many different species of grasses, leaves and herbs and so can obtain a wide variety of nutrient sources and of different nutrients according to the contents of the plants they eat. It is also unlikely that they will gorge on any one plant, tending rather to eat smallish amounts of the different ones available in their grazing area.

Although horses in large areas may roam all over that area, studies on feral horses show that they normally stay in one particular range until the grass is eaten down or loses its appeal before moving on to an area where vastly different plants may grow. Therefore, it is natural to them to have available a wide range of foods and to eat small amounts of the same foods all the time. As they migrate short or long distances to new pastures, the predominant plants will change gradually, so their digestive systems do get some warning and can adapt gradually to a slightly different diet.

Horses also have an innate sense of what they need. There have been wild, and are now feral, horses in widely differing regions of the world. Before domestication, horses were free to wander at will, restrained only by geographical boundaries and physical features of mountains, ravines, water and so on. They often ranged over many square miles of land and, in the course of evolution, migrated almost all over the world. In practical terms, they probably never had to put up with vitamin and mineral deficiencies (according to what minerals were in the soil and, therefore, in the plants in a particular area) because they could wander where they wanted to seek new nutrient sources. Feral horses and ponies now may still have many square miles to live on, or, in some cases, square acres or hectares if in formal reserves, but they are not quite as free to adjust their diets as their ranges are more and more hemmed in by man and his activities.

Domesticated horses, of course, rarely have the chance to roam over many square acres or hectares of land and almost never square miles, so have become much more restricted to what is available in a fairly confined area. Those in small over-grazed paddocks, of course, may end up with a grossly deficient diet in both quality and quantity.

Horses in general thrive on a low-nutrient, high-fibre diet. Zebras, for instance, eat the fibrous stalks of long grasses while their grazing companions, the wildebeest, prefer shorter, succulent grass. It is a fallacy that horses *prefer* short, sweet grass and will not eat long grass, as anyone who has ever watched horses with access to the latter will know. In some areas of the world, horses thrive on keep that is very fibrous indeed, and may also be sparse, according to the climate, such as our native Shetland and other ponies, the Przewalski horse in its natural range of the bitterly cold east European steppes and Asian tundra and the Caspian in its arid environment. Each type of horse evolved to suit the area in which it existed and this wide variety of members of the horse family, and their equally wide range of tolerance, or lack of it, of varying diets, still exists today; think of the well known intolerance of ponies and cobs to 'rich' grass, hay or concentrates, to give only one example.

The Digestive System

The horse has a type of digestive system unique in the animal kingdom, somewhere between our own (dealing with two, three or more meals a day, taken at intervals) and a ruminant such as a cow where the herbage is taken in and later regurgitated and chewed as cud. Instead, the horse has a large 'fermentation vat' well down its intestinal tract, the caecum, where much of his digestion takes place by means of a population of micro-organisms (fungi, bacteria and protozoa) and, along the digestive tract as a whole, various chemicals and enzymes. He is a 'trickle feeder', taking in a little food most of the time, and his digestive system has specifically evolved to work best on this system. In fact, if this system is not adhered to, as it often is not in domestication, trouble often results in the form of colic and other digestive upsets.

The system obviously starts in the mouth with the teeth, tongue and cheeks. The horse's food is pulled or torn off by the front incisor teeth and chewed and crushed up by the molar teeth at the back of the mouth, being manipulated around by the tongue and cheeks and mixed with alkaline saliva to prepare it for further action, when swallowed, by very strongly acidic digestive juices in the stomach.

It is well known that the horse has a small stomach for its size; it does not need a large stomach, unlike a lion or dog, both of which might prey on the horse in the wild, because his food, in natural conditions, arrives in small, continuous amounts, whereas his predators consume large concentrated meat meals at one go. The food may remain in the stomach for an hour or two depending on its nature and content, being pummelled about by the stomach's muscular walls and mixed with the digestive juices. As it moves on through the various sections of the digestive tract, by means of wave-like contractions of the muscles in the intestine wall, called peristalsis, it is mixed with other digestive juices and becomes more and more creamy in consistency. As mentioned, a vital part of digestion takes place in the caecum. The intestine walls are liberally supplied with blood in thread-like blood vessels called capillaries, and nutrients pass into the blood from the intestines, having been chemically broken down and in other ways 'processed' into an absorbable form.

The liver plays a vital role in the management of the horse's nutrient intake and can be called the 'food factory' of the body. Nutrients are delivered to it in the blood, and it handles them in many different ways, storing some, adding substances here and taking out others there, and passing the results out again via the bloodstream to be delivered to wherever they are needed in the body for use or storage. Bile is secreted by the liver as part of its work, and helps cope with fats (also called oils or lipids), and the juices of the pancreas are also important.

The kidneys have a rich blood supply and are responsible for filtering out of the blood many waste products of digestion and metabolism and other toxins or drugs taken into the body or formed by it.

Metabolism is the very act of living: it is the result of all the chemical reactions which occur in the body, all the chemical and physical processes which maintain the body and by which energy is produced for work, reproduction and all the processes involved in living such as the beating of the heart, the functioning of the nervous system, the excretion of waste products, maintenance of body temperature, fighting of disease, hormonal control of the body processes, growth, repair, replacement of tissue and so on.

Not all the food the horse takes in is used. Much of the fibre or roughage eaten is used physically to break up the more concentrated parts of the food to allow the digestive juices to get in and work on them. Some fibre can be digested but much is passed out, together with other unused food and waste products, in the horse's droppings, and can be seen as little splinters of woody material in the balls of dung. Other waste products are, as mentioned before, passed out in the breath and sweat and in the urine, filtered out by the kidneys.

Feeding in Domestication

Suitable Pasture

Many domesticated horses, of course, notably breeding stock, retired horses, those resting and those in light work, are given grass as a substantial part of their diet. Domesticated pasture is often unsuitable for horses, however, either because it is over-grazed and deficient in both feeding value and quantity or because it is too 'rich' and more suited to dairy cattle than athletic horses. The former is by far the less dangerous situation, although physical disorders can eventually build up due to malnutrition and deficiencies. Over-rich grazing, particularly too much all at once such as when horses stabled and working over the winter are suddenly turned out on to rich spring grazing without adequate preparation, is a well known factor favouring the development of laminitis in particular, also colic, obesity (which brings it own problems) and other digestive disorders.

Much research has gone into nutrition and pasture management for horses, particularly over the last decade, and we now know a great deal more about horses' dietary requirements than formerly. As far as pasture is concerned, it is now quite possible to purchase specially formulated seed mixes (albeit with a little pushing and a few special requests) to suit equine breeding stock of various types *and* athletic performance horses, working or resting, so that these categories of horse can enjoy the pleasure and relaxation of grazing while still receiving a suitable balanced diet for their needs.

It is by no means the case that horses 'get fat' when allowed 'too much' grass. It is the nature of the pasture and herbage that is important. Low-energy mixes which keep the horses busy without providing excessive nutrients and without causing a so-called grass belly to develop are available, so avoiding the problems which occur with too much over-rich grass. Breeding stock, which requires a higher level of nutrients, can have different mixes suited to the demands of reproduction and growth.

Balancing Feed for the Stabled Horse

It is in the area of feeding mainly stabled or yarded horses that errors are continually made, despite the fact that excellent feeds, both concentrate and roughage, are now available.

Old habits die hard and the old practices of a little bit of this, a hatful of that and a pinch or a handful of something else flourish in many establishments. It seems strange that so much money (if not enough) is spent on research into feeding and nutrition, yet when the results are made available for all to take advantage of the granddad syndrome still prevails. It is admittedly not so easy to formulate rations for animals with a subjectively assessed occupation like horses. Farm animals' nutrition can be calculated down to the nth degree for precise weight gain, milk production or egg yields, but energy, strength, stamina and athleticism are another matter. Enough is currently known, however – and new facts are emerging all the time – to produce vastly superior rations for our horses than were available even five and especially ten years ago.

The methods our fathers and grandfathers used are in some ways appropriate, formulated, as they were, over generations of experience, but for some reason we seem reluctant to employ a blend of the best of the old and the best of the new.

I feel the most common mistake made in feeding stabled horses is paying insufficient attention to balancing the diet in correct proportions of energy, protein, vitamins and minerals. Many horse owners and managers seem to pride themselves on being able to feed by instinct and take little or no notice of new, proven knowledge in this field. Given the propensity of many to take a new compound feed of some sort, either nuts or a coarse mix, fully balanced as it is, and yet mix bits of this and that as the fancy takes them, some manufacturers have produced feeds specially meant to mix with 'straights', as specific feeds such as oats, bran and so on are called. Mixing these with already balanced feeds *un*balances them, so the danger can be partly redressed by a product actually intended for mixing, provided the user follows the advice of the manufacturer as to how much of what other foods to use.

The Need for Accurate Analysis

Unfortunately, the problem, although ameliorated, does not end there. The best new compound feeds are painstakingly formulated and mixed and a decent analysis given on the bag so, with perhaps some help from a nutritionist (maybe from the manufacturing firm) or a veterinary surgeon, you do actually know exactly what you are feeding. This applies to both cubes (called pellets in the USA) and coarse mixes (sweet feeds in USA), yet time and again you can hear a horse owner or manager say, even now, something like: 'I never feed cubes because you can't see what's in them.' True, you can't actually see the ingredients, such as oats, grass meal and whatever, but you *can* read both the ingredients and the analysis on the bag, and with a reputable firm, national or regional, you can rely on such a product.

If this same person were faced with two samples of, say, oats (because oats are still such a widely used horse feed), all he or she could see was that they were actually oats. She would probably use her eyes, nose and mouth to check the physical *quality* of the oats, would know that they were indeed oats but would have absolutely no idea what was their energy level, their protein level, their fibre, fat (oils), vitamin, mineral or anything else level. Yet on a reputable brand of compound this information is laid out clearly for all to see!

I am not a nutritionist or a vet, so I am always pleased to see helpful analysis panels on feeds, feed supplements (another danger area) and other specialist products such as the carbohydrate boosters and electrolyte products which now form a regular part of any with-it performance horse owner's feed range. Surely feeding a product without knowing its analysis is too haphazard to be safe, economical or fair to the horse who has to suffer the vagaries of any diet we give him. These days, too, there is simply no need for it. The point has long since been reached when we only need to pick up a phone to check with the resident nutritionist of the firm whose products we are thinking of using, a nutritionist or management consultant in private practice, a veterinary surgeon or the equine services department of our local state or government agricultural service.*

Of course, straights will continue to be popular, but I feel that if optimum health and performance are required of a horse they should at least be analysed before being incorporated into his diet. Laboratory analysis of every new batch, if not available with the product (as it is when buying from the best feed merchants), should be arranged – probably most easily through the vet; this may sound highly impractical, but it is the only way you are going to get to know what is in the feed you are using. Oats, for example, can vary widely in their energy and protein content. Hay can vary even more: again, you can test its quality with your nose and eyes but you cannot tell just what is in it, and it certainly does not always follow that if it is of good physical quality it will be of good, balanced feeding value.

A British university some years ago provided several experienced horsemasters with various samples of hay and noted their comments and which ones they regarded as top quality. *In each case the horsemasters' subjective judgements based on the appearance and smell of the hay failed to coincide with the true quality of the hay based on analysis of feed value.* Quite a thought!

Of course, if feed is not analysed, you can make a reasoned guess at the nutrient level in whatever you have purchased, but you will have to wait and see its effect on your horse before you

* In the UK, the Agricultural Development Advisory Service's Equine Services Department, part of the Ministry of Agriculture, whose regional phone number is in the telephone directory.

know whether or not it is of high or low feeding value in general. No two batches of a single given feedstuff will have the same content and without analysis you will still not know just what is in it and whether your whole diet is balanced or not.

I feel that many cases of 'unexplained' laminitis and colic are due to horses being given new batches of feed of higher feeding value than one just finished but in the same quantities. The higher level of nutrients in the new feed and/or the slightly different constituents mean that the horse is being over-fed or the gut bacteria are not able to adapt in time, and trouble results. Of course, there are several other causes of these two common disorders of domesticated horses, but I feel this explanation is quite common and largely unrecognised.

Feed Enough Roughage!

Another common mistake in feeding horses, in my experience, is that so many owners do not give their horses enough roughage in their diets. High-level working horses such as racehorses, competition horses, hunters doing three or four days a fortnight and so on are often fed high levels of concentrates and it is generally felt that concentrates are the most important part of their diet, whereas, because of the nature and evolution of the horse's digestive tract, it is actually the roughage (hay, hayage or equivalent) which is most important.

Without going into minute details about crude protein and digestible energy levels, a good working guide for a horse in medium to hard work is to divide the total weight of the ration into one-third concentrates and two-thirds good hay. Some owners of hard-working horses may give half and half, and some authoritative sources recommend that for severe work (racing, three-day eventing and so on) the roughage should be reduced to only a quarter of the total weight of the food given daily.

It is true that horses on a high-concentrate diet will not want as much hay as others and will reduce their intake on their own. Others, however, really like their hay and will be mentally discontented and physically uncomfortable on such a diet. I personally feel that only 25 per cent hay is simply not enough, no matter what work the horse does. If the hay is of good feeding value it is surprising how few concentrates are actually needed and I have known point-to-point and racehorses working and winning races on as much really top quality hay as they wanted but with concentrates only in the single figures of pounds weight.

Horses, as mentioned, chew and digest food for a good two-thirds of the time in natural conditions. They are programmed to need the chewing action and, some believe, the specific motion of pulling grass and moving slowly about while doing so, one possible reason (apart from excitement and hunger) why so many horses sway about, stamp or kick while eating to compensate for the fact that while eating from a manger or bucket they cannot actually walk gently around as they would in nature. The view has also been expressed that the vice weaving, where distressed horses sway from foreleg to foreleg, swinging their heads from side to side at the same time, is the horse's way of compensating for the lack of ability to perform a natural motion which would occupy such a lot of his time in more natural conditions. The horse finds comfort in weaving for this reason, although there are other factors connected with the performance of vices which are discussed in Chapter 10.

The fact is that the horse's digestive system is not physically able to function properly on high levels of concentrates and low levels of roughage. The work we ask of high-performance horses is, obviously, unnatural at the levels requested and, some say, demands an unnatural diet to provide the energy needed to fuel it. The digestive system can adapt to some extent to energy-concentrated food but it is simply not open to manipulation on the level carried out by many managers of performance horses.

I know of one yard (among others) of showing and dressage horses where the proprietor prides herself on being able to get her horses to exist on only 'two slices' (as she puts it) of hay a day plus as much concentrates as they want. She does not seem able to link this weird diet with the fact that her horses' straw beds virtually disappear every night. Thankfully (for the horses' peace of mind) she has not yet got around to putting them on shavings or muzzling them. From a nutrition point of view the horses are getting a lot of fibre from the high-fibre, low-nutrient wheat straw, which will balance the concentrates. They do, though, have 'hay bellies', which is why she keeps the hay to a minimum!

The fibre part of the diet is digested low down the tract. Straw contains a high proportion of the indigestible sort of fibre which is why the intestinal tract remains 'padded out' to accommodate it and gives the appearance of a hay belly. Poor-quality hay also contains much indigestible fibre and causes a hay belly. The higher the feeding value of a horse's hay, the more of it is digested for use and the less bulk remains as the food gets well down the tract to bulk out the intestines, so the horse does not get a hay belly. Therefore, it is far better to feed a fair amount of the best quality hay you can get and build up the concentrates, if needed, on top of the hay 'foundation' for extra energy. The use of modern carbohydrate boosters for extra energy also helps avoid feeding too many concentrates and literally sickening the horse (the term 'corn sickness' being an old but graphic one to describe the condition of a horse with slight indigestion put off his feed by an artificial diet of too many concentrates combined, probably, with too little hay).

Fat, Protein – and Bran?

At one time it was held that horses are poor digesters of fat and that they need a low fat diet. In practice, following scientific research, it is now quite common to feed extra fats and oils, most conveniently and effectively in the form of corn oil or soya oil, to give extra energy particularly for stamina work such as eventing, endurance work and hard hunting. There is no need to boil linseed for hours or risk poisoning horses by using improperly prepared linseed. Some horses do like linseed, however, and if owners wish to use it as a treat as well as a feed, fair enough; however, it should really form a part of every feed (impractical!) rather than a once-weekly linseed mash the night before a rest day, the traditional way of feeding it, for reasons given below.

The required protein level of a diet is now known to be less than formerly believed. In fact, it used to be the protein figure that horsemasters used to gauge the suitability of a diet, and probably still is in some yards. A mature working horse, even a very hard-working one, does not need more than 11 per cent protein in his diet: it is the energy levels that need adjusting, in conjunction with expert advice, as the work levels increase. Extra protein is only normally needed for breeding adults (particularly mares), foals and youngstock, and elderly, sick or starved horses losing condition.

Bran is another traditional feed now known to be unnecessary and unsuitable for horses in large quantities. Bran is a poorly balanced feed, with far too much phosphorus and too little calcium, throwing the feed well out of balance when used to bulk out a diet in the belief that 'there's nothing in it, anyway'. Fed to excess it can cause bone disease, porous, swollen bones which become weak and brittle – exactly what athletic animals like horses do *not* want. A far safer alternative to bulk out a feed is chop, or chaff: chopped-up hay and/or straw, probably the type mixed with molasses for palatability.

Alternatives to Hay

Hay alternatives, usually called hayage, which, for simplicity of description, are basically a cross between hay and silage, are now extensively used by those wishing to give their horses a dust-/spore-free diet, but they are variable and come in different energy grades, which can cause some confusion. Generally, it is advised that they are fed in lower quantities than hay as they are more nutritious; this means that horses finish their rations sooner and are left with nothing to do. Alternatively, you can feed a generous amount but far fewer concentrates. If you still feel your horse has too much energy, and he is getting a fair amount of exercise, you can always switch to a lower-energy grade of hayage or cut out (or drastically reduce) the concentrates; if the horse expects something when others are fed or at a given time in his routine, you can give false feeds of chop with molassed sugar beet pulp (high in calcium) with dried grass meal or cubes. This is a fairly low-energy feed which horses seem to like. You can also use thinly sliced or coarsely grated carrots and/or apples as well as or instead of soaked sugar beet pulp.

Another way of spinning out a horse's hayage ration is to feed it in special racks or nets with small meshes so he can only get out a small amount at a time.

Hydroponically grown grass is also increasingly popular but some of the commercially available units seem very expensive for what they are. Grass is the horse's natural, nutritious and bulky feed and hydroponic grass can be fed in varying amounts (according to the seed or cereal-grain mix you use). It would be advisable to consult a nutritionist or a vet interested in feeding horses to decide on suitable seed mixes for your circumstances and horses.

A home unit can be produced (if you don't mind your house or conservatory, or a heated greenhouse, being used, as normal room temperature is needed for growth) by putting the seed thinly in layers in, say, used ice cream tubs, seed trays without drainage or old roasting tins, covering with about a quarter of an inch of water or liquid nutrient product and topping up daily. Use open bookshelves to stack the trays in a west or south-facing window, if you have one, and prepare one shelf a day. In fourteen days the first shelf should have grown enough to be fed, in fifteen days the next shelf and so on, so if you do one shelf daily you should have a permanent artificial source of the horse's natural feed which can be fed separately or mixed in with his hay, hayage or concentrates. The addition of plant lights where your shelves are will improve growth and, in winter, may actually be needed for sufficient growth to be achieved. (Plant lights emit white light, which means light from the full range of the spectrum from red to violet, like natural sunlight.)

Feed Supplements

Feed supplementation is another area where horses are often wrongly, even dangerously, fed in domesticity. Persuasive advertising gives the impression that such-and-such a supplement will make your horse a world-beater and that he can't live without it. The facts are that unknowledgeable supplementation, even following the advice of the manufacturer, can make a horse ill. There are specialist supplements, containing only one or a small range of vitamins, minerals or trace elements, and there are general, 'broad spectrum' ones which give a wide, balanced variety. Vitamins, minerals and trace elements (or micro-nutrients, as they are sometimes called) *are* essential, but if you give your horse a reputable brand of compound with good quality hay (or alternative), roots when stabled and, ideally, significant turn-out time, especially in winter when the sun is weakest (sunlight being instrumental in the manufacture within the body of vitamin D), your horse will probably not need a supplement.

Certainly you should never feed them indiscriminately, never in larger amounts than instructed on the pack or by a nutritionist or vet, and you should never mix supplements as the fancy takes you. I feel it best to use supplements only under the advice of a nutritionist or vet as some of them are very potent and vitamins are not the harmless nutrients many think they are. Overdoses can not only seriously unbalance a diet, for instance, but, in certain cases, can poison your horse. It is certainly not the case that if a little is good a lot must be terrific – on the contrary, it could be lethal. The golden rule is err on the mean side and if in doubt, don't feed the supplement at all.

There are circumstances in which 'probiotics', preparations of beneficial living organisms which help to stabilise the gut bacteria population, can usefully be given: these are discussed in more detail in Chapter 7.

Horses on high-concentrate diets, and some on not-so-high-concentrate diets, do sometimes suffer behavioural problems as a result of the build-up of acids and toxins produced by an unnaturally high level of cereal grains in their diet. Horses in the wild would, at some times, come across ripe grains but would not eat them in anything like the amounts we consistently give to artificially kept horses. Horses can, as a result of a traditional domesticated diet, become hyper-excited and bad tempered and suffer from chronic slight indigestion. One product, a montmerillonite clay supplement marketed in the UK as

'Thrive' does help such horses, according to the manufacturers, by 'mopping up' such toxins and improving the digestibility of concentrates. 'Thrive' is not meant for permanent use, however, but as a temporary supplement for use over a few weeks or months only while the diet is sorted out and made more suitable for the individual. It has helped lots of horses come to terms with a diet which is undoubtedly unnatural and, to some individuals, intolerable.

The Dangers of 'Complete' Feeds

Shortages of minerals, micro-nutrients and other substances are believed to be largely responsible for such behavioural problems in horses as eating a lot of earth, chewing rugs and tails, chomping fences, stripping bark and experimenting with poisonous plants in their paddocks. Lack of roughage is particularly prone to producing these symptoms as the horse vainly tries to appease his hunger and satisfy his natural craving for roughage and bulk and the relaxing grazing action.

So-called 'complete' feeds (usually pellets or cubes) were introduced some decades ago as a means of providing the horse with ample nutrients without having to provide hay. There were two factors in their introduction. It was an Olympic year and it was felt that a change of hay on arrival in the host country would be detrimental to the horses' well-being. Also that year, the home hay crop was not good. The Olympic team wanted to avoid transporting tons of hay across the globe and complete nuts were invented, supposedly containing all the nutrients required for hard-working horses plus enough fibre to cater for the reduced hay intake such horses would normally have experienced on a conventional diet.

At first the hayless, 'complete' diet was hailed a success for most of the horses and the nuts were marketed in Britain, eventually by several firms, but while many horsemasters claimed them to be a complete (excuse the pun) success and, of course, so very much easier than messing around with hay and its cost and ample storage facilities, other (perhaps the more obervant and caring?) soon discovered that nearly all horses on such a diet were extremely discontented and showed signs of physical and mental distress.

Quite plainly, the fibre content was *not* sufficient to cater for the horse's physical requirements and from the point of view of the horse's mental state they were a disaster. Horses were – and are, because 'complete' diets are still marketed today, mainly for horses suffering from COPD as a way of getting round the hay problem – greatly under stress through not having their hay to munch (the necessary chewing motion again) to occupy many happy hours of their boring stabled time and to give them the feeling of satisfaction and repletion which only comes from having adequate roughage. All the familiar signs of horses hungry and uncomfortable from lack of bulk and fibre came out – chewing clothing, nibbling each other's manes and tails where possible, eating bedding, chewing wood, neurotic displacement activities or stable vices such as box-walking, weaving, crib-biting, wind-sucking and general unease and distress.

Nowadays, most makers of 'complete' diets recommend that the horse be given hay at night. However, with today's established 'clean air regime' management, details of which are given in Chapter 7, there is absolutely no need to subject your horse to the misery of a hayless diet because he has COPD or due to difficulties in obtaining hay, because there are ways round the problem. By all means feed complete cubes, but *with* hay or an alternative. You may well find that the horse does reduce his hay intake of his own accord, but he will make it very plain that he does need a fair amount of it.

Cubes, in any case, tend to bore horses more quickly than coarse mix. There are high fibre coarse mixes available, and mixes for various categories of horse, as with cubes – hard-working horses, ponies, breeding stock, resting horses and so on – so you should be able to find something your horse will both enjoy and thrive on.

The 'Golden Rules' of Feeding

From the early stages onwards, children and adult novices are

taught some version of the Golden Rules of feeding horses and
ponies. Most horse-care books contain them in some form or
other, with slight variations, and they are all very important
because errors in feeding quickly upset the horse's delicate and
sensitive digestive system. They were formulated by the army
over generations of experience and, although civilians may have
also realised them in principle but not set out formally as in the
organised army, retired military personnel who had worked
with army horses frequently took employment in horsy circles
right up to the early part of this century, and disseminated
military-style knowledge. The Golden Rules are fine in themselves and would work well enough if they were followed
properly, but we often have a distorted view of their interpretation and consequently do not apply them properly in practice,
even though we may think we are doing so.

   Let's look at them and see what they really mean and where
we might go wrong when applying them, especially bearing in
mind the digestive system the horse actually has as opposed to
that we might wish him to have, and also the research into
feeding which has gone on in recent years.

   Feed little and often is probably the first rule listed and this is
excellent advice. Why, then, do most people not do so? They may
honestly believe that three feeds a day with hay night and morning
is feeding little and often, but it certainly is not. This is more like
the feeding regime of a human than that of a trickle-feeding horse.
Do a survey over several days (when you have the time available,
such as a few days off work over a bank holiday) and pay close
attention to the actual time your horse does spend eating on such a
regime. You will find it is much less than the sixteen hours out of
twenty-four which is fairly standard for horses in the wild or even
in a domesticated paddock. The worst time for many horses is
during the night. Most horses will certainly have finished their last
haynet by midnight if they were given it in early evening, as is usual
in most yards. This leaves them with no fewer than six, seven or
maybe even eight hours (a human's working day) with *no food at all*
(unless they eat straw beds). This is not only highly unnatural but
also very detrimental to their digestive systems.

Apart from all the behaviour problems which stem from hunger, frustration and boredom, the digestive micro-organisms can actually begin to die of starvation (because they, too, live on the horse's food) after only a few hours without food. Not only does this reduce the population available for digestion when next food does come along, but the dead organisms begin to decompose in the intestines, causing flatulence as gases are produced and the putrid toxins of decomposition gradually develop.

It is safer and more effective (not to mention kinder) to give horses an *ad lib* supply of good-quality hay. If its feeding value is adequate you can easily cut down on the concentrates, as described earlier. Horses do not gorge on hay as they do on concentrates and you can simply remove the hay an hour or two before work. For horses in hard work, I feel that the hay should not be reduced below 50 per cent of the total ration weight and that if extra energy is needed carbohydrate boosters and extra oils should be added to existing concentrates under expert supervision from a vet or nutritionist when formulating the ration.

The stomach is known to work best when two-thirds full and it is best not to give feeds larger than approximately 4lb (2kg) in weight, as feeding too much will mean that food may be released from the stomach into the intestines before it is ready, leading to imperfect digestion and possibly to colic. This means that if the existing concentrate ration cannot be given in three or four 4lb feeds a day, more feeds should be given rather than increasing the weight of concentrates in each feed. Six smaller feeds a day spread out from early morning to late at night would be much more in keeping with the horse's digestive system, but it seems very few yards will go to the trouble of doing this.

Hay passes through the stomach more quickly than concentrates, on to the lower intestines where most of it is digested. The concentrates need more preparation in the stomach and remain there longer. Hay is, of course, dried grass and is ideal for keeping the digestive system gently working over long periods, as nature intended, as well as providing nourishment.

Feed plenty of roughage. This principle has already been discussed in this chapter, but most people's idea of plenty of roughage is just hay night and morning, which is not often enough. If you wish to prevent your horse eating too much of his ration at once, feed it in smaller allowances but more often: this way you can adjust his intake to avoid large amounts before work. It is wrong to do what some yards do and not give the horse any hay at all on the day of hard work. As the horse will have finished his night-time ration late the preceding evening or maybe in the early hours, to give him none with or before his first feed means he will have much too long without essential roughage. A small ration at least, of about 4lb (2kg), should certainly be given. It is not a good plan to deprive horses of all roughage even before an important event, as is generally believed and done, as this will upset his digestive system and, apart from making him feel uncomfortable or even ill (when he cannot possibly work well), it could cause colic, a disorder which should never be taken lightly.

Feed according to the work done, the size of the horse and his constitution and temperament. You really must get to know your horse to put this into operation. Is he a good doer, needing little to keep weight on? Does he fret off condition with excitement or worry? Is he listless or over-excitable? Is he too thin or too fat? Is he prone to laminitis or azoturia? These and similar questions must be carefully considered when formulating a ration. It is certainly safer to under-feed a horse slightly than to over-feed him. A good rule of thumb is to have your horse so that you cannot see his ribs but can feel them fairly easily. Very fit horses, particularly those in stamina jobs such as endurance work and some three-day event horses (depending on their individual type), may look thinner than this with their lower ribs (near the hips) visible, but such horses are often of a lean type which does not run easily to fat anyway. They will still be well muscled up along their top lines, shoulders and thighs.

The two most common diseases which arise from over-feeding are probably laminitis and azoturia (see Chapter 7) and although we still do not know everything about these conditions, our

The condition of a horse can be measured by using a scoring system from 0 – 10. This measures weight displacement over the neck, back, ribs and quarters. 1 – 4 are all shades of poor condition.

1. Starvation level. *Back view*: croup and hip bones prominent and very sharp. The horse is 'cut up' behind and there is no tissue, fat or muscle definition. *Side view*: vertebrae in the neck are palpable (able to be felt) with a hollow in front of the withers. Sunken temporal fossa (hollow above the eye) and eye. Spinous processes of the thoracic and lumbar vertebrae are sharp, well-defined and easily palpable. Rib cage is prominent with all ribs showing.

2. Similar to 1 but less obvious.

3. The checkpoints (withers, croup, etc.) are still defined but less sharp. A little more muscle definition but still hollow in front of the withers.

4. Bones beginning to lose their sharpness. Front half of rib cage covered, back half still defined. Neck beginning to fill up in front of the withers.

5. Approaching normal. Withers, croup and hip bones still well-defined but less easy to palpate. Inadequate muscle definition.

6. Normal. Hip bones and spinous processes defined but not prominent, well-covered in muscle and tissue. Rib cage covered, with last three pairs of ribs still palpable. Muscles well defined.

7. Beginning to carry too much weight. As the horse gets fatter and more round, the bones become more difficult to palpate.

8. Fat. Definition of bones is lost between 7 and 9. Rib cage fills up – cannot see the last three pairs. Neck becomes hard and cresty.

9. Obese. Horse carries masses of weight on neck, quarters and back. Can feel rib cage but only just. Deep palpation is needed to feel croup and hip bones.

10. Very obese. Excessively round backside. The horse is so fat that the spine makes a hollow. Huge pads of fat on quarters and on back. Impossible to feel hip bones, croup or rib cage. No definition on shoulders.

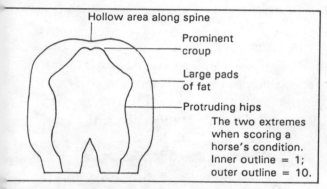

Hollow area along spine

Prominent croup

Large pads of fat

Protruding hips

The two extremes when scoring a horse's condition. Inner outline = 1; outer outline = 10.

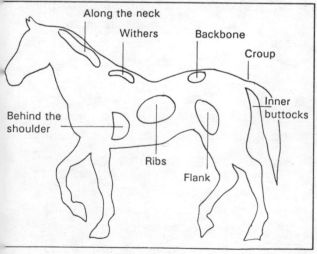

Along the neck

Withers

Backbone

Croup

Inner buttocks

Behind the shoulder

Ribs

Flank

knowledge is improving all the time. There are various causes of laminitis and different types of azoturia, but over-feeding for the exercise or work given is certainly a prime predisposing factor in both of them.

Always reduce the concentrates before the work and increase the work before the concentrates. On a day off feed no more than a single handful of his usual concentrates in each feed and that of the night before if the horse is to stand in (a very bad practice, incidentally). Try to give exercise at liberty on a day off, perhaps by turning out (which should be a normal part of his routine), either in a grass paddock or surfaced area. Leading out in hand is better than nothing, but scarcely adequate for health. If the horse is to be exercised on his day off he can have, say, a quarter of his usual concentrate ration to keep his digestive system in good running order.

Forget the bad old practice of feeding a mash (bran or bran and linseed) before the day off and possibly on the day off itself. This constitutes a sudden change in feeding (see next rule) and, as already mentioned, bran is not a good feed for horses. It is hard to digest, not easy, and is not palatable (hence the usual advice to add a little salt or a handful of oats to make it acceptable). It may have the recommended laxative effect because it irritates the digestive system, which responds by producing a mild diarrhoea, but why should anyone want to give their horse diarrhoea? To 'clear him out' is one usual explanation, but if he is on a healthy, suitable diet he does not need clearing out. Upsetting his digestion is counterproductive; best not to do it.

Make no sudden changes in feeding. Bran mashes have just been discussed. Fed only weekly, as they usually are, they constitute a complete change in feeding. Fed regularly, they are providing the horse with a grossly unbalanced diet. Because of the population of digestive organisms in the horse's gut, it is very important that some of the same ingredients should be given in each feed so that the bugs get their food, too, and remain healthy to operate the digestive process inside your horse. You can vary the amounts of the different ingredients, if you wish, but not the ingredients themselves. For example, do not give nuts for breakfast, coarse mix for lunch, oats and bran for tea and barley, maize and chop for supper. Formulate your horse's diet carefully and keep to the same ingredients. If changes are appropriate, make them very gradually over as long as three weeks so that different gut organisms have a chance gradually to die off or increase, as required.

When bringing horses up from grass, do not follow the old practice of 'mashing down' (putting them on sloppy mashes for several days after they come in, or before they go out, come to that). Instead, start giving very small feeds of what is to be their normal stabled diet while they are still in the field, and when they do come in continue grazing in hand, if no turn-out facilities are available, for three weeks. Don't suddenly cut out the grass, but taper off grazing time gradually if you are intending, or forced, to keep your horse fully stabled, and as the grazing decreases get him used to other succulent feeds to replace it.

Feed something succulent every day. This would be better written as 'feed something succulent in every feed', even if it is only a small amount. Horses do crave succulent feeds, which are natural to them. Soaked sugar beet pulp is a favourite and a good, balanced food and energy source. Carrots, apples and fodder beets (which can be very nutritious) are good and some horses will accept turnips or mangolds. With the exception of large amounts of sugar beet pulp and fodder beets, roots are not fattening. They do contain a lot of water but the horse will only take in as much water in his whole diet as he needs and will 'subtract' what he gets in his food from what he drinks, so there is no logical excuse for not feeding roots. Hydroponic grass is also good.

Keep to the same feeding times each day. Again, good advice as it keeps the digestive system in a routine, not to mention the horse's mind. Why, then, do so many people think nothing of making the horse miss an entire feed on certain working days, such as a day hunting or at a show or some other event? It is not really sufficient to take along a haynet. If the horse normally gets concentrates, a concentrate feed should be taken, too, if only a much smaller one than usual, to keep that vital intestinal tract in good order. Forcing horses to skip feeds is asking for trouble. Compounding the problem by giving a bran or linseed mash on return makes matters even worse, for reasons which I hope will now be understood. Indigestion or colic can easily result.

If going to a show or some event where you will be within easy reach of your horsebox, trailer or accompanying car, it is relatively easy to take a feed or two along, but if you hunt and will be away from your transport or stables for several hours, feed in buckets is obviously not feasible. However, there is nothing wrong with letting your horse graze or browse a little during a check (never mind 'it isn't done!'; think of your horse's well-being instead). You could also take a bit of coarse mix or cubes in plastic bags in your pocket, or a little saddlebag if you use one, and give him a handful or two when you get a reasonable chance. It's certainly better than nothing.

For horses whose owners work and, for various reasons, may be a bit late arriving to give feeds, this need not be serious provided the horse is never allowed to become really hungry; this is most easily avoided by making sure that he always has an ample supply of hay left with him in a box, shelter or field if the grass supply is poor.

Feed good-quality food only. The horse, as explained, has a very sensitive digestive system and many horses are fastidious feeders. Even greedy ones will not normally tuck into suspect food. Musty, mouldy hay, rancid oats, sour coarse mixes etc. should be thrown on the muck heap. Never accept poor or mouldy feeds from any source, farm, merchant or whatever, and do not buy more 'perishable' horse feed, such as rolled oats or barley, or coarse mixes which are often mixed with syrups or molasses to moisten them, than you can use in a couple of weeks. Use a large, old fridge, minus shelves, to store coarse mix or molassed feeds in warm weather. Certain feed supplements may also benefit from such storage.

If the horse does actually eat bad food he is very likely to get colic or some other digestive disorder. Of course, musty hay and straw can both create an allergic response in some horses and at the very least put the horse under a constant challenge even if he shows no symptoms.

Do not work a horse immediately after a full feed. This is partly because the blood supply will be somewhat diverted to cope with the sudden intake of nutrients and be unavailable to provide enough energy for work but also because the stomach and lungs are close together and will press on each other during work. The digestion taking place in the stomach will be impaired and the (comparatively) full stomach will prevent the lungs expanding as they need to during increased respiration when working. That's the idea, at any rate, and it's fair enough. It is also quite reasonable to suppose that running around after a large meal will make the horse feel unwell and queasy, as it would us. Indigestion can easily result in both species! (I have always felt that dinner-dances are arranged the wrong way round. We all eat several courses of dinner and then start hurling ourselves around the dance floor. Ridiculous!)

If the horse has only had a light feed or been trickle-nibbling hay before we arrive to tack him up, walking work for half an hour or more is safe enough. In natural conditions, the horse's stomach always has food in it yet he must have a safety margin because he may need to take to his heels at any moment if a predator threatens without going down with colic every time. Grass-kept horses, similarly, will always have some food in their stomachs yet can be ridden, slowly at first, without harm.

Water before feeding unless the horse has water always available. If he has, as do most horses these days, there is little chance he will become thirsty enough to take a long drink and, as the theory goes, risk washing undigested food out of the stomach. Many experts seem to feel this idea is a fallacy, but I feel it safest to err on the side of caution on this one! Horses with water always on hand will drink smallish amounts when they wish and many drink during and after feeding. Far from diluting the digestive juices and causing imperfect digestion, it is now believed that this actually eases the process and stimulates the production of digestive juices.

It is certainly now believed to be quite wrong to deprive horses of water before hard work. Whereas in the past water would be withheld for at least two hours before work, this is now believed to be counterproductive and actually dangerous in warm or hot weather due to the risk of subsequent dehydration when the horse starts to sweat significantly during work. Water should be available up to half an hour before work. It passes through the horse quite quickly.

Endurance riders know how important it is to let their horses drink en route to avoid dehydration. Hunters should be allowed a few swallows at any convenient source and the same goes for eventers after the steeplechase or, where there is no steeplechase, after the phase preceding the cross-country.

When work is finished, the horse should be allowed a few swallows, say about five or six, every ten or fifteen minutes during cooling down, from a convenient trough on the way home from an active hack and so on. At one time, it was advised that horses must not be allowed any water at all until they were completely cool and dry, but this is now known actually to hamper recovery: body fluids must be made up and, to this end, most competition horse managers now make available to their horses an electrolyte drink as well as plain water so they can choose whichever they need.

Depending on a horse's age, his body can be from two-thirds to three-quarters water (the younger he is, the more water his body will contain). It is essential to every aspect of life. Blood is largely water, the cells of the body are bathed in it and contain it, digestive juices are liquid, it helps transport sounds in the ear, the eye fluids are largely water, lactating mares' milk is largely water and so on.

In the wild, horses' watering habits depend on their environment. In some areas water is all around and horses can take short drinks whenever they want. In more arid regions horses may have to trek many miles once or twice a day to water holes. Zebras have been known to drink only once every four days rather than repeatedly make a long, wearying trek to a water hole. This does not mean that we should inflict this sort of arrangement on our domesticated horses: they have not evolved in the zebras' environment and are not adapted to this drinking pattern.

It is usually best to allow horses water with them all the time, but where for some reason it cannot be made permanently available, horses should be watered as often as is possible and certainly at least twice a day. They should be allowed plenty of time to drink their fill and not be harassed by equine enemies or impatient handlers. The horse will drink several long draughts of water then raise his head and appear to be resting or looking around. This is the point at which we may be tempted to pull him away. However, just stand there and watch the horse; he will almost certainly drop his head and have another long drink. He will probably move away himself when he has had enough.

However water is provided, whether from a bucket, trough, automatic container, stream, river or pond, regular checks should be made with the National Rivers Authority to check its purity; this applies particularly to 'natural' sources which may become polluted with pesticides, fertilisers, industrial effluent or other chemicals running into them with ground water. Of course, tap water (in other words, any water from the mains) is not always all it should be these days and at the time of writing two more serious incidents of mains water pollution have occurred, resulting in contaminated domestic supplies. If you have a spring or well on your premises it should be checked regularly for purity and not just assumed to be safe.

A horse can drink up to ten or twelve gallons (about forty-six litres) a day in hot weather and during periods of hard work, so don't underestimate requirements. One bucket of water, for instance, left with the horse for use while his owner is at work, or meant to keep him happy overnight, will normally be quite insufficient. At least two should be left, or a small dustbin fixed in the stable and perhaps filled by hosepipe. It's useful to have two watering points in a stable, bearing in mind the number of times horses seem to deposit droppings in their water containers, leaving themselves without a clean supply.

The Organic Movement

Producing food in a way we might call non-organically is a fairly new system. Until the Second World War necessitated much higher food production than had hitherto been possible, all food production was what we now call organic. It is nothing new but a proven, age-old system and the only one until necessity became the mother of invention, as so often happens, and super-fertilisers, concentrated, altered chemicals, highly toxic pesticides and all the other 'baddies' we have become so familiar with during recent decades were developed to enable us to grow more and more food with less and less trouble from pests and diseases which reduced yields. Hormones increase flesh in beef cattle and milk yields in dairy cows and we were perhaps rather slow on the uptake in realising that these things can and do filter out into the surrounding environment and linger in the food chain to the detriment of our own health and that of our animals.

From the point of view of cereal foods such as our horses eat, it has long been proved by marketing experts that demand creates supply. If we continue to ask about organically produced horse feeds and push for them (as in anything else) they will gradually become more and more widely available, with easy means of recognising them, perhaps by the labelling on the bag including the distinctive symbol, in the UK, of the Soil Association. At present there is no single standard to guide us, but surely *any* reduction in unnaturally manipulated fertilisers and pesticides is an advantage.

It will take time, but constant public pressure will eventually, I believe, bring about a complete return to organic methods, an increase in bio-dynamics and genuinely safe fertilisers and other products being used in human and animal food production.

One of the most worrying group of products still in use is the organo-phosphates which are based on the nerve gas used in chemical warfare. Illness in humans and animals caused due to exposure to these on food or in the environment lasts for years, leaving great fatigue and severely weakened immune systems.

They are used widely in crop-spraying as insecticides and pesticides.

It is mainly public pressure which will correct this situation.

6 Skin and Coat: A Living Envelope

The Skin

The skin is a very under-rated part of the horse. It is a multi-role organ which is essential to life. If it receives extensive injuries, such as burns, the animal concerned may well die. If its openings, known generally as pores, are all blocked, the same fate will result due to auto-intoxication (self poisoning).

The skin forms a highly elastic covering for the sensitive tissues underneath and helps, in a way, to hold the body together. It is vital to the regulation of the body's temperature, it excretes some waste products in the sweat and it gives the horse essential information by means of nerve endings which detect pressure, pain, heat, cold and touch. It is capable of repairing itself, is instrumental in the manufacture of vitamin D when exposed to sunlight, protects the body from many of the toxins encountered in everyday life, from bacteria and viruses, from excess water or dryness and from minor injuries. It also gives us a good idea of the general state of health and well-being of the horse by means of its condition and that of the coat hair, whose roots are in the skin.

Structure

Skin consists of two main layers. The outer layer is called the epidermis and comprises dead cells which flake off, eventually, in small pieces of dandruff; other cells from the sensitive layer beneath, the dermis, take their place continually. The dermis contains the sweat glands, oil glands, nerve endings, hair roots or follicles and thread-like, hollow blood vessels called capillaries. It also contains the substance melanin which gives the skin and coat (and also the eyes) their colour. Complete absence of melanin in the body is known as albinism, albino horses having pink eyes as there is no colouring matter to disguise the blood in the eye. Melanin protects the horse from the harmful effects of ultra-violet light in the sun and the skin beneath coloured hair will vary from coffee-coloured to dark. White areas usually have pink skin under them and these, without their protective melanin, are much more likely to suffer from photosensitivity (sunburn), mud fever, rain rash and the effects of skin parasites, toxic substances coming into contact with the skin and skin diseases. However, it is not unknown for white or cream-coloured horses to have dark skin and coloured eyes and there is one particular Thoroughbred strain (its most notable member being Mont Blanc) which has this colouring.

Temperature Regulation

The horse's body works best at 38°C/100°F, or very nearly, and he can keep it there quite effectively except in extreme conditions, no matter what the outside climate is doing. Exercise creates heat; so do illnesses involving fever. The temperature varies slightly according to the time of day for each individual horse. Younger animals have higher temperatures generally than mature horses, older ones lower temperatures. Fit horses usually have slightly lower temperatures than unfit ones. It is well worth while taking your horse's or pony's temperature every day for seven days under the same conditions, normally best done when the horse is quiet and relaxed and at the same time each day, so you get to know his norm and can spot trouble. If the temperature changes by more than about 3°F either way you could have problems, especially if other signs are also abnormal.

The nerve endings in the skin keep the brain informed as to the ambient (surrounding outside) temperature, so it can adjust its various mechanisms accordingly and keep the horse's body temperature fairly constant. This only happens properly when the horse is in good health and is receiving a good diet so that all his systems are working well. Weak, exhausted, sick or rundown animals (and humans) do not work optimally (like a car run on too low a grade of fuel) and in such cases temperature control is only one of many systems which will eventually suffer. The hypothalamus in the brain senses the temperature of the blood passing through it and uses the nervous system to send messages to the various body systems to warm up or cool down the body until things return to optimum.

The skin is the outlet for sweat, which carries heat well, like all liquids. When sweat reaches the surface of the body it evaporates into the surrounding air, dissipating the heat with it. If the air is itself moist there may be difficulty in achieving evaporation and the horse may cool down very slowly, if at all.

The blood vessels in and just under the skin are also important in this function. When the horse is too hot they expand, carrying more heat-containing blood in them. This function is easy to see in raised blood vessels under the skin in finely bred horses after hard work, for example. The heat in the blood radiates out through the skin to the outside air, so cooling down the horse. When the horse is cold, the vessels contract, narrowing themselves and carrying less blood, so less heat escapes.

Another temperature regulatory structure is the coat. Most of the time, the horse needs to cool down in summer and with the natural shorter summer coat this is quite easy. The coat grows at an angle out of the skin and traps air between the individual hairs. The short summer coat obviously traps less air than the longer winter one, so heat loss can be achieved. In winter, the reverse can be the case: the longer coat and thicker insulating warm air layer helps conserve body heat. This function can be negated by moisture (rain, washing the horse or sweat) which flattens the coat and also by wind which blows the hairs apart and blows away the warm air.

Horses that have to withstand cold and wet, particularly when combined with wind, can soon suffer from hypothermia. The wetness flattens the coat and the water effectively conducts heat away from the body (as in sweating) so the horse cools down very rapidly, perhaps to a lower-than-safe temperature. If conditions do not improve the body temperature will drop and the horse's life is put in danger. This can happen to healthy, plump horses in the right conditions, not only thin ones with little insulating body fat, so it should not be imagined that simply feeding a horse up to the eyeballs with concentrates in winter, but leaving him with no adequate shelter, will be enough to help him fight off the effects of cold, wet and wind. Horses can withstand cold, still, dry weather quite well, however, and even cold and a certain amount of wind; but wet as well can be the real killer. The body, is such circumstances, cannot keep pace with the demands made on it to keep up the temperature.

The opposite effect, hyperthermia, can also kill the horse. Treatment of hyperthermic horses, most notably at equestrian sporting events such as horse trials and endurance rides or races, may consist, under veterinary advice and treatment, of icing the head, throat and inside the legs so that the cold will pass through the skin to pulse areas and blood vessels near the surface, so cooling down the blood in circulation. Cold hosing applied to various parts of the body may be used under veterinary supervision but it is generally avoided over muscle mass areas such as loins and quarters as it can cause muscles to cramp up.

The skin is such an effective barrier to changes of temperature that some vets believe that cold hosing in cases of, for example, sprained tendons does little good and may point to studies done in the USA where sensors were placed deep in the leg and the leg hosed, only to result in no change of temperature at all being noted deep in the leg. The blood in and immediately below the skin was cooled, so cold treatments, including cold packs, presumably have some effect in helping to reduce superficial inflammation.

The condition of the coat is a practical guide to the horse's health. If the coat is dull and rough (rather than smooth and glossy on a supple, free-moving skin as it should be, even in outdoor horses whose gloss may be dulled because of dirt), then the horse may be under the weather or sickening for something, if not actually ill. If the coat 'stares' (stands up away from the skin) this is a sign of his trying to keep warm and is often seen in thinnish horses whose subcutaneous (under the skin) layer of insulating fat has been used up.

Each hair has a tiny muscle at its root which, by contracting, pulls the hair upwards, increasing the thickness of the insulating air layer. This is a perfectly normal and natural action and happens in healthy, cold horses, too, but if noticed at a time when the horse would not normally feel cold, and combined with a dull, rough-looking coat, it could certainly spell trouble.

Although putting clothing on horses is intended to help keep them warm, it could be pointless in unclipped horses unless conditions are severe or the horse has to cope with wind and wet as well as cold, because the rug would flatten the hair, reducing the air layer. It would be a good plan to feel the horse's belly, loins, quarters and the base of his ears carefully to check if he is chilly before assuming he is. If he's unclipped and stabled at night try him without a rug: if he's being turned out on a cold but still, dry day, again try him without a rug. He will probably be more comfortable and you will save wear and tear on his clothing. With a clipped horse, of course, clothing will at least partly replace the hair (and its associated air layer) and help keep the horse warm.

Excretion

It is important that the pores of the skin are kept as clear as is reasonably possible so that the excretion of toxins in the sweat and the regulation of body temperature are not hindered. This is normally carried out in stabled horses by body-brushing, which is effective enough at removing dandruff and excess oil and dirt if carried out properly, weight being put on the brush to get the bristles right down to the skin. In unclipped horses, the use of the body brush is less effective, but it is not impossible to keep a long-coated horse fairly clean with a body brush.

The general idea is that outdoor horses should not be body-brushed as they need oil and scurf (combined with coated-on mud and dirt) to help ward off the effects of rain and wind. In natural conditions, it falls off gradually and horses dislodge it by scratching and rubbing on trees, rocks and the like, and by mutual grooming, scraping each other with the front teeth. The skin and coat of feral horses normally work perfectly, although they can become diseased and infested with lice and ticks, of course.

Hard-working, stabled horses not exposed to natural 'shower' facilities in the form of rain do need to be groomed. Rinsing down is also beneficial, although too much soap, however mild, is counterproductive as it can dry out the natural oil and make the skin dry, prone to tiny cracks in the surface through which infection can more easily enter, and itchy, causing the horse to rub and scratch and, again, break the surface. Plain water is very effective at removing surplus grease and perhaps we should not be in too much of a hurry to bring in stabled horses turned out for a couple of hours if there is a shower of rain. It won't harm them and they will soon come and stand by the gate if they want to come in. With young, finely bred foals, however, it may be best to keep a closer eye on them during wet, chilly spells and bring them in if they start sheltering a lot behind their dams. They cannot cope with the vagaries of the weather as well as older horses whose body systems are better established.

Sensation

The nerve endings in the skin are important to the horse for giving him information about his environment, as mentioned. The skin varies in thickness, as does the coat, according to the breed of the animal (which in turn depends on where it evolved) and the part of the body, skin being thinnest and having most nerve endings on vital areas such as the head, inside the legs and on the lower half of the body generally. The coat and skin are thickest on the top of the neck, the back, loins and quarters, which receive the brunt of the weather. The horse needs the special antenna hairs around muzzle and eyes to inform him about the proximity of grasses, other food and solid objects which he might otherwise collide with in the dark. Unfortunately, here in Britain it is still widely the practice to clip them off, but more and more people are being more considerate to horses and leaving them.

It may seem contradictory to have thin skin on the legs as they are in frequent contact with scrub, long grasses, mud and so on, but the horse also needs good sensory powers near ground level to be sure he keeps on safe ground as far as possible.

When the nerves are confronted with outside stimuli the sensory nerves relay to the brain what they have detected – heat, pressure, pain, cold or even a touch on the hairs as light as a fly landing. The brain sends a message out to the appropriate part of the body down other nerves called motor nerves (because they initiate movement) to move the body away from the stimulus if necessary.

We all want a riding horse with 'light' sides and a sensitive mouth. Were it not for the horse's sense of touch and awareness of pressure and weight (ours) we could not ride or drive him so effectively and would have to rely entirely on his sense of hearing. The brain, as always, receives the messages sent along the sensory nerves to tell it what aids we have given and the horse responds, not by instinct or reflex action as is sometimes suggested, but because he mentally agrees to cooperate. Because of his training to understand our physical and vocal aids, the brain again interprets this learned behaviour and the horse, we hope, does what we want.

It is known, though, that horses become less and less responsive the harder and more frequent the aids given him. In the same way that we get used to the 'white noise' of constant background music in a restaurant or shopping mall, he can still feel the aids but they no longer stimulate him so much. His response has become dulled. He develops a 'hard' mouth (although it is also true that injury through severe misuse of the bit can damage the nerves in the bars, with the same result) and dull, insensitive sides which can make him either dangerous or unpleasant to ride. There is also a style of riding in some quarters where the legs are kept 'on', if not actively communicating, all the time the rider is mounted, which cannot possibly help matters: such horses frequently have worn or even bare patches on their sides where the rider's legs have worn away the coat hair. Similarly with a rider who does not sit still but constantly moves against rather than with the horse's movements in the saddle. The horse frequently ignores any weight or seat aids given by such a rider, again because of the 'white noise' effect.

Anyone who has contact with a horse whose sides, for example, seem to be insensitive should take the opportunity of watching that horse on a day when flies are active and see how easily and quickly he feels and deals with any insect which lands on that part of his side which comes into contact with the legs to realise that those sides are extremely sensitive, just like the rest of the body which is covered in skin.

Like other prey animals, as opposed to hunter animals, horses seem to have a low pain threshold. Not only are harsh, rough aids unnecessary in normal circumstances, they can have the result of either dulling the horse's response to them or irritating him to the extent that he becomes angry: both can result in loss of control and consequent danger. Causing the horse pain other than occasionally for discipline purposes is bad horsemanship.

Skin Repair

Although very elastic (as you can test by picking up folds of skin on yourself or your horse and pulling slightly), skin can be injured in several ways. It can be slightly grazed, maybe only involving the epidermis; it can be burnt (rather unusual in the horse); it can be torn (lacerated) as by barbed wire or thorns, cut (incised) as on glass or by a sharp blade, or worn away by friction. Wounds can occur where the epidermis does not actually break, as in some bruised wounds or pressure sores. Skin does have the power to heal itself but infection can enter the wound during the healing process or at the time of the injury, probably the most serious result being infection by the tetanus bacterium (lockjaw) to which horses are very susceptible and which usually kills unprotected horses. Even if the horse is vaccinated against tetanus and has his boosters, many vets still prefer to give a shot of antiserum to give him extra antibodies ('soldier cells') circulating in his bloodstream to protect further against infection.

Most wounds heal better in the presence of air so any

dressings are normally recommended to be porous to keep dirt out but let the wound 'breathe'.

Healing by what is called first intention involves the edges of the skin being stitched together so that they heal quickly and usually without leaving a scar, the tissue healing together under the stitching further down in the wound. Stitching obviously does not take place in the wild, and the more natural form of healing is called second intention. Healing by second intention involves the production by the body of proud flesh (more correctly called granulation tissue) gradually filling the gap up to skin level where special skin tissue called squamous epithelium grows across the wound underneath any scab which may have formed from blood and other body fluids. As healing progresses, the scab falls off and new skin is left, often leaving a scar.

Sometimes, the body is a little over-enthusiastic in its production of proud flesh and too much is produced, bulging out of the wound and actually preventing healing. Although certain dressings can be applied to prevent this, if it does happen it normally has to be removed by the veterinary surgeon and the wound stitched to prevent a recurrence. Feral horses are sometimes seen with grotesque wounds filled to overflowing with ugly, sensitive red flesh crawling with insects and maggots, not to mention serious infections. In some conditions, wounds can be the cause of the horse's death as infection can enter the bloodstream and the wound become gangrenous.

A simple guide is to call the vet if any wound penetrates both main layers of skin and is more than an inch long, so that it can be stitched and problems made less likely. Stitching should take place as soon as possible; after twelve hours the edges of the wound will not heal so well as scar tissue begins to form.

Vitamin D

Vitamin D is needed by the horse for the health of bones and teeth and, in nature, the horse, eating wild grass and leaves and exposed to sunlight, would not suffer a deficiency; neither would the fairly naturally kept domesticated horse. Those stabled or kept indoors a good deal or who nearly always wear clothing when turned out could well suffer from a deficiency at any time of year if the diet is not supplemented.

Apart from his natural food, sun-cured hay is a good source of vitamin D (in other words, not barn-dried hay, although the vitamin may be added during the production process of hayage products – check the analysis panel on the bag), although most reputable brands of coarse mix and cubes will have it added.

Vitamin D stimulates the absorption from the intestine of calcium and phosphate, and their reabsorption from the kidneys so they are not passed out in the urine, but most plant foods contain only the vitamin D precursors *ergosterol* and *dehydrao-cholesterol* and not the vitamin itself. A precursor is an intermediate substance from which another is formed (in this case vitamin D) during the course of a chemical process. The horse absorbs the precursors from his food and secretes them on to his skin, where they are converted by ultraviolet light to vitamin D which is then reabsorbed and used by the horse.

Although the horse's body is usually almost entirely covered by hair, enough light gets through to enable this process to occur unless, as mentioned, the horse is usually covered by clothing or kept indoors. However, standing a horse without clothing under full-spectrum lighting in his box (lighting which ranges, like daylight, from the red to the violet parts of the light spectrum, like plant lights) will enable vitamin D to be produced. If only ultra-violet light or light emitting only the blue end of the spectrum (such as the cheaper fluorescent lights) were used, the horse could end up suffering from what humans call 'sick building syndrome'. The fatigue, headaches and irritability suffered by employees in offices lit this way, for example, could well be suffered by horses similarly treated – who knows?

It follows, therefore, that more natural management is by far the best way to give the horse his vitamin D, although we should be aware of the circumstances which may make its supplementation in the diet necessary for health.

Water resistance

The new porous, permeable or 'breathable' textiles used in

horse clothing now are an attempt to mimic the natural function of the horse's skin. Skin lets moisture out when needed but prevents excess moisture getting in except in extreme circumstances. The oil (sebaceous) glands are sited along the hair roots and secrete into the follicle a natural lubricant called sebum which spreads along the hair and skin, making the skin resistant to water from outside and preventing too much being given out; it also has an antibacterial effect.

Excessive shampooing of the horse with any product which breaks down grease, even the mildest animal or baby shampoo, is detrimental to the health of the skin. I feel only very dirty horses should be shampooed generally, and that even where horses are expected to be very clean for exhibition purposes, plain water is usually sufficient and the coat will look sleeker and glossier with his natural shine rather than the more shallow and superficial sheen produced by topical coat dressings, some of which can actually cause skin reactions. Because sebum is a lubricant as well as a protector, objects which might scratch the skin will slide a little more easily over it and, combined with the coat, a naturally lubricated skin will have more protection against and resistance to general abrasions than a rougher, over-dry skin lacking in natural sebum.

The Coat

The coat is of great benefit to the horse, not only because of the functions mentioned but because in the wild it acted as a camouflage. Most wild horses were probably about the colour of Przewalski's horse today, beige-brown and cream with black points, or roughly like the Exmoor pony. Domestication has brought about many genetic variations in colour which would make a horse positively stand out like a sore thumb in the wild, grey being a prime example. Prey animals need to be able to melt into the background or at least mingle unobtrusively with others in the herd in order to confuse a predator's eyesight. True, we have no green horses – although a friend of mine inadvertently turned hers a pale shade of green. He was a dark palomino and she wanted his coat more golden so she treated him to a mild bleaching with diluted hydrogen peroxide. It worked well and there were no ill effects on the horse, but next time she shampooed him he turned green and stayed that colour till he cast his summer coat!

Green horses would seem, from a camouflage point of view, to blend into the background perfectly, but in practice brown is a much less obtrusive colour than green, as you can see by looking at a garden. Brown string, canes and fencing blend much better with green foliage than green ones and anyone who has observed feral horses or ponies, say on Dartmoor or Exmoor in the UK, can testify how hard they can be to spot against the multi-shade variations of brown and green on the moorland. The myth of the white stallion leading his wild herd in purely natural surroundings is just that – in reality he would soon be spotted (no pun intended) and killed by a predator. Spots and stripes, actually, are excellent camouflage, helping to break up the animal's outline and blend it into the background, as for example in zebras and some deer.

Growth Patterns

The coat has two main casting (moulting) periods per year, in spring and autumn. It will grow and cast a little at a time over a period of a few weeks until the new coat is set, and this uses up a certain amount of energy in the horse: there is a true old saying to the effect that a horse never looks his best at blackberry time. The coat grows mainly backwards and downwards away from the head but various whorls and other shapes occur. The different growth directions, such as at the hips and on the flanks, help direct water down the most convenient channels to guide it away so it drips off the horse rather than soaking too readily down to the skin, but a steady downpour will soak any horse.

Horses and ponies evolved in cold climates have excellent insulating winter coats. You can examine any native pony with a thick layer of snow on his back and find that he is warm and dry next to the skin unless the snow is the penetrating, fine, wet type. Even so, it take some time to get through to the skin.

Hot-blooded types have thinner coats, as already mentioned, and normally higher tail carriages so that the tail hairs can be lifted away from the buttocks to allow heat to escape. Colder-blooded types have lower tail carriages and also thicker, more wiry and perhaps wavy hair, which all helps to trap more air next to the body and help the animal keep warm. Hairs are hollow, as well, which increases the insulating effect.

Controlling Coat Change and Growth

Working horses are commonly clipped in winter to relieve them of their heavy, thick overcoats which would cause overheating and excess sweating. If a hard-working horse were left standing in a thick coat, the sweat having flattened the coat and robbed the horse of much of his insulating layer, body heat would pass out through the moisture too quickly and he would cool down quicker than his coat dried. Heat would continue to be lost through the still-wet coat, and the horse could not only lose condition but also become hypothermic.

Clipping is normally carried out to get round this but it is, of course, a completely unnatural state to have little or no hair in winter. Many owners do not work their horses hard enough to justify conventional clipping, some don't like doing it and even more horses dislike or are frightened of it. In such cases, hand clippers such as those used by hairdressers can easily be used to give the horse a mini-clip, say on the breast and up the gullet, which removes a reasonable amount of hair for lightly working or fine-coated animals, but the thickness of the winter coat can be controlled by starting to clothe the horse in early autumn and, as the days shorten, exposing him to light.

At the first sign of the summer coat casting, put a light rug on the horse to fool his body into thinking the weather is still warm, and at the same time ensure that he is exposed to sixteen hours of light out of twenty-four. In the stable a fairly high wattage bulb, 150w or 200w, should be left on in the evenings (the bulb should preferably be the full-spectrum sort) so that the brain picks up the light through the pupil of the eye, again with the intention of making it 'believe' that summer is still well and truly here and there is no need to grow a thick coat. Some coat will still be produced, but it will be much lighter than if this treatment were not given. As the nights get colder, increase the clothing but always ensure that the horse is not uncomfortably warm or sweaty. The natural time for the winter coat to have grown fully, or set, is about the end of November, so you can omit the light part of the treatment then, and go easy on the clothing. In practice, the coat will not then grow much more, if at all.

Conversely, if you wish the horse to shed his winter coat early in spring, again give the horse the light treatment and ensure that he is warm. This is one way to bring, for example, Thoroughbred breeding stock into breeding condition for its earlier-than-natural breeding season, combined with good feeding.

If you do decide to clip your horse it is as well to remember that if the horse is turned out a good deal it is best not to remove any more coat than strictly necessary as he needs it for protection. The area needing most protection is the hind end (and obviously the back, loins and quarters). Horses habitually stand with their tails to the weather and need the hair left on the tops of the hind legs; they should also have unpulled tails to help prevent too much heat loss. Alternatively, you could use a rug with a tail flap if you wish to clip the horse and pull his tail.

The areas which sweat most are the neck, throat, shoulders and round the tops of all four legs, so these should be clipped if your aim is to avoid excess sweating. If horses are worked in muddy conditions they will kick up a good deal of mud on their bellies and between their hind legs and should really have some protection left to them in these areas, whereas they are usually close-clipped here. Perhaps consideration could be given to doing them with leg blades which removes some hair but leaves a little on.

Legs, too, are a bone of contention. Hair is meant to protect the legs from wet and mud, especially feather on the heels, but there is no doubt that hairy legs can still get mud fever and this cannot be effectively treated unless the hair is clipped off. I find a good compromise is to clip the legs of hairy horses with leg blades and to rinse off mud thoroughly on return from work, drying the legs thoroughly with a hand-held hairdryer, then bandaging over cotton mesh dishcloths or squares cut from an old anti-sweat rug, which will provide an insulating air layer next to the legs, unlike gamgee tissue or cotton wool. Liquid paraffin (mineral oil in the USA) can be smeared on the vulnerable areas of horses susceptible to mud fever and occasionally washed off with a mild soap or shampoo. An emollient cream, such as udder cream or E45 barrier cream, is excellent for white-legged blood horses as it is heavier and very effective. This does sound like a lot of trouble, but really helps in practice.

Not all animals *are* susceptible to mud fever, of course, but I still dislike the old practice, still recommended in some quarters, of leaving the mud on and brushing it off when dry. This can cause tiny abrasions to the skin surface and actually make it easier for the mud fever bacteria to enter the skin and cause infection. Particularly with the chemical and toxic content of mud in some areas today, I feel it is best to get rid of it as soon as possible as some animals, even if they do not succumb to mud fever, can react badly to chemical land treatments and pollution.

Trimming the horse – pulling the mane and tail, trimming leg hair, tidying up the long hair under the jaw and on the edges of the ears and removing the antenna hair around the eyes and muzzle – should be very carefully done to horses under any system of management but particularly those whose owners wish to keep them fairly naturally. An unpulled tail is best, and will look lovely carefully plaited for special occasions, particularly if neatly banged across the bottom so that the horse carries it halfway down his hind cannons (perhaps a bit shorter in winter to prevent a build-up of mud and snow and so that car drivers can actually see any reflective strips the horse might have on his legs when exercising on dark roads, if this is absolutely unavoidable).

The mane does help retain heat in the neck, which is another area where considerable heat loss can occur, but tidying it up by judicious pulling and snapping off the hairs at the ends with the fingertips on thin manes will improve the horse's appearance without removing too much protection.

The hair inside the ears should, I believe, be left to keep the insides fairly clear of debris falling down and causing difficult problems: simply close the ears together and trim off the hair protruding from the edges, particularly at the base of the ear, with curved fetlock scissors.

The fetlocks can be lightly clipped or tidied up with scissors and comb, always leaving the usual little frond on the ergot to assist drainage.

I am absolutely against the practice, still common in the UK at least, of removing the horse's antenna hairs for the sake of 'smartness'. These hairs are important to the horse for direction-finding in the dark, for helping him sort his food and avoid anything which might bang him on the head, and in general act as his eyes in the dark. Horses do adjust to having them removed, but it is much more considerate to leave them in the first place. I always ask people who trim them off if they would remove their cat's, dog's or pet rabbit's whiskers (perhaps rather bloody-minded of me!) and the answer is always something like: 'No, but that's different, isn't it.' Of course, it isn't different at all, but bigotry seems to be alive and kicking everywhere!

Clothing

Modern textiles have enabled vast improvements to be made in the field of horse clothing. Traditional fabrics such as wool and jute are still used but there is no doubt that they are much more difficult to launder (and may therefore tend not to get done) and are heavier for the horse to wear than the lightweight synthetics now commonly used. Proper 'horse-shaped' rugs are now very common and I hope it will not be long before the unshaped sort cease to be made. America (with its shaped Baker blanket) and New Zealand (with shaped, waterproof New Zealand rugs) led the field generations before the rest of the world caught on, but now horses of all nationalities can have the benefit of light, comfortable, well-fitting clothing with, nowadays, the even greater advantage of permeable, 'breathable' and often heat-retaining fabrics as well.

Putting a rug on an unclipped horse on a cold but dry, still day may well be counterproductive because it will flatten the coat, reduce the warm-air layer and simply replace what it has removed. However, waterproof turn-out rugs come into their own when the weather is windy and wet as they stop the water getting in (but, if a modern fabric, can allow some body moisture out) and also stop the wind blowing the hair apart and letting the warm air escape.

Clipped, stabled horses can now be kept warmer with fewer garments and much less weight. Improved design lessens rubbing and pressure, saves the coat and increases the horse's comfort.

For turn-out rugs, synthetic fabrics, which used to be guilty of 'leaking', are now much more reliable and, although they should normally be reproofed after laundering, depending on the exact textile design and function, they have the distinct advantage of repelling water in many cases, so avoiding the horrendous weight of a soaking wet traditional canvas turn-out rug, which also could take days to dry in some circumstances.

Although completely unnatural, good, modern clothing is a definite advantage in the health and comfort maintenance of today's horse.

Horn

The subject of feet is more fully dealt with in Chapter 2, but this is an appropriate place to point out that horn is a 'relative' of skin and hair. Like them, it is composed largely of a protein substance called keratin, and grows downwards from the coronet in tubules. It can take about nine months for a complete new hoof wall to grow from the coronet to the ground at the toe.

Modern innovations have produced effective hoof dressings which help to harden and protect the horn, as opposed to the old oils which simply stayed on the surface, prevented the uptake of essential moisture and gathered dust and bits. Ordinary oils can also prevent excess moisture, which weakens the horn, from evaporating. Dressings which contain gelatine and lanolin do seem to help the condition of existing horn, and new dressings claiming to sink into the horn and improve condition appear regularly on the market. Work done in Edinburgh, however, is showing that most hoof dressings barely sink into the horn.

The horn is largely produced from the nutrients in the horse's diet, and although there is some scientific and practical disagreement on the exact nutrients needed for healthy skin, hair and horn, it seems that methionine, biotin and MSM (methylsulfonylmethane) in the diet have definite effects on their growth and quality, as does adequate calcium balanced with phosphorus, the recommended ratio at present being 1.5 calcium to 1 phosphorus.

MSM is currently claimed to be able to help hoof wall moisturisation when fed as a dietary supplement, benefiting existing horn as well as that being produced from the coronet, and as most brittle hooves are in need of moisture, not oil, this development is well worth watching and following up.

Excess moisture, such as when horses are turned out on very wet land, can cause the horn to soften and wear, also the bulbs of the heels, although some animals are more resistant to this than others. Breeds which evolved in hot, dry areas such as the Caspian, are, conversely, able to withstand baked, cracked land in summer much more easily than some others. As ever, observing each horse as an individual helps us decide what is best for him and what circumstances are likely to cause problems.

7 Health Matters: It Really Does

Good health is one of those things nearly everyone takes for granted until they haven't got it any more, and animals are no different. We cannot tell whether or not an animal, having been sick or injured, ever feels thankful that it has recovered or appreciates feeling good while remembering what it was like to feel otherwise. One thing is for sure: sick and injured animals react to their misfortune just as we do, which is not surprising because we are animals too, of course.

Monitoring the Horse's Health

Most people spot when a horse is out of sorts because its behaviour changes in some way: normally it is lethargic and miserable-looking, standing at the back of the box or away from others if out, resting a lot, maybe lying down for more than half an hour at a time, and more frequently. It may sweat (a sign of pain, shock or fever, among other things), tremble, show breathing difficulties or may look or bite anxiously at the part causing discomfort or pain, such as snatching at the flanks in colic or gnawing at a painful leg, although the latter is less common in horses, in my experience, than in, say, dogs. The horse may ignore people or other animals it normally greets and associates with, such as not coming to the gate when you visit the field. Going off food is a common sign of disorder but so is unusual drinking behaviour, either drinking too much or too little. The droppings and urine are also good signs of health or disease. A horse will pass about eight piles of droppings in twenty-four hours and their colour and consistency depend on how he is kept. A hay-fed stabled horse will pass fairly firm balls of khaki-coloured dung just firm enough to break on hitting the ground, whereas a grass-kept horse's droppings will be green and looser. Any significant variation from these two extremes such as very small, hard droppings or loose, foul-smelling ones, should alert the manager's attention. The urine does not have to be clear: it can be cloudy but should always be some sort of yellow colour. If it is dark or has a strong or unusual smell, this could indicate trouble.

The best practical indicator of a horse's health is his temperature, and this should be the first thing the owner takes when suspecting disease. The horse has an average normal temperature of about 38°C or 100°F: if it reads about half a degree Celsius or one degree Fahrenheit above or below your horse's normal average at-rest reading, call the vet for advice, at least.

To take the temperature you can buy very accurate digital thermometers or ordinary mercury-filled glass ones, the strong, stubby veterinary sort available from your vet or a veterinary chemist. Shake the mercury down into the bulb with a snapping motion of your wrist, lubricate the bottom half of the thermometer with Vaseline or saliva and insert it into the rectum with a gentle twirling, side-to-side motion to ease its passage. Tilt it slightly to one side to ensure you have the bulb against the wall of the rectum and not inside a ball of dung where the temperature will be lower. Push the thermometer halfway in and leave it in place (holding on to it for safety) for the time stated on it, usually half a minute. Withdraw it, wipe it on the tail and read off the temperature.

Obviously, if your horse is excited, worried or has just exercised you will not get an accurate reading. Pick a time when he is quiet and take his temperature when he is well under these conditions at the same time every day for a week so you get confirmation of his normal average level, then you will know for sure when something is wrong.

The pulse can also be a guide to health, although individual horses' average at-rest rates can vary surprisingly from as low as thirty beats a minute to fifty or thereabouts. Old and fit horses have slower rates (and lower temperatures) than young and unfit animals. A high pulse rate at rest indicates a problem, although the rate will increase in excitement or fear anyway. An erratic beat also signifies trouble.

To take the pulse, use your fingertips (not your thumb which is less sensitive and has a pulse of its own to confuse matters) and feel along an artery where it crosses a bone; this is normally done on the lower jaw but can also be done inside the elbow, at the side of the dock or on the temple. Leave your fingers in any one spot for several seconds before trying elsewhere as the pulse is not always easy to pinpoint. Also, at rest the heart sometimes misses a beat quite normally and this has to be accounted for.

The pulse can be related to the respiratory rate quite usefully. The rough average at rest is about twelve to twenty breaths per minute, in and out counting as one breath. Larger animals breathe more slowly than smaller ones, and fit ones more slowly than unfit ones. Again, faster-than-normal breathing when the horse is at rest and has not just been worked or excited indicates a problem. If, at any time and for any reason, the ratio of respiration to pulse approaches 1:1 you should certainly call the vet.

Even when breathing hard the sound of the air going in and out should be smooth rather than harsh or rasping. When testing a horse's wind during a pre-purchase examination the vet will note whether or not the horse 'roars' or 'whistles' on *inspiration* as this indicates a breathing problem. Difficulty in breathing out, which normally involves no effort as it is a result of relaxation of the intercostal muscles (between the ribs), the diaphragm (the sheet of muscle separating the thorax [chest] from the abdomen) and the natural elastic recoil of lung tissue, usually means that the horse suffers from COPD. Lung damage caused in this common allergic condition means that the lungs do not recoil sufficiently and the horse has to make a muscular effort to expel more air at the end of what recoil there is. This gives an apparently double beat to the expiration of air or a break in expiration, which gives rise to the popular name of broken wind for this condition.

These are the most useful practical ways to gauge a horse's general health in addition to the usual ones of bright, alert eyes and appearance, lively, bright coat with skin moving easily over the ribs, no significant discharges, particularly from the nostrils, salmon pink mucous membranes, lack of lameness and so on, familiar to most horse people.

The Immune System

Like other creatures, the horse is equipped with a very effective immune system or disease-protection system which means his body is constantly defending itself from constant attack by potentially harmful bacteria, viruses, fungi and other invading micro-organisms. These can gain access to the body via wounds and various mucous membranes such as those lining the respiratory, intestinal and reproductive tracts and can be transmitted by an infected horse, a carrier which shows no symptoms of the disease or by insects and other means. In the case of pathogens (disease-causing micro-organisms) which cause allergic conditions such as COPD, they may be present in the environment on hay and bedding and not introduced by another living creature.

The germs, to use a popular descriptive expression, enter the body and multiply either locally in one place or systemically throughout the body, according to the pathogen concerned. The body recognises the invaders and soon starts producing fighting or 'soldier' cells of various sorts, mainly white blood cells, which either engulf them or otherwise put them out of action; so there is a stand-up fight going on inside the horse's body which we may never even notice. There is an incubation period, a period of time which may vary from hours to months or even years, depending on the disease, when the horse shows no outward signs of disorder, and this is often when the disease is most likely to be passed around to other horses.

After a while, the symptoms or signs typical of that disease may start to show themselves and it is often not until then that the horse's connections realise something is wrong, although loss of peformance is now recognised as a plain warning that all is not right.

The production by the animal's white blood cells of specialised proteins called antibodies is called the 'immune response'. The horse also has other means of defending the body from attack: the skin itself is an excellent barrier, as are the mucous membranes and the acidity of cell secretions, which create an unfavourable environment for the invaders. However, if the challenge is overwhelming, if the skin is broken or the mucous membranes, say, damaged by inflammation or irritation, the germs find it easy to get a hold and the horse becomes ill.

The immune system is very complicated and sometimes it goes wrong. For instance, in COPD, a very familiar allergic condition, special defensive cells called mast cells secrete too much histamine which causes the narrowing of the airways, the inflammation, swelling, irritability and mucus production which all go to reducing the horse's airspace volume, often creating severe breathing difficulties for him. In autoimmunity the body actually rebels against its own tissues.

Normally, however, the system works very well but, like any system, the more it is called upon the more energy it uses up. It takes energy to fight off disease and younger, healthier horses are obviously better able to do this than weakened or very young or old ones. The foal, of course, is born without his own antibodies but can absorb them within the first few hours of life from his dam's first milk or colostrum. If he doesn't get colostrum he needs veterinary help to build up his natural immunity.

When horses are sick, it is the stronger, previously healthier ones who are best able to fight off a significant attack of any disease, who have not only excellent energy resources but perhaps their own natural antibodies specific to particular diseases (produced by the body in response to a previous attack of the disease, as in strangles) who will stand the best chance of recovery. The reason animals need to convalesce and are run down after disease is because their energy resources have often been seriously depleted when fighting the invaders; damaged tissues also need time to heal. The disease organisms can damage the body tissue making it weaker in future and prone to attacks by other pathogens of the same or a different disease. For instance, strangles is a not uncommon secondary infection or complication after influenza.

After a bad attack of any disease the animal, being a living system, may never really recover his former health and strength. This is particularly likely if the convalescence period allowed is not long enough.

As well as the horse acquiring his own natural immunity in response to disease attacks, we can, of course, give him immunity by means of outside help in the form of vaccinations against certain diseases. Vaccines consist of live, altered or dead germs of the type against which we wish to protect the horse. Application of a vaccine stimulates the body to produce antibodies to that disease so that should an attack occur the body will be ready equipped to fight it off without having to undergo the delay involved in producing antibodies from scratch, during which time the body can become significantly infected. In time, the antibodies reduce in number and booster doses of the vaccine are needed if protection is to be maintained, the intervals between shots depending on the disease and its habits and the likelihood and possible virulence of any infection occurring. As well as producing antibodies to specific diseases, the body also produces antitoxins aimed at neutralising the poisons produced by invading pathogens.

The horse takes a little time to build up his immunity in response to a vaccine and sometimes more immediate help is needed. In such cases blood serum (a clear liquid part of blood) can be injected which has been taken from a horse already having a strong immunity to the disease concerned. This will often happen in suspected cases of tetanus where the infected animal has not been fully vaccinated against the disease. This immunity is not so long-lasting as that produced by a vaccine, however, and vaccination should be undertaken as soon as possible on a vet's advice.

When a vet administers antibiotics this is a way of providing extra outside help to combat bacteria or protozoans which are infecting the animal. Antibiotics are drugs or substances which kill or greatly cut down the multiplication of the germs. They have no effect on viruses but are often given in cases of viral infection to combat possible secondary infection with other bacterial germs.

Antivirals are substances aimed at killing or reducing the activities of viruses, but as viruses work by invading host cells, the antivirals kill the host cell too, so are more or less toxic to the patient. Interferon is the body's natural antiviral; administered antivirals are not widely used in animal treatment as they are very expensive and risky, although work is progressing on improving this situation.

Antifungals are capable of killing or inhibiting fungal infections and some antibiotics are effective in this field, too.

Antihistamines are administered to combat the effects of naturally produced histamine, for instance in COPD, but sometimes their effect can be disappointing. Other drugs for both desensitising the horse and minimising the allergy's effects can be given on veterinary advice, and broken-winded horses can often now be returned to hard work in combination with a clean air regime (dust-free feed, bedding and environment).

So, even though the horse has a very effective immune system of his own, we can help him by keeping him in the best possible health and by good management and hygiene in his everyday care. Also, vaccines should be given to protect him from unnecessary disease attacks and veterinary treatment sought when he does succumb to disease.

Tissue Repair

As well as fighting off disease, the horse can also repair his own body tissues when they are injured – skin and flesh can heal, so can ligaments, tendons and even bones, in theory, although the size and weight of the horse makes fractures problematical, depending on the nature and location of the break.

The healing of skin and superficial wounds was partly dealt with in Chapter 6. The basic healing process for body tissues is that the blood carries away dead and damaged tissue and provides oxygen and nourishment, including various proteins and minerals, for the manufacture of new tissue. Often, however, the replacement tissue is not as strong as the original. Horses with bad tendon injuries, for example, may recover, but because the new tendon tissue is not as good as the original the horse may be prone to further tendon injuries under less stress than caused the first injury. Scar tissue on skin may lack melanin and hair follicles, and healed tendon tissue may have dis-organised bundles of tissue fibre which are weaker than the regular bundles of the original.

Because of the extra work needed to heal an area, more blood is diverted there and this results in the familiar heat, tenderness and swelling associated with inflammation, a telltale sign of injury. Other body tissues also arrive, such as fluid leaking from damaged cells and accumulating in the area, and lymph, another body fluid involved in healing and fighting disease. The skin may be very stretched and if the resultant swelling is consider-able the area is said to be congested, which does not, in fact, help healing. Veterinary treatment in the early stages of an injury is normally aimed at reducing this over-enthusiastic response of the body, perhaps with anti-inflammatory drugs and/or, depending on the vet's school of thought, the application of cold packs. Gentle exercise is now often recommended, depending on the injury, to keep the tissues 'free' in cases such as tendon and ligament injuries and to prevent the formation of adhesions or the 'sticking together' of tissues because of the development between them of fibrous connective tissue during inflammatory conditions. If adhesions are allowed to develop, as they might if nature were left to itself, the action of the part would probably be permanently hampered and should that area be significantly stressed during work the adhesions and adjacent tissues might tear and cause further injury, whereas with gentle exercise and, in many cases, appropriate physiotherapy the tissues would remain able to move freely against each other and would not tear under such stress.

Bone is often thought of as a hard, dead substance, the framework of the body. It is certainly the latter but, as anyone who has ever suffered a broken bone knows, it is certainly not dead or insensitive. It has its own supply of blood, lymph and nerves and, like all living tissue, is constantly changing. In young animals it may be about 60 per cent fibrous tissue which accounts for its comparative 'softness' and malleability, whereas in old horses its composition may have changed to 60 per cent lime salts, making the bones brittle. Although constantly changing, bone in the horse is at its most serviceable, its toughest and hardest, between the ages of about six or seven and fifteen.

In general, horses mature from the ground up. The growth plates we hear so much about in young animals are sited at the ends of the long bones, notably the cannons, and are made of a cartilaginous material, tough and gristly, from which further bone grows enabling the bone to lengthen. On X-ray, this material does not show up well and appears as a gap or opening in the joints. Two-year-old racehorses sometimes have their legs X-rayed to see if their growth plates have 'closed' which indicates, to their trainers at least, that they are able to withstand harder training. As the horse matures, this cartilage turns into bone itself and when the process is complete the bones will not grow any more, although a layer of cartilage remains to help cushion the joint from concussion and facilitate joint movement, along with a special joint fluid called synovia.

Unfortunately, the closing of the growth plates by no means indicates that the horse's legs are mature – bone troubles from concussion or sheer over-stress still occur regularly in three-year-olds and sometimes in four-year-olds. Two-year-olds frequently go down with 'sore shins' or 'bucked shins' caused by over-severe training or hard ground, both of which mean that the horse has been subjected to conditions it cannot cope with. Some experts claim that sore shins are due to tiny fractures of the front of the cannon bone, normally in the front legs as these carry 60 per cent of the weight of the horse (plus, of course, rider and tack) and so are subjected to more stress than the hind legs. Others put them down to concussion, tearing away from the surface of the bone its protective membraneous covering, the periosteum, from the inner side of which new bone grows, enabling the bones to increase in girth. When a horse throws a splint, it is because the periosteum between the little splint bone and the cannon has been injured, normally as a result of concussion, tearing of the ligament between the splint bone and cannon or perhaps a blow such as a kick, and excess new bone is produced to heal the injury.

When bone is injured new bone crystals are formed to replace the damaged ones: fractures can heal but expert assessment of any break is needed to take into account the weight and temperament of the horse. A placid horse who can stand months of being in a cast or severely immobilised will stand a better chance of recovery than one who won't keep still and, despite casts and slings, over-stresses the break, either preventing healing or re-injuring the damaged part.

Sometimes, as with proud flesh, too much bone is produced and a possibly permanent hard lump or ridge forms at the site of injury: this is why horses who have had sore shins as youngsters often have permanently 'thickened' cannon bones at the front. Diseases such as arthritis, which affects horses as well as humans, produce permanently enlarged, deformed bones and joints and a very much weakened skeleton.

Degenerative joint disease (DJD), common in competition, performance and racehorses as a result of the wear and tear of their work, has been the cause of many a horse being retired and possibly being put down for economic reasons, as well as humane ones. In inflammatory conditions such as this it has been, and still is, common to give anti-inflammatory drugs which help reduce the inflammation and pain although doing nothing to help nature heal the part: indeed, some of these drugs even precipitate the breakdown of the bone. Now, a drug called hyaluronic acid can, depending on the case, be injected into the joint. It is the main constituent of natural joint fluid and the main stabiliser of cartilage, so helps heal and protect the joint rather than just damping down the symptoms. At present, various forms of hyaluronic acid are available and some are very expensive, so treatment can not always be afforded, but from the point of view of veterinary science this is certainly a big step forward.

It is normal in the horse world, even in racing, to delay jumping horses seriously until they are approaching natural maturity. In jumpers, the spine takes a great deal of strain and post mortem examination of jumping horses often shows various bone changes, indications of stress injuries and DJD in the spine, particularly in the lumbar region (just behind the saddle). The spine may not mature fully until a horse is six or seven years of age, an excellent reason for returning to the old practice of never starting to jump a horse until the age of five and not putting him to serious work of any kind, but especially jumping, until six or seven.

Unfortunately, in this sphere the competition horse world is even worse than the racing world. It is very common to see potential competition horses as young as three jumping fences of roughly 3ft (1m) loose or on the lunge, which is doing not only their legs but certainly their backs no good at all and will certainly not help them towards a long and useful life. There are various prestigious so-called 'high performance horse' sales around the world, arranged by national organisations or private individuals and stables, aimed at showing potential competition horses to buyers who (say the sellers) insist on seeing animals of this age 'popping' (in other words, actually jumping) a fence so that style and potential can be gauged. The animals will have been schooled for some months beforehand, of course, and so will have been jumping significantly from far too young an age for safety. It is not unusual to see, in animals jumping at this age, various lumps and bumps on the legs and symptoms of sore backs already – sad evidence of a very short-sighted policy indeed, it seems to me.

Medical work in Japan with a new ceramic stronger than human bone may lead to veterinary applications, lengthening the pain-free, useful lives of various animals, including horses. The bone substitute is 'bio-active', that is, it binds with the bone and can be moulded or cut into any shape, such as a vertebra. It has been used successfully in Japan for ten years but it does not seem to be anywhere near being approved for use in other countries. It is something to anticipate for the future, however.

Like other tissues, bone adapts to the stresses placed on it, or not. During fitness programmes, bone 'remodels' or thickens and hardens in response to work in a natural response to outside stimuli, but exact knowledge of this process is some way behind scientists' knowledge of soft tissue physiology due to lack of suitable techniques for taking biopsies or samples of bones before, during and after exercise, as can be done with muscles, blood and other tissues.

Rest and Sleep

As in most creatures, the horse needs adequate amounts of rest and sleep for the mind and body to 'renew' themselves. Sleep in all species is still rather poorly understood but we do know that lack of it, in both quality and quantity, causes irritability, lack of concentration and even nervous breakdown, in horses as well as humans.

Horses, like humans, experience short-wave sleep (SWS) and what is called rapid eye movement (REM) sleep. During various states of consciousness and sleep the brain emits electrical waves of varying frequencies or wavelengths. In SWS the horse is easy to rouse and this may well be a defence mechanism due to his being a prey animal. He can experience SWS standing up due to a locking mechanism called the stay apparatus in his elbows, knees and stifles, and also when lying down propped up on his breastbone. When predators threaten, it is essential, as explained earlier, for the horse to be off in a flash to stand any chance of staying out of their reach and, therefore, alive. It takes several vital seconds for a completely recumbent horse (flat out on his side) to get to his feet and be off, and these seconds could well mean the difference between life and death. It seems the horse does not dream during SWS and, although genuinely asleep, is only lightly so and the brain is not very active.

REM sleep, however, is a different matter. From experiments on humans, it seems that it is during REM sleep that we, and probably other animals, dream. 'Guinea pigs' woken during REM sleep (when the brainwaves are long and the eyes can be seen rapidly moving around and from side to side beneath the eyelids) all said they had been dreaming and could remember their dreams vividly, and researchers all remarked how relatively difficult it had been to rouse their subjects, compared with those in SWS.

The horse can only experience REM sleep flat out on his side, when he can be seen to twitch his legs, lips, ears and other parts of his body, including his tail, and also produce rapid eye movements. It is fairly easy to approach a horse during this state and fairly difficult to rouse him. It is, therefore, an extremely dangerous condition for a prey animal to be in, but essential, it seems, for the recreational state of dreaming. Deprivation of REM sleep by preventing a horse lying flat out (such as when stalled on a long sea voyage, when supported in slings during an injury or simply given a box or other stable area too small for him to lie down like this) is known to make horses miserable, tetchy and off-colour, just as it does humans.

Horses stabled near an enemy, those uncomfortable for any reason (clothing, insufficient, irritating or damp bedding, cold or heat, draughts, rats in the stable, etc.), those in a strange stable or with a new neighbour, suffering bereavement or some kind of loss (such as a best friend having left the yard, or during weaning), in fact in any emotionally or psychologically stressful situation, often refuse to lie down flat out due to a feeling of discontentment or insecurity, and, at such times, will be deprived of REM sleep. In most situations, the cure is to remove the cause if at all possible, and it is wise to watch horses, stabled or at grass, at all hours of the day and night, to check just who seems to be sleeping well and who is not.

Healthy horses do not lie down, flat out or otherwise, for more than thirty minutes at a time. They sleep for only about four hours out of twenty-four, anyway, and never all at once, as do humans. They snatch their sleep in half-hour or shorter spells all round the clock and in herd situations there are always one or two sentries standing on watch or grazing, looking out for trouble (predators, humans with headcollars, marauding dogs, etc.). As one horse wakes and rises, another will lie and rest, at first propped up (maybe standing), and later lying flat out. Even in a row of loose boxes, it is very unusual to find all the horses lying down at once, and never all flat out.

The importance of providing adequate sleep (and suitable facilities for it) and quiet rest, plus actual playing time, for horses should not be under-estimated as a management topic essential to their health. Despite our incomplete knowledge of sleep, it is certain that it is essential to well-being. When a horse is sick he will sleep and rest more, saving his body's resources for fighting the disease. Hard-working horses particularly need adequate rest and sleep for restoring resources and as a relief from the stress of their jobs.

It is noted that when horses lie down out in the open their main requirement is a dry place so to do (this is quite different from rolling in mud, which is done partly as a protective measure) and, for this reason, it would be as well for more attention to be paid to their bedding, particularly to shavings beds which, in my experience, are rarely kept dry enough. Try sitting down on your horse's bed for half an hour (perhaps reading this book!) and note whether you can feel damp striking through your clothing. If you can, so can your horse. Horses kept out should, similarly, be provided with a weatherproof overhead shelter kept bedded down (probably an open-fronted shelter shed with its back to the prevailing wind and sited on the driest part of the field) so that they can use it to sleep in when they wish to. If free to come and go, horses rarely stale in their shelter areas; but they have no choice in a stable.

Parasites

Although wild and feral *equidae* are troubled by external

parasites they probably have much less trouble with internal ones than do domesticated horses. Most internal parasites are picked up from pasture although bots are licked by the horse from his own skin. In wild conditions, horses are free to move on to fresher, sweeter pastures when they wish and over-stocking with its attendant high parasite infestation is not a problem. Also, different species of animal graze together habitually and kill off each other's parasites when eaten with the grass. Zebras, for instance, normally graze with wildebeest and not only eat different grasses and different parts of the same grasses but graze very closely together, presumably dealing with each other's parasites as they go.

In domestication, particularly nowadays, horses are often the only animals on a pasture. They are constantly taking in and passing out larvae and eggs, reinfesting themselves and their grazing companions, unless drugs are given very regularly. In addition, they are usually confined to very small paddocks compared with their feral cousins and worm infestation on the land builds up extremely quickly. Work done at the Animal Health Trust in Newmarket, England, some years ago concluded that there should be one horse and ten cattle to one acre of land, a stocking ratio hopelessly out of reach of most ordinary horse owners. It does emphasise, however, that the advice to graze the land with cattle, either at the same time as or following on from the horses, is still sound. Not only will the cattle kill off any horse parasites, which cannot survive in an unnatural host, but they will also graze off long grass in lavatory areas ignored by the horses and deposit their own dung and urine on any 'lawn' areas (those possibly over-grazed by horses), so enriching them, and masking the smell of horse droppings, which is repulsive to the horses. A discussion with your veterinary surgeon will keep you informed of any diseases which could be passed on by the cattle, such as ringworm, and steps to be taken in such cases, but he or she will also be the source of the best advice on worming medicines for the horses.

Nature is constantly evolving, and worms are no exception. Drugs which killed acceptable numbers of internal parasites ten years ago are now no longer so effective, due to genetically resistant worms having built up their populations. When exposed to a drug a given number of worms will be killed (never all of them) and some will survive to breed again. Some will be severely disabled but a few will not be affected at all due to some quality in their genetic makeup which means they are not susceptible to that particular drug. These happy and thriving worms obviously carry on breeding unperturbed and, despite six-weekly doses of the drug, are not affected and build up their numbers apace. Eventually, a whole population of zillions of worms, larvae and eggs exists in a herd and on its pastures despite regular worming.

The veterinary surgeon can do faecal egg counts, i.e. count the numbers and types of eggs present in droppings to tell you how your horses are infected, to what extent and with what. Blood tests can also be done to detect the foreign proteins in your horse's blood given out due to the presence of invaders – in this case not germs, but worms. He or she can then recommend a suitable wormer. If, after worming, the count does not show an appreciable fall in egg numbers, or in the amount of alien protein, you'll know that your present drug is not effective against the race of worms infesting your horses.

At the time of writing the two most effective drugs against parasites, including bots and 'true' worms (mainly strongyles) are ivermectin and pyrantel. The latter is also effective against horse tapeworm. There are currently no reports that I can discover of resistance to pyrantel, although some are just beginning to come through of initial resistance to ivermectin. This is worrying, although perhaps to be expected, as ivermectin is so far the only drug which kills off larvae circulating in the bloodstream at normal dosage levels. This is a big advantage, because it is the larvae which do the main damage to arteries, weakening them and causing aneurysms (ballooning) which can burst without warning and kill the horse. They also cause blood clots which block blood vessels, cutting off the blood supply to the gut, which can cause fatal colic. Mature worms, of course, cause considerable damage to the gut lining, favouring the development of peritonitis, and bots (actually fly larvae and not helminths or worms) damage the lining of the stomach where they congregate for the winter if left in peace.

At present, it is still sound advice to worm your horse with ivermectin after the first frost of the winter, which will also kill adult bot flies due to begin operations next spring by killing off their larvae inside your horse. Of course, if all other horse owners did the same thing the bot fly would become extinct within a season. This dose of ivermectin will also kill helminth larvae in the horse and, as fewer are taken in in the winter (worms breeding most in warm, moist conditions), will significantly control the problem. In early winter give a double dose at one worming with pyrantel for tapeworm (and helminths) and continue at possibly eight-weekly intervals with ivermectin and other drugs, as recommended by your vet, throughout the year.

If you are unfortunate enough to keep your horse on premises with other horses whose owners will not worm properly or cooperate in a joint, all-at-the-same-time worming regime, which is the only way to achieve really effective control, your best plan, currently, is to use ivermectin almost exclusively, to keep down the larvae population in your horse at least. Your vet is the best person to advise you generally on the possible problems of resistance normally encouraged by not rotating wormers, changing from one drug to another unrelated drug so resistant worm populations do not get a chance to build up. Look on your wormer for the actual drug, not the brand name, and be sure to buy the right drug, although your vet will surely tell you which branded products to use.

Land management also plays a big part in maintaining the health of domesticated horses from the point of view of nutrition and parasite control. In the wild, as mentioned, horses move on when the pasture becomes eaten down (as well as for other reasons, such as more shelter at certain seasons) but the only way they can do this in domesticity is if their owners rotate their grazing. It is best to have your land divided into at least three areas so that you can use, treat and rest each in turn. Two separate areas would be an absolute minimum to allow this.

Apart from the fact that land should be rested for three continuous months each year, rotating grazing helps avoid over-grazing of the same areas all the time and, of course, the build-up of parasites whose larvae are constantly being taken in again and recycled by the horses. Expert advice on soil and herbage analysis, seed mixtures where needed and appropriate fertilisers according to the results of the analysis can be obtained from seed companies, independent consultants and fertiliser companies if you are using their products. Independent advice can be obtained, in the UK, from the Equine Services Department of the Agricultural Development Advisory Service which is part of Ministry of·Agriculture; their local telephone number is in the phone directory.

Horses are naturally selective grazers. It is not true that they only like short grass. They will certainly eat long grass but they do seem to prefer sweet grass, although as individuals they have preferences as to grass types just as humans have food preferences. It is no use sowing unpalatable grass types as horses are known to go hungry or chew fences before they will eat something they don't like. Horse paddocks, particularly those for winter use, need an element of hardwearing grass species to protect against hooves. It is the habit of horses to designate lavatory areas in their grazing grounds and to use them exclusively, unless desperate, for dunging and urinating. They also tend to perform these functions on the edges of the lavatory areas, so they grow larger and larger and the grazing areas grow smaller and smaller. Although this is one way of keeping the horses away from parasite larvae passed out in the droppings, it is also very wasteful of land and potential food. Over-grazing certain areas depletes them of essential minerals, so that what grass does regrow is poorer and poorer. Weeds and poisonous plants also thrive on poor land like this. It is also less resistant to hooves as the root-mat cushion deteriorates, and it becomes easily cut up and poached and so even less able to support a useful growth of grass. And, of course, the more larvae there are crawling around away from the lavatory areas the more your horse picks up and the more seriously he becomes infested.

The best thing to do, after dividing your land, is to graze the horses on it for a few weeks until the grass growth becomes patchy. During this time, do your level best to pick up the droppings daily – an awful chore but the best way to keep the larvae right down, and not too bad if you work out a 'droppings rota' with friends, family and colleagues. Do not follow the old advice of breaking up the droppings (with a harrow or some other way) and spreading them around to desiccate in the sun and air; this is now frowned on as the desiccation is, apparently, not as effective as the spread of larvae resulting in the scattering of the droppings. The most dangerous weather for larvae development is warm, moist weather, so if you only pick up droppings then it's better than nothing. A hard frost and a boiling hot, dry day will both help to kill eggs and larvae on the pasture.

After a few weeks, then, move your horses on to another field and, if possible, put cattle on the first field to eat down the lavatory areas and some larvae, or at least cut ('top') the long grass. The field should be harrowed hard in both directions to root out dead, matted grass and aerate the soil and, according to the advice you receive, any necessary fertilisers applied. Then shut the field up to rest and grow, not using it at all for several weeks – in fact until the grass in the second field becomes patchy and in need of treatment. If you have a third field to bring into the rota, all well and good.

This kind of rota mimics nature as best as possible during domestication and will effectively keep down your parasite problem as well as providing plenty of suitable, cheap food ideally suited to your horse's digestive system. Special seed mixes can be made up to provide 'non-fattening' grazing for athletic performance horses, high-energy/protein grass for breeding stock, low-energy but filling food for laminitic ponies, and so on. If you remember that, in general, horses cannot take rich pasture of the type suitable for dairy cattle, but do best on clean, well-managed but poorish-quality grass from a food-value point of view, you will not go far wrong.

Diseases of Domestication

Probably the three most significant and common diseases directly caused by man and his mismanagement of his horses are azoturia, colic and laminitis. There is also the allergic condition of chronic obstructive pulmonary disease. There are others which are favoured or encouraged by the horse's environment and work, such as navicular disease, arthritis and viral and bacterial diseases such as equine influenza (often under-estimated in its seriousness), strangles, equine herpes viruses, diseases of reproduction such as contagious equine metritis and so on, but the first four disorders mentioned are probably the most widespread among all categories of horse and the first three, in particular, are nearly always directly caused by man and are never, or almost never, reported in feral-living animals. Parasite infestation, in the wild, would never build up to the proportions found in domesticated populations and here special mention should be made of feral animals living in restricted environments such as the New Forest in England, where parasite burdens are great due to over-stocking of the area with ponies.

Feral and wild *equidae* could, of course, catch any viral or bacterial disease, but as they often live in isolated populations they may well not come into contact with other herds infected by any given disease and almost certainly not with domesticated horses among whom the diseases are most common due to intensity of numbers in comparatively small areas. As they spend all their lives in one particular area, unlike many domesticated horses and ponies, they build up strong resistance to whatever diseases are common in their area and probably remain relatively free from such diseases. When they do succumb, though, the results may be disastrous because of lack of nursing care and, of course, of prior vaccinations to establish protective immunity.

Azoturia
This condition is also known as equine myoglobinuria, equine

rhabdomyolysis, paralytic myoglobinuria, set-fast, tying-up, Monday morning disease (although the latter expression is also often used to describe lymphangitis) and exertional rhabdomyolysis. It is always associated with exercise but is still imperfectly understood and probably has several triggering factors. A fairly common idea is that, as it usually occurs in horses who have been kept short of exercise but still on a heavy concentrate diet, energy in the form of glycogen accumulates in the muscles. Then when the horse starts to exercise again, such as on the day after a day off, excessive amounts of the metabolic toxin lactic acid are liberated in line with the amounts of glycogen. Lactic acid causes muscle damage and pain, during which process the colouring pigment myoglobin is released from the muscle cells and is partly excreted in the urine. However, some of its molecules are too large to pass through the very fine tubules or filters in the kidneys and so accumulate there, causing kidney damage, too.

The condition can be very mild, causing the horse to be slightly stiff and pottery, and maybe to tremble slightly, or extremely serious with staggering gait, hard, swollen and extremely painful muscles of the quarters and thighs, possibly even causing the horse to fall down and be unable to rise. In mild cases the mistake is often made of keeping the horse walking gently about whereas in all cases of azoturia it is essential to cease all movement at once. If the horse is walked for any distance he could well die.

In a nutshell, this is a condition of bad management related to feeding and exercise. The rule with any horse fed on concentrates should always be to reduce the concentrates before reducing the work and to increase the work before increasing the concentrates. 'Days off' where the horse is kept stabled with little or no exercise should be forbidden in all stables! The horse can certainly be rested but not box-bound. A walk in hand 'to pick a little grass' is also quite insufficient. He should be turned out in a field or surfaced enclosure, led briskly in hand for a good half hour twice, hacked gently out for an hour or so or led from another horse. Almost anything will do so long as he receives some exercise.

His concentrates should be cut right down, maybe to as little as a single handful of his normal concentrate in each feed of his day off, to keep his digestive micro-organisms ticking over and ready for an increase after his next period of work.

Azoturia is definitely a job for a veterinary surgeon. Keep the horse still to prevent further muscle damage and put a rug, your jacket or whatever is available over him, particularly the loins and quarters, if the weather is at all chilly, and wait for the vet.

Recent research indicates that electrolyte (mineral salt) imbalance could also be a contributory factor, stressing the need for a correctly and professionally devised and balanced diet and the use of electrolyte supplements *after* work if the horse will accept them and seems to want them. Dehydration is felt by some to be a factor and electrolytes are important in combating this, but it is also vital that owners of performance horses come to realise that the old advice to deprive horses of water for hours before work, during work and after it is quite wrong. Horses can be allowed water up to an hour before hard work. Endurance riders now realise that it is vital to let their horses drink en route if dehydration is to be avoided (and the same could apply to hunters, of course, whose work is often prolonged) and horses should be allowed frequent short drinks immediately after work until their thirst is satisfied even when hot, say five swallows every ten minutes or so. Some equine physiologists recommend that horses should have free access to water immediately after work and between phases of competitions such as events (horse trials) and endurance rides when horses should be encouraged or, if necessary, trained, to drink en route.

Work is continuing on azoturia and exercise physiology in general and it will be very interesting to keep track of it.

Colic

'Colic' is a term indicating abdominal pain but horsemen generally use it to refer to digestive disorder of a serious kind. Whatever type of digestive colic is referred to (spasmodic, flatulent, etc.) it all boils down to incorrect feeding for the horse concerned and his circumstances, although it can certainly be brought on by stressful situations such as a long journey which, again, can interfere with the digestion.

Feeding has been discussed in Chapter 5, so it is probably enough to emphasise here that anything which interferes with the regularity of the digestive system, such as not feeding identical ingredients (as opposed to identical amounts) in each feed, giving the famous weekly bran or linseed mash, feeding insufficient roughage and too many concentrates, feeding poor-quality feed, using up all an existing batch of food before starting a new batch instead of mixing them for a fortnight, and so on, are all highly likely to cause colic. Giving a full feed when a horse is tired after hard work 'to restore his energy' is also wrong as his blood supply will be diverted to other jobs such as clearing away toxins, repairing or renewing body tissues and so on, and so will not be fully available to help the digestive system function as it should. A horse should be given a small feed of his normal ingredients after he has cooled down rather than a normal-sized feed, and certainly should not be given a bran mash, for reasons explained in Chapter 5.

A type of colic caused by parasites is where the larvae have blocked off the blood supply to a particular part of the gut which becomes damaged or killed off as a result. Food may be unable to pass this point or simply not be digested there, causing a blockage. Parasites can also cause an intussusception in the gut where it 'telescopes' on to itself (thought to be caused by irregular peristalsis or gut movement because of parasite activity, or by enteritis). This can cause strangulation of the gut and blockage of the blood supply, leading to gangrene. A twisted gut, where the intestine twists round on itself in a tight loop, is thought to have the same cause and result. In both conditions the affected part of the gut may have to be removed by surgery, but the outcome is by no means always successful.

Colic, again, is definitely a situation for a veterinary surgeon. I should call the vet out for even a very mild colic, rather than waiting as is sometimes advised, as time lost in giving appropriate treatment can also mean a lost horse or pony. Check with your own vet as to what management to give the horse pending his or her arrival. Normally the old advice to walk the horse is no longer thought appropriate, as it can tire out an animal needing all its resources to fight a very painful condition. Certainly all food should be removed. It is no longer advised to drench the horse with a colic drink as this can do more harm than good, or, if it contains painkillers, can mask symptoms which the vet needs to see.

Laminitis

This is another extremely painful, dangerous and common disease which should be entirely preventable and, again, is almost entirely the product of domestication. Although wild and feral animals could, in theory, get it, in practice they are very unlikely to find themselves in an environment favourable to its development. This disease, too, is not yet fully understood, but research is being done particularly by Robert Eustace at the Laminitis Clinic at the University of Bristol, England, and a good deal of work has also been done in the USA.

Often triggered by an overload of food, laminitis is also caused by jarring (by fast work, even trotting, on hard surfaces), stress, cortico-steroid drugs which may have been administered for other conditions (such as sweet itch), toxaemia (blood poisoning), digestive upset, incorrect trimming and shoeing and any condition which interferes with the blood supply to the feet.

Any animal which is obese is a prime candidate for laminitis, whatever its breeding – it is not only cobs and native ponies who get laminitis – and elderly ponies (about fifteen years and older) with pituitary tumours are also prone to it. The first sign of this condition is a failure to shed the coat, the hair of which becomes long and wavy. The pony may become diabetic and eat a lot of food yet become thin.

Cortico-steroids should not be given to animals with a risk of getting laminitis because they act by constricting the blood vessels and so reducing the blood supply: in laminitis, the blood supply is already hampered and cortico-steroids simply make matters worse. Other anti-inflammatory drugs should be used instead.

The classic laminitis stance, with the horse leaning back on his heels (front or back) to take the weight off the most painful part of the foot at the toe, is a reliable sign of the disease but the feet are not necessarily hot as the blood supply may have been lessened rather than increased. The supply is needed to maintain the health and integrity of the immensely strong bond between the sensitive and insensitive laminae inside the feet, and when the supply or the composition of the blood itself deviates from normal the laminae can begin to separate and the crescent-shaped pedal bone inside the foot becomes more and more detached from the horny wall. It is not always realised that this bond between the laminae is the only thing that is supporting the horse's weight.

As the hoof wall and pedal bone start to separate and the bone becomes loose or detached, it starts to move downwards, and if you feel all round the top of the coronet with your finger you can feel a 'ditch' or depression immediately above the coronet which clearly indicates this movement. If the bone is detaching at the front, the foot is said to be foundering. If the ditch goes all round the coronet the bone is obviously detaching all round and is said to be sinking. All cases of laminitis are urgent and need immediate veterinary attention, but sinkers need specialist care from a vet or clinic specialising in these cases within twenty-four hours if the horse is to be saved.

Another sign useful for diagnosing laminitis is the state of the horn in the white line area of the toe. The white line is where the insensitive, horny laminae and the sensitive, fleshy laminae bond inside the foot. As the bone and the hoof wall separate, a softer cheesy horn forms in the gap and can be detached at the white line which becomes wider and soft. This is most easily checked at shoeing. Animals with chronic founder may go undetected by unobservant owners and farriers and the condition may become worse as the animal continues to work. Normally the gait will be shorter than normal, the horse may appear reluctant to work and may show signs of feeling generally off-colour or ill-tempered.

Once laminitis is diagnosed or suspected, expert, specialist advice should be sought. It will probably be advised that frog supports are fitted to help prevent further movement of the pedal bone: these can be applied simply by taping folded bandages to the underside of the foot. Veterinary treatment may involve cutting away the front wall of the foot (called a dorsal wall resection) to allow healthy horn to regrow in alignment with the new position of the pedal bone, and special support shoes (heart bar shoes) supporting the bone from under the frog may be needed once their exact position has been determined by X-ray.

Management of the laminitic horse or pony has changed in recent years. The old advice to walk the animal 'to get the circulation going again' is now known to be completely wrong as it will cause further damage within the foot, as well as causing the animal unnecessary suffering. Forcing a laminitic animal to walk, maybe even hitting it to force it to move, amounts to criminal negligence, even cruelty.

Feeding is critical as the animal must have adequate nutrients, particularly those aimed at producing healthy skin, hair and horn (which are all similar substances), without being given excess energy. A high-fibre, low-energy feed is needed with balanced vitamins, minerals and trace elements, and with adequate protein. At present in the UK, Dengie Feeds produce such a range of feeds which are used and recommended by the Laminitis Clinic at Bristol, and a supplement ideal for this purpose, Farrier's Formula, is available both here and in the USA.

The old idea of starving laminitic animals, both those suffering from the disease and those which have suffered previous attacks, is now known to be quite wrong (although still widely practised) as when kept short of food animals can start using their own body tissues for nourishment: they can become seriously undernourished while still fat and even though they may eventually lose weight they lose muscle tissue, too. This is obviously no condition in which to maintain them. With a diet more closely approximating their natural diet, high in fibre (which is satisfying) and low in energy (which horses were evolved to thrive on) and which includes all the nutrients the animal needs, you can keep his weight at the ideal of not actually being able to see his ribs but of being able to feel them quite easily. The horse or pony will feel content and have sufficient dietary resources, including energy, to work well and maintain good health and tissue integrity.

An understanding farrier is essential for the maintenance of a working – indeed, of any – horse or pony, but it is particularly critical, with laminitic animals, that he is prepared to keep the toes nice and short and shoe the feet well back at the heels to provide essential support there. All too often toes are left too long and heels not rasped down enough (as the heel horn keeps growing but the toe horn stops, following separation of the laminae). This puts unnatural stresses on the foot and leg and apart from causing tendon strain it over-stresses the hoof at the toe, producing unnatural forces and encouraging the toe wall to separate gradually from the pedal bone. Sometimes a horizontal crack appears across the wall just below the coronet because of the excessive force transmitted up the toe wall as the hoof turns over with every stride.

The two factors of correct diet and correct foot trimming are well within the control of the owner or manager of the horse, and owners should request their veterinary surgeons, when appropriate, not to give cortico-steroids but to use a different anti-inflammatory drug or painkiller (laminitis is not primarily an inflammatory disease). Owners should remember that stress of any kind, such as attending a show, a journey (particularly if undertaken in a poorly ventilated vehicle and/or one driven inconsiderately so that the animals are thrown off balance), discontent in general, etc., can all trigger laminitis, particularly an upset digestion which, itself, can be caused by these things.

Chronic Obstructive Pulmonary Disease

This allergic condition has already been discussed in Chapter 4, so it will probably be realised that it is a disease of domestication and should, with proper management, be largely preventable apart from the effects of respiratory diseases or pollen in some horses.

Veterinary assistance and treatment can be given both to allay symptoms and to protect the horse against their occurrence. From the management point of view, placing the horse and any adjacent stabling on a clean air regime can keep the condition at bay to the extent that previously badly affected animals are able to return to quite hard work. One thing is sure: the condition is progressive, so the longer owners put off treating it the worse it will get and the harder it will be to effect a 'cure'. In fact, the animal may always remain susceptible to it but with good management may never actually suffer the symptoms.

Clean air regimes are an excellent idea whether a horse has wind problems or not. Most high-class competition horses are on such regimes whether they have shown COPD symptoms or not and lung function tests and general performance prove that they improve horses' work and well-being.

What is needed is to establish as near as possible a completely dust-free atmosphere by placing the horse on dust-free feed and bedding and in a dust-free atmosphere. Whether the dust in question is just that, physical dust, or fungal spores, which are more harmful, it is still deleterious to the horse's condition.

For bedding, shredded paper kept on a semi-deep-litter basis or mucked out daily is suitable, as are vacuum-cleaned shavings or straw. These can be bought ready vacuumed or machines can be bought so that yards can vacuum their own hay and straw bedding. The machines currently available are not suitable for 'home cleaning' of shavings. Obviously, sawdust and peat, which contrary to popular opinion is a very dusty bedding, are not suitable for this management system.

Hay can be soaked for up to twelve hours either to damp down dust or to swell spores to such a size that they cannot be sucked down into the horse's airways where they cause such damage. However, soaking hay longer than this can result in the leaching out of essential nutrients, so significantly reducing the quality of the hay when eaten. Even apparently clean samples of hay should be soaked, but those which are obviously dusty or mouldy should not even be used for bedding down field shelters.

Other forage sources to provide horses with their roughage

and bulk are available should hay be a problem. There are hayage products available in vacuum-sealed polythene sacks, which, in layman's terms, come halfway between hay and silage – long grass semi-pickled and preserved in its own juices – and other similar products, such as Hygrass in the UK, produced in a rather different way but with a similar result: clean, nutritious forage. These products come in different energy grades for different categories of animal, children's ponies, performance horses, breeding stock and so on, so it should be easy to choose a suitable product for your animals. The nutritionists at the firms making them are always willing to give advice. There are also various makes of bagged, molassed chop (or chaff) available and the forage range marketed by Dengie Feeds which fulfils the same purpose. Hydroponically grown grass (grown in units with only water and sometimes special nutrients, but no soil) is also a valuable part of a clean air regime diet.

Concentrates, if fed, should be damped before serving, but cubes (nuts/pellets), and coarse mixes (sweet feeds in USA), being moist compound feeds, are also suitable. Both come, again, in various energy grades and all are expertly balanced as regards nutrients. ('Complete', hayless diets are quite unsuitable for the horse's digestive system and mentality.)

These bedding and feed products, together with very well ventilated and regularly vacuumed-down stabling, constitute a clean air regime, the nearest one can get in domesticity to the sort of environment the horse would enjoy in the wild.

Drugs and their Origins

Like many creatures (though perhaps not humans), horses often seem to have an instinct for the foods they need. Palatability trials have shown horses known to dislike a particular grass or herb positively picking it out when they are off colour presumably because it contains something they feel they need at that time. So many drugs come from plants, fungi and naturally occurring minerals and other substances that it is surprising that so many people still regard herbal, homoeopathic and other so-called alternative medicines as witchcraft or something akin to it. Apart from the comparatively modern realisation that lifestyle and freedom from excessive stress exert a great influence on mental and, often therefore, physical health, the use of the earth's natural products as medicines, whether employed in conventional or alternative medicine, is nothing new, of course.

Many of these substances are available readily in nature and as such could be regarded as nutrients. Many supplements are sold as nutrients for both human and animal treatment because our laws forbid them to be labelled as medicines, even when they are being used as such, without a great palaver over licensing, testing and proving that they do what so many people already know they do.

Much more emphasis is placed today on preventive medicine and management, in contrast to the older scheme of waiting for something to go wrong and then calling in the vet. Veterinary surgeons and other 'modern' experts are invaluable in formulating a health maintenance plan for our horses and it is becoming more and more common for vets, nutritionists, farriers, physiotherapists and others to work together cooperatively instead of separately and competitively for the benefit of the horse, particularly in enlightened competition yards. There is still scepticism, not only among horse owners and managers but also among members of the various professions themselves, not least, in my experience, some vets, but I feel the general atmosphere today is one of more open-mindedness and an increased willingness to work together which has in part been brought about by intelligent and perhaps more caring owners (who foot the bills) wishing to adopt a wider view of their horses' health and well-being and wishing to try all means at their disposal, to take advantage of the 'new' sciences of, for example, exercise physiology and nutrition, in order to keep their horses in the best condition possible – even if it *is* only to win prizes!

It is not natural, of course, for one species intentionally to interfere in the health of another and, in this sense, human and animal medicine are unnatural practices, but this is one of the benefits to the horse of domestication as opposed to a purely natural life. Although, in the wild, horses may treat themselves by seeking out certain plants or herbs which they feel they need (and so 'know' instinctively that this is what they need just now), horses can acquire a craving for something harmful and poisonous, such as acorns, which are addictive – as, for example, humans do for tobacco and alcohol – so the horse's taste is not infallible. This normally happens if the horse has experimented with something bitter or otherwise unpleasant, such as ragwort, because he is hungry: another excellent reason for feeding horses properly and ensuring that they have a satisfying diet which provides all their requirement without overloading them.

'Alternative' Medicine

In addition to veterinary medicine (and human medicine) there are other sources of treatment sometimes still regarded as 'crank' areas, such as homoeopathy, chiropractic, osteopathy, herbalism, acupuncture and acupressure, massage, hydro-therapy, radionics and so on. Some of these fields may come under the general heading of physiotherapy which is now a recognised and accepted part of human and animal treatment. Herbalism and acupuncture, in particular, are very old forms of treatment known to be of benefit, yet people are sometimes still sceptical about them.

All forms of alternative or complementary medicine have their enthusiasts and denigrators. Personally, I am in favour of anything which works even if there is no scientific proof that it does so. Until fairly recently, there was no actual scientific proof that smoking caused cancer and this point was played on *ad nauseam* by the tobacco companies. Those who stated publicly that they believed it did were ridiculed and run down in the way that some complementary medicine practitioners are now. A common remark about non-conventional treatment is: 'That sort of thing does no good, the horse would have got better anyway,' but the same can be said of *any* treatment, surely. Antibiotics may well help overcome a bacterial disease but, left to its own devices, the horse probably would have 'cured' itself in time, although the disease may have run a longer and more virulent course and left more serious after-effects and a weaker horse.

I hope the present climate of more open-mindedness continues, that research into all forms of treatment will be undertaken and that humans, horses and all creatures will be able to reap the benefits of both conventional and complementary/alternative medicine.

'Dr Green'

For generations, a cure-all has been to refer a horse to Dr Green, in other words to turn him out and let grass, sun and fresh air work whatever cure was needed. A large part of Dr Green's treatment was, and is, rest, with the associated relaxation, freedom from stress, a more natural lifestyle, company (with luck) and time. There is no doubt that this combination really does constitute a genuine tonic and rest cure for many conditions caused by over-work, excessive demands and over-confinement.

Stress is now recognised in human and animal medicine alike as a triggering factor in many seemingly unconnected disorders and although we may not be able to teach our horses meditation and relaxation techniques, it is very true that adequate liberty, preferably at grass and in congenial company with kind weather, works the same magic on our horses and should be a regular part of every horse's routine, not a rare or occasional treat. It is as much a part of preventive medicine or management as vaccinations and worming programmes.

Probiotics

Everyone has heard of antibiotics; now probiotics are becoming familiar to those interested in their horses' health. There are beneficial bacteria and harmful ones, as well as those in between. As described in Chapter 5, beneficial bacteria and other micro-organisms in the horse's intestines help digest his food, and the maintenance of a healthy population of gut 'bugs' is essential to health. Many situations can upset this delicate balance in an equally sensitive and delicate body system – stress, disease, the administration of drugs (including antibiotics which, not surprisingly, may kill off gut bacteria which is why they so often cause diarrhoea) and bad feeding practices can all do it. In such situations the temporary use of a probiotic can certainly help restore the balance and, so, the horse's well-being.

Many first-time foal breeders are dismayed to see young foals eating their dam's droppings, but this is a perfectly natural device aimed at populating the foal's gut with digestive bacteria to help him cope with his forthcoming diet. Convalescent horses sometimes do it for the same reason, although if the practice continues (it is called coprophagy) it indicates a more long-standing dietary deficiency or problem.

Probiotics are preparations of beneficial living organisms which have a stabilising effect on the population of gut bacteria by outnumbering harmful bacteria, competing with them, restoring numbers of beneficial bacteria and also helping digest carbohydrates in the gut which creates conditions which are unpleasant to harmful bacteria, also providing the horse with much-needed energy to restore his health and strength after stress, sickness, hard work, a long journey and so on.

An old practice was to put some droppings (which contain gut bacteria) into a cloth and soak it in water, then using this water either to drench the horse or to damp his feed. Nowadays, this is quite unnecessary as commercial preparations are available, such as Transvite in the UK, which can be given according to veterinary instructions or on the advice of the makers of such products. The times when they are advised to be given normally are shortly after birth (to both foal and mare), at weaning when bereavement and a change of diet stress the youngster and maybe the mare, after gelding, after sickness, during digestive disorders frequently, when a horse is deprived of grass, during hard work, when a horse's routine is being changed, such as being brought up from or turned out to grass, and particularly before and after a stressful journey (which may be only half an hour with a bad driver).

Probiotics are not meant to be given all the time, only when the digestive bacteria have been at risk for whatever reason. They form a valuable addition to the feed room and medicine cabinet in an up-to-date yard.

Formulating a Health Plan

Your veterinary surgeon is a valuable ally not only when your horse is ill or injured but in advising on preventive medicine and management, too, and can help you work out a yearly programme designed to keep your horse in good health and so able to stay fit and able to work or breed for you. Even – or rather, especially – older animals need an annual veterinary check, particularly if they are still in work, to monitor their well-being. It is good management practice and the timings of such things as vaccinations and wormings can be critical to performance.

For instance, it is known that vaccinations sometimes make a horse feel a little below par for a few days and that they should not be worked at all hard for about ten days after vaccination. Worming can also affect horses slightly – the drugs are, after all, poisons – and so it is wise to arrange such things when the horse is not going to be required to perform at the peak of his abilities.

As well as vaccinations and worming, horses should have their teeth checked regularly, every six months for young or old animals and every year for others, and, if necessary, the sharp points and hooks should be rasped smooth, depending on how the individual horse wears them during chewing, to enable him to eat properly and to prevent injury to his cheeks and tongue. Sharp points on the back teeth, when the bit may press against them and pinch the cheeks and tongue, can be a cause of horses being difficult to handle and reluctant to work, not surprisingly, and even if the horse does not actually quid (drop partly chewed food out of his mouth) it does not mean his teeth are in perfect order.

In the wild, far more horses and ponies reach a natural old age than in domesticity, and if they are not eaten by predators they tend to die of starvation due to the teeth wearing out or becoming sharp, hooked (at front and back of grinding rows), broken (which may enable the opposing tooth to grow into the resulting space and, as horses' teeth do, continuing to erupt until the animal cannot chew properly or close his mouth) or decayed. The teeth erupt from the jaw throughout the animal's natural lifespan and eventually the roots themselves erupt and the grinding surfaces of the teeth become smooth, which means the horse cannot grind up grass, leaves and so on, and so gradually dies of starvation.

The vet can check the horse's heart either simply with a stethoscope or with more sophisticated equipment such as a heart monitor, while the horse is working, or an electro-cardiograph. The wind can be listened to or a full lung function test performed. Blood samples can be taken to check the horse's general health and/or fitness and it is amazing what unsuspected disorders these can reveal.

Generally, a good time for a check is at the end of a horse's season (if he works seasonally) or just after his busiest time, to give time for any necessary treatments to be given while causing little or no interruption to his work or to give them time to take effect before he goes back into work, but there is a lot to be said for a check before starting a fitness programme, too, to ensure that the horse really is healthy enough to start one. This is particularly important with old horses, who may deteriorate purely because of their age.

Competition horses will need a recorded vaccination pro-gramme or they will probably not be allowed on to the competition premises. A vaccination given even one day late can mean the horse being turned away and having to start a complete new vaccination programme, even though your vet may feel he is adequately protected against disease. Vaccination certificates are needed and, in certain cases, passports for the horse with full identification signed by the vet, so all this has to be considered in appropriate cases.

The most important reason for a health plan, however, is obviously to keep your horse in the best health possible by taking advantage of all the advances of modern veterinary science available to your veterinary surgeon and other specialists. In domestication, if horses and ponies are not put down for economic reasons (being unable, for some reason, to work), they can live to a much older age than wild and feral ones, provided they enjoy the benefits of domestication such as shelter, proper feeding and veterinary care.

Transport

Transporting horses is well known to be the biggest cause of stress most have to undergo in their lives, yet so many of us think so little of it. Fortunately, serious research is currently going on in this field and it is hoped that the full effects of travel on horses will soon be documented and available to all concerned.

Unfortunately, this is another of those areas where so many people ignore the evidence even when it is there in front of them in the form of a colicked horse, a 'tied up' horse, a sweating, nervous wreck or a horse showing all signs of travel sickness except the actual vomiting (horses cannot vomit unless there is something very seriously physiologically wrong with them).

Most horse transport vehicles do not allow for the fact that horses carry two-thirds of their weight on their forelegs and are not anatomically suited to facing in the direction of travel in a moving vehicle. If they can travel tail-to-the-engine they can keep their balance much better and are much more relaxed both physically and mentally.

Consider, for a moment, the effects of forward motion, acceleration, braking and cornering on a living body shaped and balanced like a horse's. As the vehicle starts off it lurches forward, throwing the horse's weight on to his hindquarters – the very part not designed to carry much weight. This necessitates a hard bracing of the muscles of back, loins, quarters and hind legs and a wide-legged stance completely unnatural to the horse except for short periods such as when staling or *momentarily* keeping his balance. As the vehicle sways and moves from side to side, again the muscle-bracing and wide-legged stance are needed and can, in a fairly short length of time, cause significant muscle fatigue, cramp, weakness and stiffness. As the vehicle brakes, the horse's weight is thrown forwards on to the forelegs – which can take it better than the hind legs, but this, to the horse, puts his vital and sensitive head at risk of being hit against the front wall of the vehicle. Then, when the braking stops, the weight is thrown back on to the quarters. Dr Sharon Cregier of the University of Prince Edward Island, Canada, who had done probably more research on this subject than anyone else to date, has described this feeling as constantly having the rug pulled from under your feet.

When the horse travels tail-to-the-engine many of these effects are negated. During braking he has no fear for his head as his padded hindquarters can take any impact there may be. During acceleration his weight is directed on to his forehand (acceleration is usually much less 'violent' than braking) and the horse has less fear for the safety of his head. Forward motion, of course, continues for most of the journey but, facing backwards, the horse is much better balanced to cope with it and the wide-legged stance and constant muscular effort which are so physically stressful and damaging are greatly lessened. The metabolic toxins which build up during unremitting physical effort such as conventional travelling do not arise so much and the horse arrives at his destination in a much more fit condition to work.

Poor ventilation in much horse transport is a definite cause, particularly on long journeys, of the formation of disease-causing organisms which cause the condition known as 'shipping fever' and also encourage a feeling of nausea which the horse is quite unable to relieve or tell us about.

Many 'small' horse owners have trailers in which to transport their horses as opposed to the more expensive (both to buy and to run) horseboxes. Trailers can never provide as stable or safe a ride as a horsebox but, if well maintained and driven, can be acceptable. In the UK, at least, and I understand in most other countries, nearly all trailers are built to travel the horses facing forwards. If do-it-yourself attempts are made to convert the trailers internally so that the horse can travel rear-facing this actually dangerously unbalances the trailer, because the heaviest part of the horse is then at the back of the trailer behind the axle. This has the effect of tipping the trailer and lifting the towing vehicle off its rear wheels, at least partially. A few manufacturers are willing to cooperate in producing rear-facing trailers to order and in North America and New Zealand I believe some are made as part of commercial lines, 'ready made', as it were.

Of course, these problems do not arise in a horsebox and it is a fairly simple matter to convert and rearrange the internal stalls. If you have to hire or borrow transport or hitch a lift with friends, do your best to get a rear-facing stall for your horse.

I sometimes hear reports from owners that they tried such transport but their horse did not like it. This was always in connection with horses who had been travelled for many years facing forwards, and so were obviously unused to the new direction; but experience shows that after a very few short trips they quickly come to realise how much easier and less stressful 'balanced' travel is and previously bad travellers become calm and willing to load and travel.

I hope fully comprehensive reports, and accurate conclusions free from the bias occasioned by tradition, will soon be available to all concerned with transporting horses, and be acted upon for their benefit.

In conclusion, the best tip I can give is Dr Cregier's advice, no matter what type of transport vehicle you are using – drive as though you had no brakes.

8 Reproduction: Life Must Go On

Almost everything the horse does is aimed at one thing – the survival of the species – and the horse has survived as a species very well indeed. It is often said that if it weren't for the horse having proved useful to man, it would have become extinct, but the very fact that it has proved adaptable enough to *be* useful to man is a major point in its favour. It has also retained the ability to revert almost within days to a 'wild' life when the opportunity arises. Research workers in France who turned horses completely free and unfettered by even such things as yearly round-ups were surprised to find that within five *years* they had reverted to a wild-type herd hierarchy and survival mechanism. I can only assume that the researchers had no previous significant knowledge of horses because any reasonably experienced horse owner would have expected this within days or, at most, weeks.

The adaptability of the horse has ensured that its breeding activities can be manipulated by man, too, and so its usefulness increased even more. The breeding of horses in domesticity is usually far removed from the way it happens in nature and although this results in lower fertility than feral horses would produce it still maintains a domesticated horse population of millions worldwide.

Nature's Way

The horse is a 'photoperiodic' breeder, in other words a seasonal breeder; to be more exact, its breeding cycles, in both male and female, are controlled mainly by light and, to a lesser extent, by temperature and food availability. The word 'photo' being Greek for 'light' and periodic being self-explanatory, it follows that the word photoperiodic simply means that the horse breeds periodically (as opposed to all year round) depending on day length. Its natural mating/breeding seasons runs, in the northern hemisphere, from April to September, the horse having evolved to fit in with the increasing availability of food during that time and the rising temperatures of spring and summer.

The horse's natural gestation or pregnancy length is eleven months. In wild and feral conditions mares do not have a foal every year: if they did the foaling date would get earlier and earlier each year until it became out of sync with the natural scheme of things. As may be expected, man has already interfered with nature by declaring that the official birthday of all Throughbreds and some other breeds is 1 January of any year and virtually busts a gut each year to make sure such horses foal as near to that date as possible.

This system was introduced for economic reaons. Impatient as ever, man did not want to wait until his horses were three or four years old before their appearance on a racecourse (with its attendant possibilities of winning races and money, earning prestige for their owners and providing excitement and entertainment for racing enthusiasts) and wanted them to be able to race as two-year-old babies. As horses are still growing significantly at two years of age (they don't naturally mature until six or even, in a few cases, seven years of age), it was realised that the earlier in the year they were born the more growth and strength they would have attained by the time the flat-racing season started in their two-year-old year, and it is a fact that 'early' two-year-olds do win more than 'late' ones, even allowing for individual differences in type, 'forwardness' or 'backwardness'. By the time the animals are three, any real differences have been ironed out and the advantage of early birth has been negated.

The mare stops coming into season, which she does about every three weeks during the breeding season, about October and begins cycling again about mid-April. Her cycles are controlled by hormones which are stimulated initially by light or the lack of it. In the male, similar stimulation takes place. The main hormone which enables the horse to 'tell the time' on a yearly seasonal basis is melatonin, which is produced by the pineal gland in the brain. When melatonin levels are low the horse 'knows' it is the breeding season, and vice versa. Much more melatonin is produced by night than by day and as the days become significantly shorter during the latter part of summer and in autumn the mare gradually stops cycling and the male's breeding hormones similarly reduce. During winter, when most melatonin is produced, horses do not breed, but once the days start to lengthen gradually in midwinter this fact is registered by nerve endings in the eye. Light falls through the pupil on to the retina and neural messages are transmitted to the brain to tell it to start triggering the production of breeding hormones. As the day length increases (which also stimulates the growth of grass and other plants), the weather eventually warms up, natural food becomes more available and, again in response to hormones and temperature, the horse's winter coat starts to cast and be replaced by the summer coat. Eventually the stallion's sperm count has risen in time for his mares' increasing interest in him and the natural breeding season begins when mares actually come into season.

Mares will drop the foals resulting from last year's mating when the weather is kind and nutritious spring grass available in plenty to feed both the new foal and the lactating mare, milk production being very energy-demanding of the mare. It is all very finely coordinated after millions of years of evolution. The spring grass also helps maintain the stallion in good condition for the production of sperm, the serving of mares and the fighting off of rival stallions out to steal his harem, all of which are extremely demanding and frequently result in a very tired and battered stallion by autumn.

Natural mating behaviour consists of a good ten days' courtship between mare and stallion during which time the mare flirts with the stallion, rubbing against him, parading in front of him (and he her), and they nuzzle and groom each other, but it is the mare who decides when actual mating will take place, which is towards the end of her season. The stallion will serve her frequently once she permits it, usually to the exclusion of other mares. The mare gives off certain scents (pheromones) which 'tell' the stallion when she is ready to mate and at her most fertile. Once she has conceived, these pheromones change and the pair lose interest in each other, the stallion turning his attention to another mare, and so it goes on.

A mare will come into season again some days after foaling and technically be ready to mate again then, but matings at this time are less likely to be successful than at subsequent seasons. In natural conditions, mares sometimes fail to conceive in the summer after foaling, so giving themselves a year's rest, but this is no good to man who exercises all the ruses and veterinary advances at his disposal to ensure that mares produce as far as is possible a foal every year, although, again, this often does not happen.

In herbivores, such as the horse, actual mating is accomplished quickly but tends to continue for three or four days, particularly towards the end of the mare's season, until she goes out of season. The tendency now in commercial studs is, through the skills of veterinary science, to discern exactly the most likely time for a mare to conceive, even down to the hour in some cases, and to serve her once then, rather than following the older practice of serving her twice or more during her season until she goes 'off'. With the present-day single-serve tendency, the stallion's resources are greatly saved, obviously, and he can serve many more mares (and earn many more stud fees) in a season than in the past, when the traditional figure was about forty. When domesticated stallions run with their mares they follow the natural behaviour of concentrating all their energies on one fully in-season mare, usually to the exclusion of others.

In-hand stallions in general have much lower fertility figures than those able to run with their mares, and there is no doubt that both stallion and mares are much happier, calmer, more relaxed and sexually hyped up than animals mated in hand and so much more likely to produce a pregnancy. Unfortunately, the monetary value placed on many breeding animals today, particularly stallions, dictates their being used in hand, so that the actual mating process can be very closely controlled and possible injury to the stallion (and, to a lesser extent, the mare) prevented as far as possible. It is known from observation of both wild and domesticated animals that courtship, usually denied in domesticity, is an essential part of the mating game and some species are unlikely to conceive without it. I once did a personal mini-survey of breeders known to let their stallions run with their mares and all those I spoke to confirmed that fertility figures were much higher and even notoriously 'difficult' mares (difficult to get in foal) conceived quickly. They also confirmed that none of the stallions had sustained a serious injury from a mare during this natural type of mating – and those 'polled' included breeders of Arabs, Anglo-Arabs and Thoroughbreds as well as other breeds and ponies.

As stallions are well known to be highly accurate in choosing the right time to serve a mare (when she is fully ready and most likely to conceive), it seems reasonable to assume that, to prevent numerous and seemingly unnecessary matings of one mare in a herd, once a mare had been seen to have been served she could be removed from the field and fairly safely be assumed to be in foal. This method would only involve one reliable observer watching the herd at a time and is much less labour-intensive than having several people attend one mating, as happens at present. This was, in fact, done at the Irish National Stud some years ago when they tried 'natural' breeding methods with a Throughbred stallion and it worked well. Many of his mares were actual 'no-hopers', yet he got them in foal. When the horses were brought in at night, the stallion was stabled in the same yard as his mares where he could keep an eye on them, rather than being segregated unnaturally into a separate stallion shed with other, rival, breeding stallions, something which would never happen in the wild but is common on commercial domestic studs.

Again, in wild and feral conditions, the stallion stays with his

9a. Outdoor surfaced maneges are ideal for turning out horses for exercise. Two or more horses or ponies can, of course, be turned out together, if they are compatible, but other animals make welcome playmates, too!

9b. And a photographer is better than nothing!

10a. For those who would like their horses to go *au naturel* for whatever reason, it is quite possible to learn to trim your own horse's feet yourself. The diagrams on page 64 depict the foot balance to aim for (although horses with feet naturally different from the standard would be better left to a good farrier who can adapt to them). To remove a shoe, place a buffer (or the end of a strong screwdriver) under the clenches and tap them up with a hammer so they are no longer holding the shoes on.

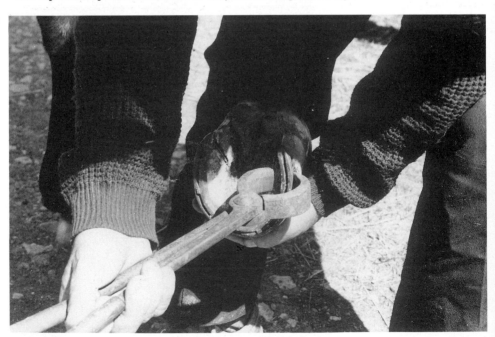

10b. Lift the shoes a little at each heel with the pincers . . .

11a. . . . and then carefully grip each nail head (which will rise when you flatten the shoe again at the heels) with the pincers, being careful not to snap off the head. Draw each nail out so that you can remove the shoe. Often the shoe will fall off of its own accord.

11b. You may wish to wear a tough pair of jeans or leather chaps for trimming your horse's feet. Hold the foot between your thighs, as shown, and rasp off excess horn from the bearing surface as needed, having first familiarised yourself with the balance you are aiming for. The most common fault is to remove too much heel horn and too little from the toe area where horn is thicker and the work harder!

12a. Aim for a smoothly rounded finish, rasping away flared-out areas, if appropriate, and smoothing any chipped or uneven areas, with the rasp angled slightly in and down, as shown here.

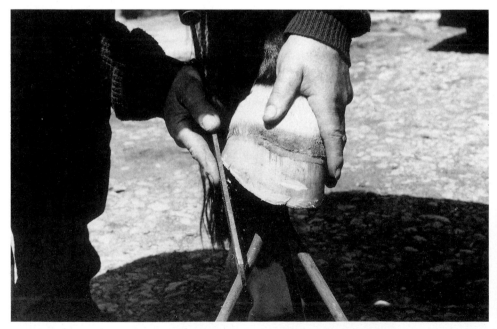

12b. Smooth off the outer surface as well as the underneath bearing surface, if needed. It will make your job easier for this stage to use a proper farrier's block or tripod (as used here) but some people manage quite well just resting the hoof on an upturned bucket.

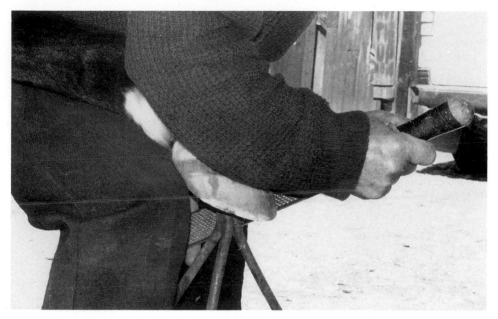

13a. Get used to manipulating the rasp according to how you find it most comfortable and whether you are right- or left-handed. If, say, you are right-handed, it is normally best to keep the handle in your right hand, using it in different positions rather than changing the handle from hand to hand.

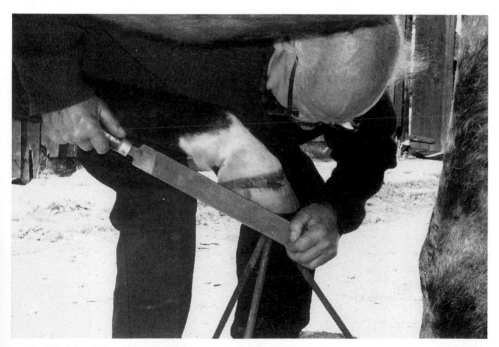

13b. Finish off by rounding the edge of the bearing surface with the finer side of the rasp to help minimise chips and cracks.

14a. Use a proper farrier's draw knife to remove loose flakes of horn from the frog . . .

14b. . . . and bars so that they cannot grow and form overlaps under which dirt can lodge and encourage the setting up of infection. Always go carefully and gently with any tool at first as, initially, it is better to take away too little material than too much.

15a. A good range of clothing can certainly make life easier and pleasanter for horse and owner. Good turn-out rugs, in particular, or light rain sheets in warm weather, enable a horse to be turned out a good deal, with all the benefits this entails, while still remaining warm and relatively clean. An owner will have few qualms about turning his or her horse out all day if it has good clothing and shelter, depending on the time of year.

15b. Most of the excuses owners and grooms give for not turning out horses simply don't hold water! It is especially common for fit, in-work competition horses to be turned out alone because their owners are frightened they will get up to high jinks and injure themselves. However, there are always ways round such excuses: this is a fit, in-work steeplechaser who, along with the other horses in his yard, is turned out daily with his pony companion. The pony is very calm and stolid in temperament and provides companionship, which keeps the horses content and prevents them possibly charging up and down the fence looking for a way out to find company and maybe even trying to jump out. This particular pony also has a fairly dominant personality and won't stand any messing about from his much larger companions.

15c. The competition pony in the middle of this small group is wearing a well-designed New Zealand rug (well shaped and with no surcingle) and speedicut boots to protect her legs during any high jinks in the field. These precautions are obviously optional and many people do not believe in 'wrapping horses in cotton wool'. However, it is far better to do this and let the animal go out than keep it in and deprive it of social company, freedom, fresh air, grass and exercise at liberty.

16a. Circus horses are an excellent example of the horse's acuity of perception, of his liking for habitual practices and routine and of his excellent memory and willingness to please people when he feels confident and secure. These Arab liberty horses, trained and here presented by Mary Chipperfield, are all stallions (as are most circus liberty horses). As the music played during their act mostly prevents their hearing their trainer's spoken commands, they rely  on memorising the movements required in strict order but also keep a very close eye on Mary, who uses body language and careful positioning of her whip and stick to indicate to the horses what she wants them to do. They also react to the music, memorising the tunes and 'automatically' performing certain movements and routines to specific parts of particular tunes. Changing the music creates havoc! Selecting music for a new act may also cause problems, as if the horses have worked a different act to it years previously they may lapse into that instead of the new one.

16b. Hunting is one of the jobs horses enjoy most as they find it most natural. They are in company, there is a good deal of coffee-housing on the part of their riders, which gives the horses a chance to stand about doing their version of the same thing, if permitted; depending on the day, their work may vary from fast work over fences to waiting around during checks and hacking from one draw to another, all done in company. They are out in the open, moving around, enjoying company, just as they would in the wild. No wonder a season's hunting is often prescribed for some sour, over-the-top competition or racehorse as a sure-fire sweetener.

herd all year round, obviously freely mixing with maiden, barren and in-foal mares as well as those with foals at foot, weanlings and youngstock. In domesticity, this is even rarer than natural mating but it does occur. Most stallions are known to live quite calmly with their families in this way, forming non-sexual friendships with mares (who, of course, are in season for only a short time out of a whole year) and with youngstock, and taking a tolerant and affectionate interest in the foals.

But there are exceptions. Occasionally it has been known for stallions to kill male foals conceived to another stallion the previous year and, therefore, not their own. This has been observed in domestic herds and in wild and feral ones, too, although it is not very common. Presumably the stallion is able to recognise by smell that the foal is not his own and kills it as it does not carry his genes for continuing his line, a view put forward by several zoologists and behaviourists. However, female foals represent future mates, whether they are his daughters or those of a previous incumbent. As useful vehicles for carrying on his genes and continuing his line, they are left unharmed.

This sort of behaviour has been described in domesticated breeds, Camargue horses and Przewalski horses, among others, yet these same stallions were positively affectionate and nurturing towards their own male foals, only becoming aggressive when they reached puberty, became potential rivals for the harem and, as is natural, were literally kicked out of the herd to wander in bachelor bands until able to acquire herds of their own.

In-breeding, close-breeding and line-breeding are all natural processes in nature. Many of the younger mares in a herd will be the daughters of an established stallion and he will mate with them just the same. However, as wild and feral stallions will probably not be in their prime for more than about five years, and so hold on to a herd for only a fairly short time, the amount of in-breeding over the years is not sufficient to cause trouble, just to fix in the herd those genes favourable to survival in its environment.

In domesticity, close in-breeding such as father with daughter, brother with sister, is normally avoided in horses these days although it was widely practised in the past. It can be extremely risky and can fix prepotent undesirable genes for generations, producing all sorts of faults. Expertly done, line-breeding (the mating of less closely related individuals) can fix into a stud's stock good qualities while eliminating bad ones, but the breeder has to be very certain that the good qualities he or she is aiming for really are prepotent (dominant) over less desirable ones, by closely studying the stock produced by both the mare and the stallion he or she is considering mating.

Domestic Breeding Systems

By far the most common way of mating horses in domestic conditions is in hand. The mare and stallion are both held by attendants and the mare may or may not, depending on the stud's policies, be twitched and hobbled – twitched to keep her still and hobbled so that she cannot kick the stallion. The stallion is led in to the covering area and may be allowed a few seconds' courtship (as opposed to nature's ten days), or he may not. He may be held back by his attendant to 'get him ready' and usually mounts the mare almost immediately instead of enquiring of her first from the side or even nuzzling her tail. When mating is completed, the mare is led round to prevent her straining and perhaps getting rid of the stallion's ejaculate, while the stallion is led straight away to recover in time for his next assignation.

This procedure is obviously completely unnatural and has been described by ethologist Dr Marthe Kiley-Worthington, expert breeder the late Marguerite de Beaumont, and others as rape, particularly in view of the fact that, even when in season, the mare may well not be quite ready and, therefore, is unwilling. Even if she is fully ready, she is allowed no chance at all to get to know the stallion or even to smell, touch and see him properly before mating. This method persists, though, due to the human desire to avoid kicks to the stallion and to make the best use of his energies, despite known lower conception figures.

Running stallions with their mares is most common among pony breeds but others, even Thoroughbreds, are bred this way and some studs operate both systems depending on mare owners' requirements.

The numerous examinations of mares to see whether they are ready to serve, in foal, progressing normally and so on, usually still done by means of rectal palpation where the vet inserts an arm into the mare's rectum and feels what is happening within the breeding organs through its wall, are done to keep a check on the mare so that when things go wrong treatment can be given, another service from the stallion arranged or whatever, to ensure as far as possible that the mare will produce a live foal next spring. Many experts, both vets and breeders, dislike rectal palpation as they claim, probably rightly, that it can upset some mares so much that they abort. Ultrasound scanning is becoming increasingly carried out, is very effective and does not upset the mare.

Weaning is another unnatural procedure the way it is usually carried out on studs. In the wild and in domesticity, the foal grows and develops both physically and mentally and will naturally take less and less milk from the mare but may still be suckling very occasionally, taking into account the mare's also naturally diminished milk supply, several months after weaning would have taken place on a stud, usually around six months of age. It is not uncommon for a previous year's foal to still be around its dam and taking a very occasional suck when the new foal has arrived on the scene. Female horses, in particular, form very strong bonds within the family herd and this practice is fairly common and quite harmless. In some cases, however, the mare will naturally wean her offspring but not normally significantly until it is nine months of age or older.

It is a very common system on studs for mares and foals to be suddenly separated at about six months, but wise stud managers will at least stagger the process, weaning 'forward' foals first and others later. There are other methods of lessening the sometimes great shock of separation, amounting to bereavement, by separating mares and foals for initially short periods, increasing them until full separation is carried out with little effect on mares or foals. Another system involves putting one or two 'nanny' mares or geldings into a herd and gradually removing the dams of the most forward foals first, and so on, till the foals are left with only the nannies.

Stud staff often say that foals and mares get over weaning in a few days or a couple of weeks at the most but the fact is that very many foals go back seriously in condition because of the mental anguish of losing their dams at an unnaturally early age. Some experts believe that this leaves mental scars and other psychological effects which damage the horse's future outlook on life for the rest of its life, as happens with orphaned children. In cases where a mare is not a good mother or where a foal is very bombastic and is pestering and genuinely upsetting her, there may be a case for early weaning, but not otherwise.

Once separated from their dams by whatever system, it is common for foals to be kept singly for a week or so, psychologically a very damaging process, or to be put in pairs for company, but even this latter process is not ideal as one will always turn out to be the boss and may become unacceptably aggressive to both humans and other horses while the underdog may suffer all the traumas and disadvantages, including lack of ability to socialise, undue defensiveness, lack of confidence etc., which that condition causes.

When foals are all kept together in a herd of the same age they have no natural discipline from older horses and do not learn herd manners which, incidentally, not only helps them relate to other horses but makes them easier to handle from a human viewpoint, too. Things are better when older horses (nannies again) are left with them, provided the latter are not actually aggressive, but the most effective system, which very nearly mimics the natural one but which is rarely used in domestic situations, is to leave all females of any age and colt foals together, separating out the males when they become sexually mature as would happen in the wild. This also ensures that unwanted pregnancies in the herd do not occur. In situations where entire males (and maybe geldings, too) are brought up together and used to this sytem, there is no significant fighting, just normal youthful horseplay, and the animals develop a healthy respect for both peers and elders, again as happens in the wild. Mature serving stallions rarely get the chance to be turned out in company, but here again, I have known of several examples where stallions had companions, usually non-breeding mares, and formed firm non-sexual friendships with them, and were much happier and more sensible as a result.

Teasing is another practice which is unnatural the way it is practised on studs. An entire horse or pony of low monetary value is often kept to try mares and gauge whether or not they are ready for mating by the serving stallion. This is obviously extremely frustrating and unkind to the teaser who rarely gets any mares himself. Many studs operate without teasers, allowing stallions to do their own teasing by various means; this system works very well and must surely be preferred by the mares when actual mating time arrives. Although a feral stallion may be somewhat frustrated by a mare who is 'hard to get' he does 'get' her in the end and the whole process is natural and acceptable to the horses.

Artificial and Natural Selection

The subject of natural selection is one which is taught in probably every school in the course of general science or biology lessons, its essence being that although animals are free, within natural social mores, to mate with whatever other animals they choose, those which will best thrive in their environment are those physically and mentally best fitted to do so. Animals, both as individuals and as groups, will evolve with the best physical and mental characteristics to cope with their surroundings. Characteristics which will hamper their survival there will eventually be bred out of the population as those animals possessing them will not survive to pass them on to their offspring.

In domestication this does not happen. Matings are artificially selected – often with no regard to the suitability of mare or stallion for each other physically and with no real idea, on the part of the mare owner, what market the resulting foal is aimed at. Although certain hereditary diseaes are listed and avoided in stallions by most breed societies and other registries, faulty conformation, bad temperament and similar faults are not discriminated against to the same extent by all organisations. As an example, in the Thoroughbred world a conformational fault has been firmly bred into the female population in which the anus is set back from the vulva so that the latter is constantly infected by faeces whenever the mare does a dropping. This leads to vaginal and uterine infections and although they can be treated by a vet to ensure, as far as possible, that an infection does not prevent the mare conceiving or satisfactorily carrying a foal, the fact is that in natural conditions this fault would never have been established as it would not have been passed on, the mare possessing it being unable to conceive and bear offspring due to constant infection.

This is only one example; there are many others which are tolerated in the Thoroughbred world where the only requirement, really, is speed. If the horse is shaped like a camel it doesn't matter so long as it is fast!

Breeding for fashion can also cause problems in domestic stock. In the Quarter Horse showing world some years ago considerable problems were encountered in the hooves of animals which had been bred to have small, 'dainty' feet which, in practice, were not, therefore, up to carrying the weight of the horse. The Quarter Horse is a chunky sort of horse anyway, with well developed muscling (as are flat racers bred for sprinting) to provide power for a lightning getaway with tremendous propulsive thrust and, therefore, muscular effort. Breeders were breeding heavier and heavier topped horses with big muscles and tiny feet. The trend is now reversing but, as horses live a fairly long time, it will be some time before the trait disappears.

In the Arab showing world, the problem at present is backs and toplines like tables with no proper 'horse' shape — flat withers, short, straight backs, level croups and high tails. This can produce problems in saddle fitting and actually keeping a saddle in place and, because it is an unnatural shape, problems of action, physical weakness and a tendency to 'topline' stresses and strains which can lead to bone and joint disease such as arthritis.

In the early years of this century, when Arab importations from the Orient were taking place, sickle hocks were a problem as breeders who did not know their horses bred any Arab to any Arab, and the reputation of weedy, sickle-hocked animals fit for nothing still persists nearly a hundred years later in non-Arab sections of the horse world. As explained, serious faults such as those often deliberately bred into a breed or family by man would never be passed on in the wild because they would disadvantage their possessors so much that they would be unlikely to survive to pass them on.

Nature's Clock

Naturally and ferally bred animals have all the time nature intended to grow and develop to maturity but, as mentioned, this is often not good enough for man who does everything he can, in many cases, to attain early physical maturity and size with a view to selling his stock as 'well matured' or to putting them to work. To this end, many breeders and producers of youngstock have, in the past, grossly over-fed their stock with the view that the more they eat the faster and bigger they will grow. In practice, they don't. Youngsters have had gross amounts of oats pumped into them, excessive amounts of protein (even allowing for the fact that youngsters are among the categories of horse who need more protein than mature horses) and ended up with hot, painful, swollen joints and 'contracted tendons'. The excessive protein and unbalanced diet has adversely affected the growth plates (also called epiphyseal plates) at the ends of the long leg bones and ended up with epiphysitis (inflammation of the epiphyses) and bones growing so unnaturally fast that the tendons cannot keep up. The tendons, being attached at the top to muscles in the forearms and at the bottom to bones in the feet, are 'pulled' between the two to their fullest extent, not allowing the legs to straighten out normally. This results in knuckling over at the fetlock (in extreme cases so that the youngster is actually walking on the front of the lower leg, the coronet and front of the fetlock joint) and bent knees, so that the poor creature is crippled. Sometimes surgery can save the day and sometimes, if the problem is caught early, a correctly balanced and professionally formulated diet can gradually correct the condition as the horse continues to grow.

It has to be said, though, that this sort of physical disorder so early in life must result in some permanent weakening of the leg and joints and is a significant disadvantage to an animal who is probably intended to be put into work, if a flat-race Through-bred, when it is barely eighteen months old in order to get it racing in its two-year-old year. Even in animals, Thoroughbred or not, being broken to work at a later age (say three years), this sort of disorder must be a serious disadvantage.

Getting youngstock 'over-topped', in other words too fat, so they appear in 'good condition' and carrying plenty of flesh (fat) with a mature appearance, is similarly damaging to the animal's physique. Obesity at any age is dangerous, but a heavy body on top of immature legs will stress those legs beyond the limits of safety – and if the youngster has been fed in such a way it will probably have a degree of epiphysitis, too, compounding the problem. Sadly, youngstock in this state are all too common, even now with our advanced knowledge of balanced nutrition and the horse's real nutritional needs, at prestigious sales of young Thoroughbreds and other breeds. As a very experienced Thoroughbred stud manager said to me ten years ago: 'One of the worst things you can do to a youngster, particularly a foal, is prepare it for the sales.' He admitted it was extremely difficult to get them looking well grown and in good condition without their developing leg problems. 'A real tightrope act' was how he described it. Even today, with our greatly increased knowledge of appropriate diets, so many people do not take advantage of modern knowledge and still have the old traditional problems which feral horses and ponies, and those raised more naturally, do not experience.

Tinkering with the Clock

It is not very difficult today to get artificially kept stock in breeding condition outside the natural breeding season, to comply with a 1 January birthdate. Light is the main key. By exposing stabled mares and stallions to sixteen hours of light in twenty-four, probably a combination of daylight and artificial light, you are more than halfway there. Even just leaving a 150 watt ordinary electric light bulb on in the stables in the evening to extend the daylight hours can do it, but plant lights which give out a full spectrum of the colours comprising white light or true daylight do seem to be even more effective and not so jading as red-spectrum candescent light or blue-spectrum fluorescent lights. The 'light trick' also works if you give just one hour's extra light than normal but at around 2 a.m. to 3 a.m.

Good feeding combined with clothing, and maybe heating as well where it can be afforded, completes the picture, although some 'stubborn' mares may still need hormones administered either by injection or in the feed to get them cycling regularly.

The light/food/warmth system also gets stallions in the mood and here it is interesting to point out that some stallions are not keen to serve mares who have been induced into season with hormones.

Getting back to Nature

Every now and then, articles appear in the racing press pleading with the 'authorities' to let the Thoroughbred world return to a more natural official birthday, such as 1 May or at least 1 April, giving all the logical reasons why this would be better for the horses and the industry (not the same thing, of course). Horses would be allowed more time to mature, they would be easier to breed from, being more inclined to do what comes naturally, and this would save large amounts of money currently spent on extra electricity, veterinary attention and treatments, a long stud season (which could end in July or August) and the employment of extra staff during that season. Of course, as horses would be born later this would mean that two-year-old racing would be virtually abolished or undertaken only in the autumn of the animals' two-year-old year, but as this would avoid the billions of pounds/dollars of wastage in young animals which currently takes place, the industry would ultimately benefit.

All this is true; so why doesn't it happen, not only in the racing world but in those other breeds where the official birthday is 1 January? It doesn't happen because most people in the horse world don't want it to, for reasons already given. They are impatient to see their painstakingly bred horses out there working – racing, competing, winning trophies, medals and money – and to do this they need the earliest, 'best' start in life modern technology, research and knowledge can provide, so the system will continue as it is until most people involved want things to be otherwise, and I'm sure that will never happen. Scientifically devised diets which produce early maturity without physical problems are already becoming available. I hope somewhere along the line Mother Nature will put the blocks on so we shall not see the Classics being run at two or million-dollar races for yearlings. Remember, in the early days of racing it was unthinkable even to back an animal at two, never mind race it. And these trends are slowly but surely infiltrating the competitive worlds of other breeds too, under the umbrella of the title 'performance horse'.

9 Coordination and Perception: Who's in Control?

As a prey animal, the horse has survived as well as he has because of his finely tuned sensory systems. His senses – feeling, sight, smell, taste and hearing, plus the more controversial one of extra- or, as I prefer to call it, super-sensory perception – are usually much more effective and highly developed than, and sometimes rather different from, their human equivalents. They are finely coordinated and linked to the nervous system to give the horse lightning reflexes to keep him safe and warn him against danger. As in most creatures, his reaction to what his senses tell him is, at times, almost subconscious: he will almost instinctively run from something startling without thinking about it. The sight, sound or even just the smell of something dangerous or merely unfamiliar can send him off at a seemingly blind gallop. Only when he feels he is out of its reach might he turn and investigate.

Because we tend to think he perceives his world and reacts to it in pretty much the way we do, we often make mistakes in understanding his reactions and this can result in inappropriate treatment or riding on our part, so let's look at his six senses to see what might really be happening.

Feeling

The most obvious interpretation of the word 'feel' is the ability to sense through touch. Whereas we use mostly our fingers, the horse uses mainly his muzzle. But there are other sorts of feeling, too. There is an inner sense of feel which detects discomfort, internal pain, lameness or a general feeling of being unwell. There is also proprioception, or a sense of awareness of body position, the sense of balance and feelings of need such as hunger, thirst, fatigue and the need to stale, to defecate and to mate.

The Nervous System

Inextricably linked to all the horse's senses is his nervous system, although we tend to think of it more in connection with feeling than with the other senses. The skin covers almost the whole horse and is continuous with fine mucous membranes in certain parts such as the insides of the lips and eyes. Horn and hair are insensitive themselves, but stimuli such as a fly landing on the coat or someone banging on the horse's hoof are felt by means of shock waves transmitted through the dead material to the sensitive structures beneath.

The nervous system consists basically of the brain and the spinal column running from it down the spinal canal in the vertebrae. Branching out from the spinal column are forty-two pairs of nerves serving different parts of the body, and these branch out again and again so that virtually the whole body has a nerve supply. The nerve endings are specialised to detect stimuli such as pressure, pain, temperature and so on. When nerves called sensory nerves detect or sense a stimulus, they send chemical or electrical messages to the brain via the spinal column; the brain analyses the information and sends other messages back down motor nerves, which initiate movement, telling the horse what to do, all in milliseconds.

The parts most generously supplied with nerve endings in the skin are those with the thinnest skin, such as the muzzle, the underparts such as the belly and the insides of the legs, around the genital organs and so on. The skin acts as a protector for the sensitive under-tissue, so it is logical that where it is thinnest it should have more 'information sensors' to provide extra protection to make up for the thinness of the skin.

The horse can feel even a fly landing on its coat. The

movement of the hair as it lands activates a nerve ending which flashes a message to the brain: 'Something irritating has landed.' The brain flashes back another message saying: 'Flick skin to dislodge it,' and the horse normally does so. This is less likely to happen if the fly lands on the longer, tougher mane or tail hair, of course, but there are other hairs which are much more sensitive than the ordinary coat hair roots. These are the antenna-type whiskers around eyes and muzzle and the bristly, tactile short hairs around the lips. We rarely interfere with the latter but some people do clip off the whiskers, quite wrongly.

These whiskers are very important, especially so as the objects and areas the horse investigates with the muzzle cannot be seen. Because of the shape of the head and position of the muzzle below the eyes, the horse has a blind spot under his chin, so relies upon his whiskers and nose to tell him if there is anything there. I have known horses go completely off their feed for a few days when the muzzle whiskers were clipped off, and start banging their heads when deprived of the eye whiskers, particularly in poor light. Many people say that this does not bother their horses and even if it does they soon get used to it. This is no reason for depriving the horse of one of its most important means of touch and information. It is quite possible to have a horse looking neat and tidy by trimming the under-jaw hair and that protruding from outside the edges of the ears, particularly at the base, in winter. I think that horses shorn of their antennae give away the fact that their owners or managers either do not understand their bodily functions or simply do not care enough.

Nerve endings tend to be specialised, some being responsive to touch, some to pain, others to temperature and so on. There are different specialised cells or groups of cells known as receptors sensitive to different sensations. As the coat and outermost layer of skin are themselves made up of dead tissue, the horse does not live in a constant state of hypersensitivity. We can safely stroke, ride and handle our horses! When thin, raw patches of skin develop for any reason, such as are caused by the friction of badly fitting tack, cut or torn wounds, the nerve endings themselves are less well covered or exposed and intense sensitivity and pain arise.

Under normal circumstances, 'touch' nerves become less and less sensitive to constant use. This is why horses subjected to constant firm bit pressure or unceasing kicks from their riders become worse to ride, dull and hard-mouthed, rather than more responsive. This can happen over a long or short period of time. For instance, if a horse is taking a strong hold or bolting, the least effective thing to do is take a constant, steady pull in an effort to stop him. It is normally more effective to vary the pressure on the bit with 'give and take' to keep the nerve endings responsive. Similarly if a horse is ridden over a period of weeks or months by a heavy-handed rider who hangs on to the bit, keeps the leg 'in contact' with the horse's sides when riding to the extent that bare patches are worn in the hair, or constantly kicks and kicks, not only will the horse's nerve endings become less sensitive (and in the case of the mouth may be even injured), but so will his brain, and he could turn into an uncontrollable, hard-mouthed horror or a 'plug'. It is far better, with an unresponsive horse, to apply strongish aids if necessary, and then stop, and also use the voice, then reapply the aids again if needed. This gives the horse a chance to respond and to learn that if 'a' is happening he's expected to do 'b' and if he doesn't 'a' will happen again. There's no reward in responding if the aid or discomfort never stops. He eventually becomes immune to the 'white noise' of nag, nag, nag from the rider because this is how his nervous system works.

The horse can also detect by touch indirectly applied pressures in the form of vibrations, most commonly through the ground via his feet and legs and can tell when a person, or a predator in the wild, is approaching – hence the stealthy gait of an approaching wild dog or cat looking for a meal. Having said that, this is only one means of such detection and some horses seem to be quite bad at it.

Other feelings do not involve touch at all. Special sensors in various parts of the body detect pain which may be due to swelling or pressure on the appropriate cells or nerve endings, but it is noticeable that when we feel ill but not in pain, we say just that – we *feel* ill. Horses would use the same expression, and can certainly detect when they feel unwell though not in pain.

Proprioception

One particular 'feel' sense is that of proprioception or the ability to know without looking and assessing all the time the position of the body and where the limbs are placed. Proprioception involves specialised receptors, groups of cells sensitive to movement, pressure or tension within the body. They are present in the muscles, tendons and ligaments and detect from the stretching of various parts of a leg, for example, whether and how it is flexed or extended, and so on. The horse can, therefore, 'feel' what position he is in. These proprioceptors are essential to body coordination when the horse is moving and the main-tenance of posture and balance, and are just as essential to humans for balanced, harmonious riding and ordinary, every-day living.

There are various reasons for lack of coordination in horses. One not uncommon cause is 'force-feeding' youngstock, par-ticularly Thoroughbreds during sale preparation, which can cause bone disorders. If the vertebrae are affected they can press on to the spinal cord, hampering the motor nerves and causing movement and coordination problems. Bad coordination and lack of this vital sense of proprioception is also sometimes inherited and obviously steps should be taken to check the cause before breeding from an affected animal.

The horse's organs of balance, closely connected with pro-prioception, are in the inner ear and consist of three linked semicircular canals filled with fluid. These canals have special receptors responding to the state of the fluid in the canals. If you ever spin round and round very quickly or do anything which unduly sets in motion the fluid inside your balance canals, the receptors cannot cope and you feel dizzy and uncoordinated. Normally, they can detect and, via sensory nerves, inform the brain of whatever movements you make and positions you adopt, so you always know which way up you are facing, and so on. These canals work just the same way in horses and it is hard to imagine any ordinary circumstance in which they might become dizzy, horses not being prone to circling repeatedly unless forced!

Paralysis

Horses, and other creatures, can become paralysed as a result of injury or disease. In the horse, diseases such as tetanus and herpes virus can cause paralysis. Another not uncommon injury causing partial paralysis happens when a horse gallops along a fence line where the rails are on the outside of the posts, leaving them exposed. The horse can easily bang the point of the shoulder against a post and cause injury to the radial nerve in the shoulder, resulting in a 'dropped' elbow and difficulty in moving the affected leg.

Because a horse is paralysed does not mean he can feel nothing: sometimes it is the motor nerves (along which instructions for movement travel) which are affected by the disease or injury, not the sensory ones (which carry sensation messages). This means the horse can still be in pain. His handlers should look for other signs such as patchy sweating, a distressed attitude or facial expression. If a horse is partially paralysed, the vet might prick him lightly with a pin in the suspected part and look for signs of movement in other parts, such as the head or other limbs as the horse attempts to react to the slight pain of the prick.

Any injury to a nerve can be serious as recovery prospects are not good. However, new nerve tissue can infiltrate an area in some cases to take over the work of the damaged nerves and the end result may be adequate or, for all practical purposes, as good as the pre-injury performance.

There is still a lot to be learned about the nervous system and precisely how it works and controls the body and mind. A few things are certain, though. If you spot even slight signs of uncoordination, don't pass them off; watch for a repetition and don't delay discussing it with your vet. The nervous system affects the mind as well as the body. Like humans and other animals, horses can suffer from psychosomatic illnesses, so don't dismiss the importance of a contented mental state in your horse. Because so much is unexplained in this field, apparently strange or undesirable behaviour should not be automatically punished or denigrated: there could be very good reasons for it which require us to give the horse the benefit of the doubt and treat him with understanding.

Sight

Probably of all the senses vision is the one we should least like to lose. To the horse, a prey animal for millions of years and still possessing a prey animal's mentality, vision is crucial to its survival in natural and pseudo-natural environments.

As a prey animal, the horse's eyes are positioned differently from those of predators such as humans, cats and dogs. The latter have eyes on the front of the face while horses, cattle, sheep, antelope and so on have eyes more to the side, giving them all-round vision. The only areas the horse cannot see are directly behind him and directly beneath his chin and muzzle. He can maintain this near all-round vision in most positions. The horse's long neck and long head enable him to reach the ground without having to buckle at the knees (as sheep and goats often do) to eat his natural food, and to reach up and browse leaves to some extent. With a slight turn of the head and/or neck, he can see right round him, too. The legs are long and thin, built for speed, so with the virtual all-round field of view, they provide the perfect protection for a grass-eater in open country vulnerable to predators. The legs do not block the field of view significantly and the horse has every chance of spotting an approaching predator in time to give himself a head start. As his maximum speed of roughly 30 mph is about that of predators (maybe a little less than some), he will usually get away if he can start running soon enough.

Another feature of the horse's eyes which aids all-round vision is the horizontal oval shape of the pupils, which contributes to the narrower but wider plane of vision than the daytime slit of cats or the porthole-type view of humans and dogs.

You may also have noticed two black or brown lumps on the edge of your horse's pupils. These are the *corpora nigra* (dark bodies) which are thought to increase the narrowing of the pupil in response to light shining into it. They probably also act as built-in sunshades, again to prevent the horse being blinded by sunlight which would prevent his spotting predators.

Focusing

For many years it was believed that the horse had a so-called 'ramped retina' which accounted for erratic head movements when he was trying to focus on something. It was suggested that the horse brought objects into focus on his retina (the 'screen' at the back of the eye) by moving his head to adjust the light rays entering through the pupil and shining on to the retina. It was thought that this compensated for the horse's poor ability to focus by altering the lens of the eye as we do. Because the horse had a sloping (ramped) retina, it was believed, the upper part of the retina was used to focus on near objects and the lower part distant objects.

Research has now disproved this theory. Electroretinography, the study of electrical impulses in the retina in response to light, has shown that the middle of the horse's retina allows the sharpest, clearest vision and that because of the shape of the pupil, the horse has to look through the upper part of the eye to bring objects into focus in this central area.

This becomes obvious when you look at a horse grazing with his head down. You will also have noticed him looking through the upper part of his eye when you are with him in his box and have something in your hand he wants to see. He arches his neck and brings in his muzzle, focusing the top part of his eye on to your hand as closely as he can. Horses can see things in the far distance by simply raising their heads, without having to arch the head or draw in the muzzle. To see something in the middle distance, or close up, however, these movements *are* necessary. It is clear that in order to see properly the horse's head must be allowed free movement. Those riders who hang on to the horse's mouth, restrict his head with reins or martingales and generally work against his natural physical function are making matters worse for themselves and the horse by partially blinding him, maybe at some critical moment like taking off over a jump.

The rather poor performance of the equine eye's less flexible lens is not helped by the fact that most horses seem to suffer naturally from some degree of astigmatism, which impairs simultaneous horizontal and vertical focusing. This means that the horse can see things but cannot define what they are until he has had time and opportunity to focus on them properly. In a prey/predator situation there is no time to focus – the horse takes off first and may stop and look from a safe distance later. This accounts for many horses' apparent flightiness, shying at harmless things like paper bags (which could be a small predator or nasty domestic terrier), a vehicle approaching fast from the rear (a lion) and sudden movements by humans nearby (something about to spring on him). This makes it all the more heartening that so many horses live quite calmly in a man-made environment, trusting their owners not to place them in danger despite not being able to discern clearly what is going on.

On Not Necessarily Looking Where You're Going!
The horse also differs from us in that he receives two separate views, one from each eye. Because he only focuses with *both* eyes on objects directly in front of his head, his brain is receiving two quite different pictures from the individual eyes, not two slightly different views of the same thing as in humans. The arrangement of the nerve fibres to the brain permits their reception and assessment. This again is most helpful when looking out for predators and implies that the horse is quite capable of thinking, if superficially, about two things at once!

Side-on vision is good for perceiving the presence of objects but not good for depth perception. The width of the forehead decides just how good a horse is at this. Horses can only judge depth when they can see an object with both eyes at once. This suggests it might be a good idea not to buy a horse with a very wide forehead for jumping. (It would be interesting to learn, from measurements of this area in top showjumpers, just how much, if at all, this really affects jumping success.) Side-on vision is also better at discerning movement than precisely defining an object, which is why horses tend to shy more at things seen from the side or behind with one eye rather than swerving away from clearly seen things in front of them.

To see directly and fairly closely in front, the horse must lower his head and neck – another reason why it is important not to restrict this movement when approaching a hazard. If you watch horses who do have freedom of the head, you will see that they lower the head to inspect where they are going, not so much to smell the area as to see it accurately.

Colour Vision

Another old belief recently scotched is colour-blindness in horses. It is now known that they have similar colour-discerning cells to ours (called rods and cones) in their eyes and can see yellow very well, plus orange, red and green, but probably have difficulty with blue and violet.

Smell

Of all the animals we come into contact with, or the wildlife which surrounds us, humans probably have the worst sense of smell. Our fellow primates have a better sense of smell than we do, but when it comes to dogs, deer, cattle, cats and horses, we're non-starters. And because we do have such a pathetic olfactory system we naturally tend to under-estimate just how important smell is to horses and how much they use and rely on it in their daily lives.

In wild conditions or even just in a domestic paddock, horses use their sense of smell all the time: they purposely put it into action smelling their companions, grasses and plants, fences, droppings, urine, the air, just about anything, whereas we often only use it when something actually assails our sense of smell. In other words, we use it only passively, when smells confront us, whereas horses actively go out of their way to take advantage of their olfactory abilities.

Greetings!

The very first thing horses do when greeting each other is to put nostril to nostril, breathe in and out, snort a little and generally smell each other's breath. Then they may have a nose-and-tail smelling session, particularly if they don't know each other well. As the hierarchy phenomenon comes into play, they may also strike out with a foreleg and squeal, trying out each other's status. Once status is confirmed, up or down, the smell of the new horse is remembered by the herd and it is the animal's smell rather than its appearance which is the main aid to recognition in future.

If you watch horses in their nostril-to-nostril pose, you will see that they arch their necks and bring in their noses so that the very edges of the usually flared nostrils meet full on so they can take full advantage of the smells involved in a close exchange of breath. They do not position their heads head-on but stand at a slight angle so right nostril meets the opposition's right, or vice versa. Two friends re-establishing their bond in the field, at freedom, often stand next to each other and turn their heads slightly so one left nostril meets a right one, again with heads drawn in and ears probably pricked.

Humans often fail to allow horses to carry out this basic and natural form of greeting and inspection, presumably because we don't go around doing it ourselves when greeting another person. As ever, we try to instil human-type manners, standards and dominance on non-human animals. We often go straight up to a horse, perhaps talk and offer him a titbit and stroke his neck (the senses of sight, hearing and feel being used here) and totally ignore the horse's most important and informative sense where introductions are concerned – his sense of smell. Non-horsy people are, understandably, even worse. They usually go right up to the horse and try to give it a pat on the forehead or even between the ears, the equivalent of patting a dog on the head. Even dogs don't like this (if you ever observe them closely enough to take note) and horses hate it, can be frightened by it and often simply won't tolerate it. Patting a human child on the head is a sign of friendly superiority which is similarly often resented and to do it to a potentially dangerous animal like a horse or dog is patronising, unnatural and stupid.

The most effective way to introduce yourself to a horse, and play safe while doing so (also the most natural as far as the horse is concerned) is to approach at a slight angle so he can see you properly and stand a little way away from him but within reach of his nostrils, standing quite still, talking quietly, perhaps (although horses don't 'speak' until after their initial smelling session), and letting him smell you as he wishes to satisfy himself as to who you are (stranger or familiar) and maybe also whether or not you are bearing gifts, as visitors should!

Next, raise your hand quietly to his nose and let him smell it, and then move it to his neck and stroke him there and/or on his withers which is a horse contact point used in mutual grooming and bonding. If you get to know a horse well enough for him to attempt to scratch *your* withers this is, in fact, a compliment indicating trust and acceptance, but few humans seem to allow this, probably to the disappointment and puzzlement of the horse concerned.

What Makes Smell a Physical Thing?
Air is drawn into the nostrils while the horse is breathing, or purposely drawn in more forcefully in a series of strong little inward breaths, sniffing. The smell consists of minute particles of matter given off by any article which has a smell to it (and, remember, we humans are extremely poorly equipped to decide what smells and what doesn't). This matter can be solid or consist of gases. Inside the horse's nose, the nasal passages leading into the windpipe and then on to the lungs are lined with very thin skin which secretes mucus – the mucous membranes or nasal mucosa. Special cells in the mucosa have tufts of hairlike structures. The inhaled particules are dissolved in the mucus and, as far as we can understand at present, act chemically with the tufts. The olfactory nerves which connect the nasal area with the brain pick up the particular smell and send a lightning message to the brain to tell the horse what it is.

Different animals are 'switched on' more easily and in a

different way by different smells. Horses are very sensitive naturally to the smell of herbivorous foods such as grass, leaves, herbs and, in domesticated horses, grain, hay and so on. Meat-eaters may be able to smell them, but are not interested: it is the smell of meat (live or dead), blood, offal and so on that really turns them on and they follow the smell on the ground or in the air to get to what may be a food supply.

Herbivorous animals are often terrified by such smells, even when they have never witnessed a kill in the wild. They, of course, are natural prey animals and horses living wild and their relatives understandably associate the smell of blood and flesh with the death of one of their number and remember it as a sign of great danger. Domesticated horses would also be frightened by them, probably through instinctive 'memory' or sense. Herbivores awaiting slaughter in an abattoir certainly exhibit fear and even terror, as reported by some researchers and other observers. So much for 'humane' slaughterhouses.

Long-distance Detection

The horse's highly developed sense of smell enables it to detect its enemies at great distances. Studies on zebra have shown quite conclusively that they can detect a freshly killed animal, or a predator which has recently killed and therefore smells of blood, two miles away if the wind is favourable. Almost certainly, this is why you can be quietly hacking along a lane with the wind in your face and your horse suddenly stops and appears nervous for no apparent reason – not a wilful jib but a definite uncertainty. He could have detected an unpleasant smell, or a frightening one, from a farm, an abattoir, hunt kennels or a wild kill. Stallions can detect mares in season in the same way from similarly considerable distances. Like other animals, mares give off specific odours not only from their vulva area when in season, but also from their urine and around their flanks. These are called pheromones, a pheromone being a chemical substance produced by one individual which affects the functioning or behaviour of another.

When a stallion detects in-season mares' pheromones, he'll

approach the particular mare and have a good sniff, then, on an 'in-breath', will hold up his nose and lift his top lip, curling it up so that it closes off the nostrils trapping the odour-laden air inside the nose. This action is called flehmen and always arouses amusement in humans, who take it as a sign of repulsion in the horse. What is actually happening is that the horse is trapping air inside his nasal passages so that it can be closely examined by his Jacobsen's organ, a structure with two tubes which run from the floor of the nasal cavity to the level of the second, third and fourth cheek teeth. This is exceptionally sensitive to smells and also helps the animal determine what food is in its mouth by smell rather than taste. Horses normally only perform flehmen for particularly interesting or unusual smells.

Marking Territory

Although migratory animals by nature, horses do mark their territory if in competition with nearby herds or in confined spaces. If a wild *equid* smells droppings or a patch of urine on the ground and decides they belong to a rival he'll do his own droppings or stale on top to disguise the smell from his mares and mark the territory as his. Even domesticated horses do this and will often mark out their own territory by instinct when new bedding is laid in a box, infuriating their owners or grooms! Removing the droppings, however, will not upset the horse as fragments will be left and the bedding will still smell of him.

When bringing a new horse into a yard it is best to clean out his box thoroughly first, using a mild equine disinfectant, rather than promote insecurity in his mind by putting him, imprisoned, into another horse's territory. The box will still smell entirely of the previous occupant and may do so for a long time despite the new horse doing his best to mark it as his own. The system in some yards where horses are constantly moved around for no apparent good reason does absolutely nothing for their sense of security. Once it has been found which box a horse likes, he should be allowed to keep it.

Smelling Fear

There has long been a saying in the horse world that horses can smell fear, and it seems that this may well be true. A few years ago, researchers working with mentally handicapped people discovered unusual peptides, chemicals, in their urine and deduced that if they were in the urine they must be in the sweat, too. When we are frightened or nervous we create specific substances in our sweat which we give off in fear. The air movement around us passes these odours to the horse who takes his cue from us. He'll either become nervous if he's a 'follower' type or maybe aggressive if a 'leader' type. Some schoolmaster horses may, for example, refuse to jump if they sense the person on top is frightened of the activity, as will a novice for reasons of doubt. The smell resulting from fear is obviously not the same as one resulting from excitement, as a keyed-up rider, keen to get on with the job, often 'psyches up' his or her horse, too, and the two may well give a better performance because of it. The adrenalin is flowing and both bodies are geared up for action – the old flight-or-fight mechanism – and in such a condition are often capable of things they couldn't do in cold blood.

Maternal Bonding

Mares and foals rely greatly on smell to establish the vital maternal bond between them. As soon as the foal is born the mare smells and licks it all over to familiarise herself with its smell and taste and the foal, knowingly or not, absorbs the smell of his dam. Her milk, too, has its own individual odour apart from the normal milk smell, which helps the foal identify her. Unfortunately, some foals try to suckle any mare, smell notwithstanding, and often get a battering for their naïvety.

With orphaned foals and lambs it is standard practice to use the skin of a mare's or ewe's dead offspring to disguise the smell of the orphan and so encourage the bereaved mother to accept it as her own. Some horse breeders say this can be helped by smearing Vick inside the mare's nostrils to lessen the efficiency of her sense of smell so she doesn't detect the strange smell of the foal. Others say that this can so disorientate the mare that she doesn't even recognise the foal as a horse and that this can result in her being aggressive towards it.

Satisfying Natural Curiosity

I feel we should pay much more attention to the importance of smell to our horses by letting them smell us, their surroundings and other horses much more than we do. It is not such a great crime to allow ridden horses to smell others. If we keep them side by side any striking out they may do will not make contact and the horses will settle with each other much more quickly than if they are not allowed to establish each other's identity from the start.

Also, when a new horse is brought into a yard, it should be led round the boxes and the inmates allowed to have a least a quick sniff, and the newcomer likewise. Keep the new horse side-on to the doors and keep level with his shoulder and he will settle into his own niche much more quickly than if not allowed this introduction and mutual satisfaction of natural equine curiosity. Stallions and mares are regularly teased or tried over a barrier in this way yet people think it sacrilege to let, say, two geldings smell each other over a stable door. After all, they're only doing what comes naturally, and what they need to do, and done sensibly there is no harm in it.

Taste

The horse's sense of taste is closely linked to its sense of smell and, like smell, it is extremely sensitive. Even though some horses will eat virtually anything, many of us know how difficult it can be to get a horse to take a 'doctored' feed or even his usual rations when they are made up from a different batch of ingredients, or to drink when away from home because the strange water has an unfamiliar smell.

Distinguishing Tastes

Like other vertebrates, the horse distinguishes taste by means of small pads of sensitive tissue on the tongue – the taste buds.

These are chemical receptors sited mainly on the upper surface of the tongue but also on the base of the tongue, on the soft palate and on the epiglottis, a flap of skin which covers the entrance to the windpipe during swallowing, directing food down the gullet instead of into the lungs where it would choke the horse.

From each taste bud runs a nerve fibre which transmits to the brain information on whether the substance encountered is sweet, salty, bitter or sour – the four tastes the horse is capable of differentiating. Horses like sweet and salty things but not bitter or sour ones. Titbits such as mints and sugar lumps are usually liked but sour or bitter ones don't normally find favour. However, bitter plants such as most poisonous plants are occasionally eaten if a horse is desperately hungry, and some animals actually acquire a taste for them with fatal results. Normally, though, a well fed horse can graze a field infested with ragwort for years and come to no harm because he ignores it. I hasten to add that I'm not recommending the practice – but it is a fact.

Very strong tastes like onions are also usually spurned, as are feeds which are going 'off' as the chemicals produced during decomposition or fermentation are either bitter or sour, or a combination of both.

The horse's dislike of bitter tastes means that bitter aloes is a very effective and cheap, old-fashioned remedy (but increasingly hard to get) that stops horses chewing rugs and stables.

Salt

If any food has one single taste almost to the exclusion of all others it soon palls on the palate and the horse can go off such a feed. Salt is an example. Horses only need a limited amount of this strong-tasting nutrient and too much added to feeds will put a horse off that particular feed. Performance horse owners can reach their wits' end trying to get their athletes to take electrolytes (which apparently taste disgustingly salty when you don't need them but like nectar when you do). The horse is usually the best judge, and will take them when he needs them.

Horses who like to lick people's hands could be after the salt in their sweat because they are short of salt in their diets. A salt lick should, of course, always be available but sometimes, in hot weather, or if the horse is working hard, he cannot get enough salt from the lick and makes his tongue sore on it, which in turn puts him off his feed. It's as well to check on the salt content of whatever you are feeding in such circumstances and add a little to the diet by means of, say, a dessertspoonful to each feed, more or less, according to the horse's reaction.

Smell and Taste Interaction

As described, the horse can detect the smell of food in his mouth by using his Jacobsen's organ in his nasal cavity. The 'smell' chemicals drift up the tubes to the organ where the horse detects the nature of the taste and smell. Normally, horses smell food before the tongue gets a chance to taste it. The horse's teeth normally meet closely at the front and the tongue doesn't get a chance to protrude unless the horse actually parts them. I did an experiment once to see just what the procedure was. I used a not particularly finicky feeder as a guinea pig to see what would happen when he was offered various different foods.

The horse was slightly hungry, having just been worked. A friend and I took a small piece of ragwort leaf about an inch square and offered it to him. He sniffed it, decided it smelt all right and picked it up with his lips. He did not open his teeth at all, therefore his tongue did not have a chance to taste the ragwort. After only a second in contact with his lips, he dropped the ragwort, having somehow detected, after smelling and approving it, that it was bitter. He could only have done this by means of detectors in his lips. (Incidentally, this confirmed an identical trial done years before on another horse.)

We then offered him a Fox's Glacier Mint – different from his usual Polo mints. He smelled it and picked it up cautiously with his lips, opened his teeth and appeared to roll the mint around with his tongue for a few seconds. He obviously realised it was not a Polo as he did not start to crunch it up until he had paused to do this, but he subsequently decided it was good and swallowed it, looking for more.

We then offered him various coarse mixes, all of which were wolfed down after a cursory preliminary sniff. He then took part of a corned beef sandwich, spent much time sniffing it first and manipulating it in his mouth, and ended up by spitting out the corned beef but swallowing the bread and butter. As corned beef sandwiches are fairly greasy and not easy to separate, this showed considerable oral dexterity!

I once visited a stud and had cheese and onion sandwiches before being shown the horses. Almost every one sniffed my hands, licked them and then did the flehmen action to assess the flavour on my hands further. Some horses, particularly young-stock, did this more than once.

It is well known that horses, being natural grazers, are capable of sorting out minutely different grasses in their paddocks. They find some grasses much more palatable than others, so these patches are grazed right down to the ground while others, not necessarily lavatory areas, are left completely alone. The senses of taste, smell and touch are all used to obtain a composite picture of the food offered.

Fussy Feeders

Some horses are fussy feeders and others positive gannets. Just like humans, horses are all very individual, and they may have their reasons for refusing food. It is easy to put a horse off his feed by mixing it with hands smelling of liniment, antiseptic, disinfectant or other chemicals. It is, therefore, a good plan always to wash and rinse your hands thoroughly before mixing feeds. Decaying food caked on the sides of feed containers or mixing utensils will smell and taste sour and can taint the whole feed, which is why containers and equipment should really be scrubbed after every feed and certainly once a day, apart from general hygiene.

Similarly, water left standing in the stable all day can absorb ammonia and other gases given off by decomposing matter such as urine, droppings and soiled bedding, and become thoroughly unpalatable. Automatic waterers can also have disadvantages, not because of the principle involved but because of the habits of some people who use them. Even if there is a plughole in the bottom, they are often not emptied and cleaned as often as buckets, with the result that the horse rarely has properly fresh water but water tainted with absorbed gases, bits of bedding, stable dust and hairs, bits of food and saliva from his mouth.

When cleaning out water containers or mangers in which the horse has done a dropping, be careful what you use to clean it. I find the best and most innocuous is sterilising fluid used for babies' feeding utensils, although there are some equally bland but effective disinfectants on the horse market now. Some manufacturers also make special disinfectants for stable use which do not leave strong odours or tastes and these are certainly much to be preferred to strong and potentially dangerous products commonly used in some yards.

Damp or Dry Feeds?

It used to be felt that horses should be given dry feeds as it was believed that damping food diluted the horse's digestive juices which process the food and make the nutrients accessible. Also, dry feeds were more likely to be chewed thoroughly and mixed with saliva than damp, some felt. However, horses' natural foods are usually high in water and many horses do have more difficulty coping with dry feed than damp feed.

Nowadays, horsemen and nutritionists alike seem to feel that damp (not wet) feeds are better as they mimic the dampness of grass. Damping a feed with hot as opposed to cold water certainly makes it more palatable in winter and brings out the flavour better. The taste buds in the tongue need the substances they are assessing to be dissolved in a fluid. This could be one of the purposes of saliva, the other being to set off the chemical breakdown of the food.

Natural Taste Tests

A stallion gauging a mare's receptiveness will first smell her, as described, but will subsequently nibble and lick her, gaining more information about whether she is really ready for mating. The smell and taste must differ very slightly from one stage of the mare's season to another because most stallions will not, left to themselves, serve a mare in the earlier stages, even if she accepts them.

The mare's bonding to her foal is partly achieved by taste as well as smell, as you can see from the sniffing and licking process after birth. After this initial period of smelling and tasting, the mare will always recognise her foal among many others, but will not spend much time licking it, as do, for example, dogs and cats.

The senses of smell and taste are so closely linked that at times they seem inseparable, particularly where food and mating instincts are concerned. They are acutely sensitive, too, and account for much apparently strange behaviour in our horses. I feel we should do well to realise that strange equine behaviour may well be due to the horse possesing senses which are much less sensitive in us humans.

Hearing

Like their other senses which are used to aid their survival in the sort of environment with which they evolved to cope, hearing was and is vital to horses to detect predators, enemies or other people and animals approaching them. As prey animals, acute hearing is part of their makeup.

Sound travels through air, solids and water by means of waves of different frequencies, or lengths, creating vibrations. High frequencies mean high sounds and vice versa, and horses are known to be able to hear much higher and lower sounds than humans. Not much work has been done on horses' use of and reaction to sound but some studies are now being done in America and England which should help us understand this topic better.

How Horses Hear

The funnel part of the ear, or pinna, which we can see, can move almost right round to give the horse nearly 'circular' hearing. By moving his head he can, of course, direct his ear towards any sound at all coming from any direction, much more effectively and easily than we can. The pinna directs the sound waves and vibrations down inside the head where a complex arrangement of bones, cavities and the eardrum transmit them and amplify them. Special sensory nerves detect them and send the messages received to the brain which then assesses the sound vibrations and 'decides' what to do about them.

If the sound is one associated with danger or anything unpleasant, the flight-or-fight mechanism is set up in the horse and he may show alertness or fear. If the sound is familiar and signifies nothing much to the horse he may not bother much about it, but if it signifies something pleasant such as the feed-room door opening and buckets rattling, the horse will show signs of anticipation and pleasure.

Strange sounds do not necessarily frighten horses, although they will show more alertness than with a familiar, non-dangerous sound. Often, sounds we may expect to terrify them do not, such as blasting from a quarry, a pneumatic drill or a police siren, yet something like a rustling bag, or the rustle of nylon clothing, can really frighten them. (The latter can be overcome by adding fabric softener to the final rinsing water.)

Because of the very long and accurate memories of horses, sounds once experienced, and perhaps associated with a particular happening, will be remembered more or less permanently. We use this quality all the time in our handling and training of horses by giving a certain command, as simply as possible (preferably one or two, and no more than three, syllables) such as 'walk on', 'over' or 'back'. To teach a youngster or, indeed a horse of any age a new command or movement, we say, for example, 'whoa' while giving it restraining aids such as pressure on the breast or the noseband of a headcollar. Eventually, the horse connects the sound (for that's all it is to him) with the action and aid, and will soon stop on hearing 'whoa' or, separately, feeling the aid. When the time comes for him to be ridden, aids for 'whoa' from the saddle accompanied by the sound soon convey to an averagely clever animal that this new circumstance also means 'she wants me to stop', and most will do so.

It is the sound that matters, and the way it is said, not its meaning in English or any other language, of course. If, for example, you consistently said to the horse 'trot on' while giving him the aids to halt, he would come to think that the sound 'trot on' meant 'stop' and would do so. I once knew a former circus pony who, as part of his act with clowns, had been taught to obey reverse vocal aids. When the clowns yelled 'stop, stop' at him he would gallop like mad round the ring, bucking and plunging as well, and when the lead clown scratched his head the pony stopped at once. It took me a few practical 'lessons' – the hard sort – to learn the pony's circus language and overcome my own forgetfulness that 'walk on' meant, to this pony, 'lie down'!

Horses also seem to have sharper hearing than humans, as well as a wider range. For instance, they can pick up sounds from a greater distance, and hear extremely faint sounds better than we do. It's quite common for horses and other animals to recognise the sound of their owners' car engines and react accordingly. When I was keeping a horse at livery, most of us owners were delighted at our individual horses' reactions when we rolled up in our separate cars, but it used to distress us to see one horse's reaction of retreating to the back of his box when he heard his owner's car and, particularly, her voice.

Horses can also distinguish between dialects and different accents and languages. A friend of mine has an American Saddlebred gelding, a beautiful, intelligent horse who simply could not take to her English accent. When she starting putting on an American accent he became a changed horse, but now understands both English and American equally well! A Welsh Cob stallion, sold to France, soon learned the new sounds to which he was expected to respond – in about three weeks – but when visited by a group of Welsh breeders (which did not include his own breeder) became aggressive at the sound of his mother tongue. He had obviously not had a very happy upbringing.

The tone of voice is also important to the horse as it changes the sound completely from his point of view. Horses dislike intensely screaming, screeching, raucous noises and may react by panicking or becoming aggressive or frightened, yet we all know how effective a soothing tone of voice, regardless of the actual meaning of the words, can be to an uptight horse, particularly if accompanied by a soothing stroke on the neck. I am sure horses, incidentally, prefer to be stroked than patted. It is more soothing and rewarding, whereas a pat which is anything more than gentle equates to a kick in horse language. The fact that horses dislike hard pats and thumps can be seen in the flattened ears and angry expressions of performance horses who, having done well, are thumped hard on the neck by their delighted riders. Obviously not much of a reward in the horses' eyes.

As for soothing a horse, it's as well to get him used to a particular sound always said in a particular way, even though tone is very communicative. For example, 'easy boy' said in a low, drawn-out way can come to convey to him that there is nothing to fear. On the other hand, never say 'good boy' to a worried horse who is playing up as, having learned 'good boy' as a reward, presumably during early training, he will think he is being praised for playing up, which is the last thing you want.

Music

Music has a considerable effect on horses and it is clear from studies done in Ireland and America that horses prefer soothing, melodious music to, for example, rock. One Texas horseman reported that his horses' favourite music was Puccini, particularly *La Bohème*, while rock music resulted in 'faeces everywhere'. To produce excess droppings the horses really must have been pretty upset as this sort of reaction is usually associated with quite significant excitement or apprehension, such as on entering a showground or hearing a sound associated with something frightening such as an oncoming train or a plane overhead.

Horses must obviously pick up our 'vibes' to respond to tone as well, I feel. How else can a horse on the end of a lunge line possibly react with a pleased little swagger at the sound of 'good boy' when having performed some movement well?

Years ago I did try a small experiment in a private yard where I kept a horse and found that whereas heavy rock noticeably hyped up the horses and frightened some to the extent of producing tightened facial skin, ears back, head up and worried expressions combined with stamping and tail-switching, Benjamino Gigli, an operatic tenor with a particularly light, effeminate and effortless voice of a type which seems rare today, produced relaxed, half-asleep attitudes, super-calm horses and contentment only otherwise noticed during late-night checks.

Although people often have radios playing in stable yards, I do feel much more care should be taken over this. For a start, they should not be left on nearly all the time as they so often are, as horses do like peace and quiet, and programmes should be chosen with much more care – musical programmes are preferred by horses to speaking programmes, and, as mentioned, calming, 'uplifting' music is better than loud, heavy rock, screeched lyrics and banal disc-jockeys' garbage in between. Gentle country music is liked by many horses, as are ballads and moderate big-band sounds – and please, keep the volume down! We are often all too ready to confuse what we like with what has a good effect on horses – not always the same thing at all. Remember, they are prisoners and can't turn it off.

Travelling

Canadian equine transport expert Dr Sharon Cregier reports that noise can have a very significant effect on how well a horse travels. Both horseboxes and trailers have the defects of rattling bodywork, vibrations, engine whine, the drone of tyres, the roar of the engines of passing traffic and banging and clanging of ramps being put up and down. All these disturb the horses, some more than others.

It may sound like a lot of trouble, but it is well worth trying to install sound insulation under the floor and on the walls and ceilings of vehicles – without blocking ventilation outlets, which are vital in maintaining a healthy atmosphere inside to discourage the rapid breeding of bacteria which can cause transport sickness or shipping fever. Sheets of various materials can always be removed and put into a new vehicle, so are not wasted. Thick, damp sawdust bedding about six inches thick insulates the floor very well as well as giving a really secure footing and, of course, stuffing the horses' ears with cotton wool during the journey can certainly help without hampering their balance mechanism. As mentioned, soothing music playing at a low level, at intervals, will also calm many horses.

Aircraft Noise

We often read reports in horse magazines and papers about horses being badly frightened by aeroplanes, jets, helicopters and so on buzzing over their fields and, as there seemed to be some clear practical evidence that mares beneath an airport flight path aborted their foetuses more often than those not near jet noise, the University of Florida, funded by the United States Air Force unit of noise and sonic boom impact technology, set up a research study funded by the latter, to help pinpoint any health or behaviour problems affecting the horses from such noise. This is not a new area of study but the problem continues. Humans can be very troubled by jet noise, and so can horses and other animals, so we obviously cannot overlook what is bound to be an increasing problem in future.

It is felt that mares in late pregnancy may be more susceptible than other horses to aircraft noise, particularly to low-flying aircraft. Stress itself, by producing flight-or-fight hormones in the body from whatever cause, is enough to bring on abortion, as many readers will know to their cost. The researchers in the study mentioned felt that stress resulting from jet noise may also adversely affect the quantity and quality of antibodies in the mare's colostrum and maybe the foal's own ability to absorb them, which only lasts for eighteen hours anyway. Without these antibodies, foals are at great risk during their early lives of contracting any of a number of potentially fatal diseases. By exposing horses to bursts of recorded aircraft noise of differing

types and by using heart monitors, scanners for foetal movements and videos of the horses' reactions to noises, researchers
hope to come up with some concrete scientific evidence as to the
extent of the effects of such noise on horses. Apparently, it is
expected that the horses will adjust to some extent to the noise;
the experiments may be continued later with real-life flyover
studies.

Super-sensory Perception

I have called this final section of this chapter super-sensory
perception as the term more generally used, extra-sensory
perception (ESP), seems plainly inaccurate to me. SSP or ESP is
one of those grey areas which has not been proved to exist by
conventionally accepted scientific means. However, just
because something has not been proved, it does not mean it is
not so, of course, or does not exist. Many years before cigarette
smoking was known to cause lung cancer it was suspected of
doing so, as was radiation. Similarly, years before the insecticide
DDT was banned, doctors, scientists and environmentalists (in
those days called 'cranks') strongly suspected it of having
damaging, long-term effects on the health of humans and
animals, wildlife and crops, but it took many years and, finally,
hard proof before the vested interests of manufacturers, agri-
culturalists and politicians were finally overcome.

I have found that only the most open-minded horsepeople,
and those interested in equine or animal psychology and
behaviour, are willing to talk about SSP in other than a
dismissive way. Through my fourteen-year connection with the
Equine Behaviour Study Circle, an international group of
enthusiasts from all walks of life, scientific and non-scientific, I
have been able to talk to and correspond with other interested
parties and several items on the subject have appeared in the
EBSC's newletter, *Equine Behaviour*, over the years.

Sceptics will say that there must be some other explanation for
apparent phenomena. I agree that we should explore all avenues,
consider all possible explanations, but we should not give

credence to one explanation while dismissing another out of hand. If we always reacted thus, some of the greatest discoveries of our time, such as the control of fire and the fact that the earth is round, would never have come to light. As it is, the science of modern genetics was held back for decades because Gregor Mendel's work was dismissed out of hand and was only rediscovered and confirmed early this century. Thousands of people and animals could have been saved the suffering of genetically carried disease had his work progressed, uninterrupted by the religious and scientific establishment of his day.

(Incidentally, he started his work with mice, not the peas with which he continued it, but the church stopped him as some of its senior figures considered that breeding experiments with mammals were just too close to home – humans – and constituted blasphemy! Plants were considered ecclesiastically less sensitive. While you may wonder what on earth this has to do with horses, apart from the connection with genetic disease, it is my experience that a similar attitude is still rife in some sectors of the horse world, particularly when it comes to peripheral and somewhat elusive topics like super-sensory perception.)

Tonic Immobility

Members of the Equine Behaviour Study Circle have in recent years contributed to their newsletter articles and letters on a state called tonic or catatonic immobility in horses. Some members, including myself, felt that their horses appeared to be 'tuning in' or listening to some 'vibes' or sounds outside human sensory powers. Members reported a rock-solid, rooted-to-the-spot and completely unreachable and immovable state in their horses during similar spells.

Scientific contacts all stress that such a condition indicates extreme fear and that any animal can become 'rooted to the spot' in fright. However, it was obvious to me, members of the EBSC and other people who commented on it that fear is *not* part of the reaction we have noticed, and so many people have had the same impression – of horses relaxed, not rigid with fear but supremely alert, receptive and totally diverted, albeit not to us mere owners attempting to get them to move on out of sometimes very inconvenient situations such as a stream of impatient cars! – that I personally am sure that either sound or some kind of super-sensory perception is the cause.

Some reported that after the horse 'came down' from his trance he walked on and very quickly another horse came into view, thus suggesting that the horse had detected the sound, or maybe even the smell, of the other horse which his human rider had not. This has not happened in all cases, however, but, of course, this does not mean that another horse had not been in the vicinity and had turned off somewhere and never come into view or human earshot. In other cases the horses concerned had been in wide open spaces with views for miles all round but no other horses or animals in sight likely to cause such a trance-like state. So far the matter is still a puzzle.

This apparently common state occurs in all sorts of horses and ponies under varying circumstances and people have different opinions as to what exactly is happening to the horse at the time. As fear is definitely not part of the state reported by EBSC members, we should really think of a different term for it. My own experience is that the horse seems to be tuned in to some communication beyond my own senses. We have already seen in this chapter that the horse's senses are much more highly developed than ours, so it is difficult to say, for example, that a horse is *not* sensing something that he can detect as a matter of normality for him, but we cannot. I tend to feel that such horses are receiving some kind of vibrations, for want of a better expression, outside the normal five senses. This condition has happened to horses of different types in my presence on several occasions, and once they have snapped out of it (and they do so suddenly) they have continued on normally, not in an excitable, sluggish or preoccupied state, and I have obviously never found an explanation.

One EBSC member, however, reported that her mare went into tonic immobility in this way at exactly 1 p.m. when out on a hack. The woman knew the time as she had just looked at her watch, having been later than usual setting off. The mare remained transfixed and seemed tense but not frightened for about five minutes before her owner could move her on homeward again. The mare continued eagerly, which her owner put down to the fact that she knew a feed would be waiting for her and they were later returning than usual.

When she finally got home thirty minutes later, the mare, on being released loose in the yard as was the normal practice, went not to her own box as usual but to that of a particular equine friend, stuck her head over the door and seemed to communicate with her, using slightly agitated whickers, sniffing and ears sharply pricked forward, not the normal relaxed greeting. Her owner found that while they had been out hacking the horse-friend had had a slight accident in the field and had fallen while cantering round. When the friend's owner was asked what time this was she said: 'It was exactly one o'clock because I was just going to watch the news on TV when I saw her fall in the field.' Apparently, the horse had lain winded and slightly shaken for about five minutes, just the length of time the first mare's trance had lasted. I can think of no explanation for this other than that the mare out hacking had received some kind of mental message from her friend in distress. She was too far from home to hear even a loud whinny and, anyway, the 'faller' had made no loud noise at any time.

Another instance involved two horses, constant companions, who were separated temporarily while one was anaesthetised for an operation. The horse left behind was extremely agitated and had to be stabled with the top door shut during his friend's absence. However, he quietened down completely at about the time the general anaesthetic on his friend took effect, and gradually became upset again as his friend (ten miles away at the vet's) came round. The writer of this tale concluded that the anaesthetic had broken the mental link between the two friends but that once it wore off their mutual agitation was felt and responded to.

It is easy to say that this is all hearsay from 'unreliable sources', but I have had many similar reports from people I know to be very down to earth, even cynical, who could not possibly reasonably be accused of romanticising the situation.

Response to Mental Illness in Humans

Horses and donkeys are known to respond differently to mentally handicapped and mentally ill humans, and differently to both from the way they react to other humans. It is common for horses, particularly experienced ones, to be gentle and careful with children and novices but to play up when a 'good' rider mounts and they think they can get away with a bit of fun. It seems that horses appear to recognise that mentally handi-capped people have brainwaves of differing lengths from non-handicapped humans and seem to regard them as chums and not bosses. Again, I have no proof of this and don't know if electroencephalograms have been used in this connection, but it would be most interesting to try it to see if the brainwaves 'click'.

It seems that horses respond with fear verging on panic when presented with mentally ill patients, depending on the actual illness. One patient who was known to become suddenly violent was scheduled to be tried on a very calm mare known to be particularly good with mentally handicapped (as opposed to ill) riders. The mare became terrified and actually broke away from her handlers before the patient could be mounted, standing trembling at the far end of the indoor school.

The following week the mare was being used in a lesson when this patient again arrived in the car park, a couple of hundred yards away from the school, having come along to watch. The mare was being brought out of the school by two handlers by the time the patient reached the building, having become 'upset and panicky' about the time the patient's car had pulled into the car park. Had she smelled or heard the patient? Her handlers thought this impossible, given the distance and the fact that a lesson was in progress in an enclosed building. Had she associated the sound of the engine (having heard it only once the week before) with that particular rider, and why had she panicked the previous week at the very closeness of this patient? There seems to be no answer other than that she somehow knew him to be sometimes violent.

An interesting related point that has been reported to the EBSC is that the best horses for mentally or physically handicapped riders are very fit Thoroughbreds, mentally and physically finely tuned and alert. They apparently sense the rider's difficulties extremely well and plod along quietly, amazing though this may seem.

Homing Instinct

The topic of a horse's homing instinct is also interesting. Some horses, like some people, have this instinct in generous amounts; the EBSC has received several reports about horses in strange localities getting their riders home or at least into familiar territory. Not all horses or ponies have this ability, however. I was caught in a sudden and rapidly rising river mist one autumn and 'threw the reins' on my very intelligent horse's neck and told him to get on with it and get us home, only to realise that he was as clueless as I! Pigeons find their way by sensing the earth's magnetic field through a special device above their beaks, dolphins and whales echo-locate, but it is less clear how other mammals do it and why some have better homing instincts than others.

One particularly impressive report consisted of a woman who had boxed to a hunt meet fifty miles outside her normal area and become isolated and alone while trying to keep with hounds. She could find no one to ask and in the end gave her horse his head. The horse got her back to the hired box – only to find it had gone. By then she had a rough idea where they were and gave the horse appropriate directions, but found that he was trying to take a direct line across country, in the dark, at a relaxed canter, the gait horses naturally use in the wild when moving from one grazing ground to another. They got home at around midnight and she swore that it was more the horse's homing instinct than her own sense of direction which was to be thanked.

In the famous book *Black Beauty* by Anna Sewell there is a vividly described instance of a horse refusing to cross a bridge in the dark, which subsequently proved to have broken. The author may have got this from real life because reports of horses refusing to do similar things are quite common, although as horses see better in the dark than us it is quite possible that horses could see the danger whereas accompanying humans could not.

. . . And Now It's Getting Ridiculous!

While talking of super-sense in a book about natural horse management, why not talk about the supernatural? Reports of horses becoming terrified in haunted places are, again, not uncommon and while this may verge on the fanciful, I can't resist telling this one true story.

I have a very commonsensical, feet-on-the-ground friend who used to live in a house with a poltergeist in it. Her family suffered several instances of tragedy or 'bad luck', both in and out of the house, and sold it again fairly soon – no one ever stays there long, to this day. Their bad luck stopped as soon as they moved out.

A while ago I was talking to a girl new to the area who said she could never get her horse, also new to the area, past that house while out hacking and had had to stop using that route. The horse's attention had, apparently, definitely been fixed on the house and not on something innocuous or ordinary in the road or elsewhere which you would normally expect to make a horse shy.

I do not know whether or not anyone else in the district had had the same problem, but the girl I spoke to knew nothing at all about the house's history and reputation – so it makes you wonder whether horses really do have a sixth sense.

10 Behaviour and Psychology: It's Mostly in the Mind

The behaviour of horses results from a mixture of evolution and the conditioning they receive during life, whether that life is a natural, wild one or one almost completely controlled by man. Chapter 1 dealt with evolution and the type of animal it has left us. That animal is one we regard highly if only because of its usefulness to us: many humans simply exploit the considerable suitability and usefulness of the horse without caring about his well-being, but others also have great respect and affection for horses. His speed, strength and general tractability are what we find most useful about the horse, but many of us are slow to understand his mind and therefore why he behaves as he does.

Instinct

Instinct can be defined as a complex inborn pattern of behaviour that is typical of all normally reared individuals of a species. The horse is born with certain predetermined behaviour patterns, but upbringing can over-ride them. Foals reared in a bland, unstimulating environment, deprived of contact with other horses, never experiencing frightening or worrying situations, do not show the normal healthy sense of self-preservation characterised by a degree of nervousness common to all prey animals and certainly to horses. They are slow to learn when put into training, they cannot relate to other horses or animals and seem to possess no flight-or-fight reaction, which is the horse's overwhelmingly major instinct, the one which enabled him to survive for millions of years in the wild and which we often find disconcerting and difficult to deal with.

If it were not possible to influence horses, to 'damp down' their instinctive inclinations to behave in certain ways, it would be impossible to train them, of course, and they would not have become so extremely useful to us. Not all wild animals have been domesticated, obviously. A horse relative of ass type, the onager, was initially domesticated by the ancient Babylonians and controlled by means of a cattle-type nose ring (really!) but the onager's temperament was, and is, unsuitable for general domestication and handling, let alone working, by man, being unwilling and nasty, so it was ditched in favour of the horse. The African ass family is a different kettle of fish and most of our domesticated Neddies are descended from wild African asses. Most people I know who have a lot of experience of both horses and donkeys say that donkeys are far more intelligent than horses, more affectionate and more dog-like in their loyalty and devotion, horses being more cat-like and independent. Horses do bear grudges and many, particularly Thoroughbred and, most particularly, Arab types, will not tolerate idiots or being pushed around, although there are exceptions. Continental warmblood breeds, for instance, have been specifically bred to be submissive (although again there are exceptions) to rather dominating riders who want a servant rather than a partner. This seems to suit Scandinavian and Germanic peoples in general, whereas Latin types, especially the French, but also the Russians, prefer a partnership and a freer, lighter style of riding. Where that leaves the British and those of English/British descent I'm not sure, as we have a lot of Scandinavian, French and German blood in us and many of us currently seem to prefer the Germanic style of riding, although this is slowly but surely starting to change, as can be seen in some of the younger generation of competitive dressage riders who produce a happier, more flowing style, often, than the foregoing generation.

Whereas a horse's instinct may be to panic and/or fight back under pressure or when in doubt, a donkey is more likely to stand solid and seem impenetrable, which is why it was dubbed 'stubborn' and 'stupid', which it certainly is not. Its ease of handling and quiet temperament has made it, tragically for the donkey, the beast of burden of choice in the Third World.

A horse's primary instinct, then, is to flee from anything frightening or confusing, only standing to fight as a last resort when cornered – and a horse in a mind to defend itself is a formidable opponent indeed. This is just one very good reason why quietness and confidence must be cultivated when handling horses and ponies, to convey safety and leadership to the horse and, if it is a 'leader'-type horse as opposed to the more usual follower, the fact that the human is dominant and should be cooperated with on the whole.

Reflex Actions

A reflex action is one which is performed without thinking in response to a stimulus, one which does not necessarily require consciousness and, biologically, takes place without the brain being involved but using instead what is termed a reflex arc. This involves a stimulus being detected by sensory cells at the end of a sensory nerve. This message travels to the spinal column (an extension of the brain) and a message goes straight back down a motor nerve to take appropriate action. These sorts of action, sometimes more complicated than that described, are nature's way of getting the horse, or part of him, out of danger before more damage is done.

An example might be a horse trotting along and treading on a sharp stone: he instantly moves his foot away and may limp for a few strides to ease the foot. Another instance might be a horse backing into a prickly bush or leaning over a barbed wire fence to get at grass on the other side and pricking himself on one of the barbs. Without thinking, he jumps away.

The horse also has reflex actions which are connected with his perception of danger. If he sees something move suddenly with one eye, particularly at the limit of that eye's range in position, such as nearly behind him, he doesn't think about shying or careering off, he just does it. Most other creatures have these reflex actions, of course, including humans, but some of us may think horses have more than their fair share of them! It can become quite difficult to decide when, for instance, a horse is shying out of genuine reflex or fear or whether he is behaving like this out of freshness or high spirits or because he feels like playing and thinks this particular rider will let him get away with it.

Reflexes of the latter sort, as opposed to those caused by physical pain, can be overcome by training, police horses being prime examples of this. So-called 'bombproof' horses and ponies are of great value for beginners or nervous riders, their psychological reflexes having been well damped down by good training and/or years of experience plus, usually, a very laid-back temperament. But put a nervy horse with a nervy, rough or thoughtless handler and his reflexes become even more sharpened and frequent, the horse jumping at everything, although not always reflexively.

Logic and Reasoning

It has long been a standard saying in the horse world that horses have no reasoning power. I do not know who first decreed this but he must have been unobservant in the extreme because it is so obviously untrue. Some of a horse's actions may take place because he has found out how to do something by accident or been shown how by a human or another horse or, in one instance I observed with great fascination myself, by a dog, but horses certainly are capable of thinking some things out for themselves. If they weren't, they could never have survived this long, particularly in the dangerous environment in which they evolved.

The incident with the dog is worth retelling. It involved a dog showing a horse how to open a feed-room door which was too heavy for the dog to manipulate. The dog was a terrier, Titch, who slept in the feed room at night to keep the rats away. He had left a bone in there and had been pawing at the door, which opened outwards towards him and, this day, was off the latch, but he was not strong enough to open it wide enough to get in. A horse with whom he was quite friendly was ambling loose about the place, as he was often allowed to do, and the terrier stood by the door barking to the horse. I was about to go out and open the door but, on seeing the horse walk purposefully over with an inquisitive look on his face, decided to see what happened. The dog turned back to the door, got his paw around the edge and tried to pull it outwards which he only succeeded in doing about a couple of inches. He couldn't seem to manage the rest with his nose, as he did in the house, due to the spring closure on the door, but the horse watched him a few times then, when the door was slightly open and the dog trying to get his nose inside, he fiddled it open with his muzzle. This happened again on two occasions, after which it became a yard rule to clear the feed room of Titch's bones and keep the door properly fastened. The horse himself never managed to get in but did not seem to want to. Once he had let his friend in he walked away.

I always admire horses who let themselves out of their boxes and then go along the row letting out all the others, too, although I have never known one do it with doors having kick-over bolts at the bottom as well as the normal stable-door bolt on the top. People say that horses learn to let themselves out by accident, through fiddling with the bolt, but I don't see why the horse cannot be intelligently trying to find out how to escape, just as we might puzzle out an unfamiliar gadget to see how it worked. Subsequently to work the other bolts from a completely different angle and let his companions out is surely not an accident but requires intelligent thought.

Learning

Reasoning is a large part of learning and although most people, including scientists, feel that horses learn through the association of ideas, I feel it is true that they also think about what they are being taught and do not learn solely by repetition. When teaching a child you can say, in some language the child understands, precisely what you want him or her to learn. You cannot do this with the horse, but you can get him to respond to particular sounds (words or phrases) said at the same time as physically, say, lifting his feet or pushing him backwards or stopping him. He then links the idea of the sound with the idea of the movement and learns that the two go together.

However, as horses gain more experience they get out and about and meet situations not encountered before which they do have to think about, such as how to get through a hazard safely or how to keep their balance on a slippery road, something we cannot possibly teach them. All but the most stupid horses will learn to take shorter steps and use their heads and necks, if permitted, of their own volition and so learn how to cope with this situation in future.

Elizabeth Svendsen of the Donkey Sanctuary told me of an instance of a particular donkey – not, apparently, an especially unusual one – who was being used to give riding lessons and simple mounted tasks to physically handicapped children. One task involved the child riding the donkey, collecting a 'letter' from one side of the indoor school, walking the donkey round to the other side and 'posting' it in a box.

The child tried and tried to pick up the letter to carry it round but could not manage it. The donkey, who was well used to this task, picked up the letter and walked round to the other side of the school, where he waited for someone to take it from him. This cannot be called learning by association of ideas because the donkey knew that the child, not he himself, was supposed to pick up the letter. He did know, however, that the letter had to *be* picked up and taken round to the other side and realised that the child, for some reason, was not doing so. The fact that he finally did so himself indicates intelligent thought and reasoning power.

It is only in recent years that ethologists and other scientists interested in animal behaviour and intelligence have started to devise intelligence tests for animals which actually suit those animals and not humans. In the past (and this does continue today) such tests have often been based on maze-type tests in which the horse has had to find his way to the middle of the maze where a food reward would be waiting. Other sorts of tests have been used such as giving horses covered boxes containing food and seeing how quickly they recognised certain signs indicating where the food was; but although these might be suitable for animals used to having to search for food, such as squirrels and birds, they are totally inappropriate for horses whose food, in the natural conditions in which they evolved, is all around them. They would never encounter a maze or anything like one in the wild, so the tests, at which horses performed rather poorly and so got the reputation of being low down on the intelligence scale (humans being at the top, of course!), were pointless.

The true measure of intelligence is how well an animal learns to cope with the environment in which it was 'designed' to live and, so, how well it survives in it – how well it learns that shrubbery, cliffs, trees and so on provide shelter, his or her position in the herd hierarchy, what constitutes food and so on. Were it not for man having hunted wild horses out of existence and taking their habitats, the horse would still be surviving very well indeed as a truly wild creature. As it is, he is surviving in domesticity due to his adaptability and intelligence having made him useful and pleasant for us to associate with.

Communication

Horses communicate with themselves and each other mainly by means of body language, attitudes and facial expressions, not mainly with their voices as do humans. They treat humans just the same as fellow horses, from this point of view, so it is as well that we learn their language if we want our association to be a two-way one, since they so readily learn ours.

If a dog puts his ears back, stretches his head down and out and wags his tail it means he is pleased to see us, but novice horsepeople would be in for a nasty shock if they read the same meaning into identical actions by a horse! These are all signs of aggression in horses. It takes a little experience to learn to recognise a nasty face or other signs of displeasure in a horse, but those who say horses do not have expressive faces are quite wrong. The ears flick freely back and forth, both together and independently, and give a good indication of where the horse's attention lies. If they are both pricked forward he is intent on something ahead of him, but if they are directed loosely back he is listening or watching something behind him. If a ridden horse has one ear ahead and one back he is watching where he is going and paying attention to his rider at the same time. Ears flat back mean aggression or that a horse is trying his hardest, for example in a race or jumping against the clock. The nostrils are normally relaxed but will flare to a circular shape in excitement or when the horse is distressed or breathing hard. If they are pinched up and back and wrinkled this indicates pain or anger.

The tail actions mean the same in any breed, although its natural carriage varies greatly from breed to breed. All horses will hold the tail more out and perhaps up when in action, particularly when excited. Some Arab horses bring their tails right up and over their quarters in great excitement, and many hold them straight up like a flagpole. A tail held proudly arched indicates a feeling of well-being, pride maybe, or mild excitement but one clamped down between the buttocks indicates resentment and anger or an attempt to protect sensitive areas. Switching the tail hard from side to side certainly shows anger and distress.

If a horse shows the whites of his eyes it does *not* mean he is vicious but is simply the conformation of his eyes as an individual. A little practice will teach a novice how to recognise a soft, affectionate look in the eye, an inquisitive look, a bad-tempered look and one indicating sickness or depression.

Horses use their heads and muzzles as we use our hands and fingers – to nudge us or other horses for attention or to express some desire or need, such as an uncomfortable bridle or rug or a scratch being required somewhere, in which case the horse may well point to the area with his muzzle or offer up that part of his body for scratching. Head and ears up means alertness and 'at attention', head up and ears back means frustration or dislike. If the head is tossing up and down, this, too, can mean frustration or mild fear or anxiety. If it is down, ears back and maybe teeth bared, this certainly means the horse is seriously thinking of biting.

Learning what the horse's body language means makes a great improvement to our relationship with him, not to mention our safety. Who wants a one-way conversation?

Vices

Actions such as crib-biting, wind-sucking, weaving and box-walking are all neuroses brought on by unsuitable management for the individual concerned. Horses are all individuals and blanket statements about specific breed characteristics do not always hold true. Not all Thoroughbreds are scatty, not all native ponies are sweet-natured, and so on. It is true that some horses and ponies will take not too badly to being kept short of exercise, to having to stand in a box for much of their time and being allowed little if any liberty, but most dislike this sort of mismanagement and, bearing in mind their evolution, it is not surprising.

Stereotypies, as professional psychologists and behaviourists call neuroses, are exhibited in farm animals, zoo animals, horses, dogs and, indeed, all creatures, including humans, having to tolerate unsuitable surroundings and physical or mental distress. I think there is no sadder sight, generally speaking, than a clipped, rugged-up, corn-fed, thoroughly cosseted horse miserably moping at the back of his cell, marching trance-like round his box, gulping down air, weaving or chewing whatever is convenient, just for something to do or as a displacement activity to try to ameliorate the distress he is feeling.

One of the results of constant and seemingly useless activity is the release into the bloodstream of the body's own natural tranquillisers and painkillers, endorphins and encephalins, and many workers in the field of animal behaviour believe that animals gain some sort of release from their distress by this means. Attempts to cure crib-biters by using the drug naloxone, which blocks the effects of endorphins and encephalins (related to opiates), have not so far been permanently successful in horses although they are used in treating human drug addicts. The drug is known to cause great nausea and whereas human patients can vomit to relieve themselves horses cannot. I understand this avenue of research has been abandoned.

It is unknown for a hardened crib-biter or wind-sucker to have been cured by any method (normally all ledges are blocked off in a stable and the unfortunate horse made to wear a cribbing strap which has a metal projection to stab him in the throat every time he arches his neck to crib-bite or wind-suck) although more success has been achieved with weavers (who swing their heads from side to side like an equally distressed zoo animal) and box-walkers (another action akin to caged zoo animals pacing their cages or enclosures) simply by putting the animals on a more natural regime – more liberty, congenial company, plenty of interest and so on. (Simply physically stopping a horse performing his vice removes his release and distresses him even more.)

A roughage-deficient diet causes considerable discomfort in horses and can certainly bring on vices, particularly crib-biting and wind-sucking, where the horse attempts to get air inside himself to relieve his hunger and indigestion. In such specific cases a more suitable diet results in the vice stopping.

Vices, although the horse's only means of relief from his distress, are counterproductive in the long term. All use up energy; crib-biting wears down the incisor teeth and both it and wind-sucking *may* actually interfere with digestion. They are without doubt brought on by unnatural management methods, over-confinement, mental distress and physical discomfort and, because of this, there is *no need* for them to occur. If horses were kept more suitably and humanely they would disappear.

Discipline

Many behavioural problems are caused by lack of discipline, or the wrong sort, unnecessarily harsh, erratic or unjust.

When raised by equine dams in a natural herd environment

horses learn herd manners, as mentioned earlier. They quickly learn their place in the hierarchy and are content with their niche. Horses raised this way are easier for humans to handle, too. If we cannot arrange this, at least let our discipline be what it would be in nature – instant, so that the horse links it with what he has just done, and consistent, so that he is punished for real misdemeanours or rewarded for good behaviour *every time*. Otherwise, if the horse is only sometimes rewarded or remprimanded and sometimes not he will never know where he is and will never learn just how we expect him to behave. This will breed resentment and insecurity in the horse, resulting in defensive (dangerous) behaviour.

With consistent, just treatment and training, horses can, obviously, be conditioned to the unnatural way of life we usually impose on them, but we can never get away from their basic needs of a suitable diet and water, the need for company, ample exercise (preferably a good deal of it at liberty) and space, not only wide open spaces to exercise and work in, but respect of the horse's own personal space. It seems that most horses have a personal oval-shaped space around them which they regard as theirs, extending to roughly 14 feet around them (about 4 metres). This obviously extends beyond the walls of a normal loose box, so it is not surprising that some horses readily bite passers-by, or kick the wall of a box housing a disliked next-door neighbour.

When feeding horses in a field, feeds should be spaced out to about 16 feet apart at least, so that they can all feel reasonably secure, although close friends may happily eat out of the same container. Invading a horse's personal space, particularly that of a strange horse, is asking for trouble, so keep an eye on that body language if you want to be sure of your welcome or lack of it.

Diet

Much has been said about this in Chapter 5, but in the present context it should be stressed that 'difficult' behaviour can certainly be the result of an unsuitable diet, as much in horses and other animals as it is now known to be in young humans; not only allergies from human junk foods, but 'fizzy' behaviour in horses from feeding high levels of a largely unnatural food – concentrates. The excess metabolic toxins these create have an irritating, intoxicating effect on horses, producing erratic, hyper-energetic behaviour and physical disorders such as skin and coat problems, chronic indigestion which does not always actually become colic, and learning difficulties simply because the horse is so above himself with 'nervous' energy and feeling physically out of sorts that he is unable to concentrate or cooperate.

Fewer concentrates and more roughage is the answer for most horses. As our knowledge of nutrition improves, diets are being produced which provide the horse with as much energy as he needs but in a more acceptable form for his digestive system to absorb. High-energy roughages (forages) are probably going to be seen more and more in future, where the horse gets his energy from digestible fibre rather than concentrates, and those who are using them report greatly improved behaviour and well-being. In the UK, Dengie Feeds are the first to introduce this type of diet in variations for different categories of animal, from children's ponies to racehorses.

It is also up to owners to push more and more for organically produced horse feeds free of the artificial chemicals, pesticides, fertilisers and weedkillers which are known to infiltrate our own food and create physical and mental problems such as allergies and violent behaviour in humans. If they are doing this to us there's no reason why they aren't doing it to our horses, too, putting them and their riders and handlers in danger from hyper-energetic behaviour and surely making the horses feel below par as well.

Commercial markets are driven by demand or lack of it. Constant 'nagging' of manufacturers and suppliers inevitably provides what consumers want eventually – so let's all get nagging!

The Horse Has Two Sides

The horse's brain, his nervous control centre, is, like that of other mammals, divided into a conscious part (the larger front part called the cerebrum) and a subconscious part beneath it and to the back (called the cerebellum). In addition, the cerebrum is divided by a deep cleft into left and right hemispheres, joined by a cord of fibrous tissue called the *corpus callosum*. Stimuli detected by the left side of the body are dealt with by the right side of the brain and vice versa, and in humans each side knows what the other is doing – they keep track of each other. In the horse things are a little different. There is little exchange of information in the brain from one side to the other and, in consequence, the horse has to learn everything from two sides.

This is why, as much as for equal physical development, it is important, for example, to work horses evenly on both reins, and why horses used to being led exclusively from the near side, mounted and dismounted from the near side and so on so often kick up a fuss when you try to lead or mount them from the off side. It is common for riders to comment on the fact that a horse may, for example, shy at something seen out of his right eye, say a dog running out at him, and to continue to shy on that rein and in that place permanently afterwards, but not to react at all when passing the place on the left rein and seeing the spot, and maybe the stationary dog, out of his left eye. In addition, he will get a different view of the place out of his left eye and may not link the two in his brain.

When doing anything unpleasant to the horse, such as giving him injections or treating a painful wound, the horse will soon learn that this sort of thing can hurt and next time you try it may object, but if the same thing is done to the other side of the horse he has to learn this all over again, which makes life a little easier for his handlers in this case, at least initially.

Memory

The horse's brain is just like a holographic data storage system.

He has a very clear, *very* long memory and once something is securely stored in the brain the horse will remember it. Horses certainly remember other horses very clearly and although they must surely remember humans, too, they do not always acknowledge them as enthusiastically as horses or some other animals. They remember each other after many years' break, for better or worse, and remember aids, movements and tricks taught to them by humans after almost a lifetime's gap.

One ex-racehorse who had been broken in by a lady as a yearling fresh from the sales – a lady who had her own special way and technique of doing this – was returned to her after not only his racing career but many years at stud, to retire. There was nothing much wrong with him and she decided to work him on the lunge and long reins to give him something to think about. He immediately fell back into her methods as if it had been only yesterday he had learned them, and no one had worked him in this way since then.

On a trip by the Equine Behaviour Study Circle to visit the internationally famous circus trainer, Mary Chipperfield, at home, she demonstrated a movement on a Clydesdale horse – lying down on request – which he had not been asked to do for five years, and he instantly complied.

This superb memory means that training the horse is easy from the point of view that once he has learned something he does not need mental refresher courses, it's there for good; but it also obviously means that bad experience, poor training, the development of undesirable practices and so on are just as firmly remembered and can cause considerable problems. Once a horse has undergone a frightening journey, had an accident at a particular type of fence or been savaged by a dog on a particular route, for example, he will certainly remember these things and may well be frightened to repeat those circumstances, refusing to enter the trailer, jump that sort of fence or go down that road again.

However, it is also true that many horses do *not* subsequently give trouble in those circumstances and, given the nature of the horse, I wonder why this is. Possibly such horses have developed such trust in humans and developed the habit of cooperation to such an extent that this overcomes their memory of pain and fear.

Rolling

This is something which often causes a good deal of amusement among non-horsy people, and among horses themselves. They really enjoy it and it is obviously an important part of their personal toilet and social life.

Horses roll for various reasons apart from pleasure. They often roll in mud in winter so that when it dries it forms solid protection against debilitating, chilling winds. Mud, or dry dust and soil, in the coat discourage skin parasites and 'soak up' excess grease, so help with natural grooming, strange though this may seem. It is noticed that horses usually choose one or two preferred rolling spots and it is believed that this helps coat them in the 'herd smell' and re-establishes herd and family bonds, aiding recognition in the wild. Zebras and wild asses make quite a ritual out of rolling, taking turns and watching each other, queuing up to use the spot. Domesticated horses rolling also do so to stimulate their skin and help dry it off after sweaty work and, it is thought, to coat new bedding with their own smell. They usually do it after a bath, perhaps to rid themselves of the unnatural scent of shampoo, and many good yards have a sand patch for horses to roll in when they cannot be turned out for any reason. It is always appreciated and worth installing.

Although rolling under a rider is obviously dangerous, every chance should be taken to let domesticated horses roll, relax and enjoy themselves. It is important and beneficial to them. Most horses and ponies will roll on the surfacing of an indoor or outdoor school, if permitted, and may indicate their desire to do so when hot by pawing the ground. What an enjoyable way to end a lesson! Remove their saddles, bring the reins over their ears and stand at their heads out of harm's way holding the reins while they do just one of those things which still comes naturally to feral and domesticated horses alike.

Behaviour During Illness

When people or animals are ill they often feel lethargic and dopey and wish to sleep more, and these symptoms also occur during over-stress, anxiety, unhappiness and sub-clinical (barely noticeable) disease. Recent research work indicates that the chemical substances which seem to cause the natural unconsciousness of sleep are linked to the body's immune system. Work done in France and America indicates that a chemical called 5-hydroxytryptamine (5-HT), which moves messages around the brain, also causes sleep when released into the brain. Another protein substance, a peptide, stimulates macrophages ('soldier' cells) to fight off invading bacteria during illness, and the macrophages give out chemicals which not only help the body fight disease but also promote sleep.

The link between them is that the 5-HT and the peptide both have to 'lock on' or bind to the same spot on the macrophage to be effective. Both keys open the same lock and do the same job, in other words. Therefore, together they may induce sleep by stimulating the immune system. This could certainly explain why animals need to sleep regularly. It's all part of the daily battle which goes on inside us all to fight off invaders before the animal even realises they are there (by feeling ill or out of sorts). This could be one reason why animals suffering sub-clinical disease sleep more and why they sleep a good deal more when actually sick. Horses which are over-stressed may suffer more from both sub-clinical and actual disease. They may also have the patterns, quality and amount of their sleep disrupted, which may explain why they sometimes appear to sleep more than in less stressful conditions.

A drug newly discovered in human medicine, Ondansatron, reacts with 5-HT and research is going on to see if it can help addicts to tobacco, alcohol and also cocaine and heroin (an opiate related to the already mentioned endorphins and encephalins produced during the performance of stable vices by horses). A drug already used in human medicine for depression and anxiety, Buspar, also reacts with 5-HT; one day perhaps this work will be extended to horses with vices. Who knows?

11 Exercise and Fitness: Life on the Move

The horse is one of those animals evolved to be born, to live, eat, sleep, mate and die on the hoof. It truly has a life in motion, not tied to a lair or den, with its home and food supply all around it. Although a horse's environment determines just how much he moves about (the less forage there is, the further he has to go for it), he doesn't thrive on a life of inactivity. Many stabled horses who get two hours' or less work or exercise a day seem content enough, but my experience is that their owners often do not recognise the subtle signs of stress caused by this sort of lifestyle. Some horses show their distress more openly by developing 'formal' stable vices or simply what we call undesirable behaviour, becoming difficult to handle, uncooperative in work and so on.

Studies done on Welsh Mountain Ponies out on their native hills showed that they often did not take much strenuous exercise and, although they kept to specific ranges, most of their movement was at the walk, often a gentle amble from one grazing spot to another, a wander over to a friend to pass the time of day or to a stream for a drink. Of course, they are not subject to predation like feral *equidae* in other parts of the world, where horses have to exercise all the instincts they have to watch for predators and to get off to a lightning start to escape.

In natural conditions, feral horses and ponies are on the move, mostly at a walk, most of the time. In domestication, stabled horses in particular usually get only two hours' or less exercise or work a day and although we all have the benefits of slow gaits drummed into us, we often ask our horses to canter, gallop and jump during their two hours for (to the horse) no good reason. Their work occurs in short, strenuous spurts compared with what they would take left to themselves.

The Deadly Duo

Probably the two most common and trouble-causing mistakes most owners and managers make with their horses is to exercise them too little and feed them too much, at least too much of the wrong sort of food (concentrates) with, often, too little of the right sort (roughage). As discussed in Chapter 5, this results in dangerous obesity, laminitis in particular, colic, azoturia (or set-fast, or whatever you prefer to call it) and erratic, sometimes violent, behaviour.

Ideally, horses should be fed and exercised according to *their* requirements and natural capacities, not what is convenient to their human attendants, this being particularly important when you get the extreme of, say, an owner buying a highly strung type of horse full of natural nervous energy who needs to be on the move, but who is imprisoned in a stable all day with, if he's lucky, perhaps an hour's exercise, because his owner has to work all day in order to keep the horse and himself. If an owner really cannot exercise such a horse adequately and arrange for him to be turned out in suitable conditions to take his own exercise for long periods, he or she should be buying a placid, lazy type of horse who can take being forced to stand in one little space for over twenty-two hours a day so long as he has some hay and water – and even this situation is far from ideal.

The Mind–Body Connection

There is an old saying, 'the best thing for the inside of a man is the outside of a horse.' Association with horses brings tremendous mental benefits as well as physical exercise for us, because riding and the jobs involved in caring for horses are quite hard physical work. Perhaps another saying could be coined, 'the best thing for the inside of a horse is the great outdoors,' because there's no doubt that well exercised horses, those exercised within their capacities and inclinations rather than worked beyond them, are mentally balanced, content, outgoing, cooperative and pleasing characters.

Not all horses are what we would call athletic, although we try to make them so. Horses in our society have to work or produce workers and we may forget that, as in humans, some like less physical activity than others, but few like virtually none at all. The ideal exercise is that taken at will, not under duress, and many human psychologists, now that the frantic aerobics craze of the eighties is over, together with the self-imposed high-achievement standards of that decade, are pushing the idea that exercise must be mentally enjoyable to be physically beneficial – if you feel physically drained after exercising, and find it taxing rather than fun, they say, your mind and body will perceive it as pressure and over-stress and react accordingly.

As far as horses are concerned, many obviously enjoy the work we ask of them, enjoy hacking out, being turned out with friends, working at strenuous activities such as cross-country work or endurance riding, show jumping, or, less often, competitive dressage. Whatever we expect of them, it is up to us to be honest and judge what type of work the horse likes best and is, therefore, most likely to do well at.

Fitness

It is also up to us to see that the horse is in a fit state to do that work. The body gets fit, in our terms, by reacting to stress placed upon it. Even ancient civilisations soon realised that what we now call fitness programmes had to be gradual affairs and that it could take weeks or even months for full, hard physical condition to be built up. It has been well known for thousands of years that if you work a horse too hard for his state of fitness you get injuries – tendon injuries, concussion injuries, joint injuries, back injuries – and also a soured temperament and sickened mind.

Feral horses are fit enough for what their bodies have to do all the time, with the exception of newborns or the sick, injured or old. The regular, similar stresses placed on them 'instruct' the body how much to react to strengthen itself, how efficient the heart and lungs must be to provide energy and nutrients and remove waste products, and, so, how to cope with existing conditions. If those conditions include fairly regular harassing by predators (human or otherwise), this, too, is part of life and they can usually cope. On an attempt to round up feral mustangs in the USA in an area where their keep was poor and their range wide, the mustangs were harried and (successfully) chased over more than twenty miles and the cowboys noted that they were not even sweating or breathing very hard, compared to their own mounts who, admittedly, had heavy saddles and riders to cope with, but were used to working cattle every day.

Horses who receive regular, long, steady work with short spells of faster activity stay very fit; and, contrary to popular opinion, there is no need to 'let down' a horse at the end of a hard season. A simple change of the type of that horse's work is all that is needed to keep him mentally sweet. A let-down is often more for our convenience than the horse's and can result in unreasonable stress for the horse once he is brought back to work, plus what many humans consider a long, boring fitness programme to be gone through again. Horses brought to peak fitness will 'go over the top' or become stale if attempts are made to keep them that fit, but there is no need to let them down altogether for months at a time. Their bodies retain fitness for several weeks, not days, so, similarly, there is no need for gnashing of teeth or anxiety if a horse needs a week or two off work due to some minor injury or indisposition of his rider.

The horse's natural capacity for fitness varies between individuals. Each horse has a genetic ability to reach a certain level of physical fitness, beyond which, no matter what we do, he cannot go. Endurance riders are familiar with the 'plateau syndrome', as some call it. During training programmes they note that despite continuing with their planned programme, the horse reaches a plateau and does not seem to be getting any fitter.

But after a few days or weeks at that level, he suddenly increases in fitness again, having adjusted to that level of work, and you may be able to take him further.

Any type of fitness training, traditional or more modern (such as interval training), starts with (in a completely unfit horse) about three to five weeks of walking for increasingly long periods, usually working up to a couple of hours a day and most often done on the roads, this being easier for the horse (if you put your horse on the grass verge and give him his head he will often go on to the road of his own accord). This gets the message through the body via the brain that the constant little concussions inflicted on the limbs because of the hard going are calling for remodelled bone (more of it, harder and denser) and this remodelling takes time. Tendons and ligaments grow stronger in response to the stress of constant reasonable demands and the whole body 'tones up' and gets what we call fitter.

There is an increased blood supply to the muscles because they are working harder, using energy and creating waste products which need to be cleared away. At some point around now the horse may feel stiff and a little crampy, which a sensitive rider will feel. If and when this occurs, it is a clear sign not to increase the programme at this time: this is enough, and right for this horse at this time, so carry on till these symptoms disappear. The legs should be hard and ice-cold before you progress. If they are warm and softish the horse is not responding enough and is not ready to progress. This is his first plateau.

From then on, proceed with the programme as planned, constantly feeling and keeping an eye on his demeanour and those legs, and his general muscular condition, and spot if and when he reaches his next plateau. You cannot push the horse faster in a fitness programme: whatever discipline you are involved in, the horse will tell you if he is responding (provided you know your fitness programme is a good one – and perhaps you will call on expert help in devising it). If he is not responding and getting fitter, don't push on, but stay where you are until the horse progresses. At the earlier stages he undoubtedly will progress, but once more strenuous work, going further and faster, comes into it, he may reach his genetic limitation before you are satisfied – and there's not a thing you can do about it. You've simply got the wrong horse for the work you want to do.

Traditional or Modern Methods?

Everyone is familiar with the traditional fitness programme, and the most common modern method developed from human athletics is interval training. This takes the concept of response to stress a little further by asking the horse to perform timed, measured stints of fast work at repeated intervals *just before* his pulse rate indicates that he has recovered from the last stint, so making specific demands on the body to strengthen itself to cope. Interval training is loved by some and spurned by others. Those who say they have known horses break down because of the repeated stress of interval training either don't, I feel, know how to apply it properly or are not keeping a correct, knowledgeable eye on the horse's physical condition and his legs. It is an excellent method but it's true that it doesn't seem to suit some animals mentally.

Depending on whom you talk to, in addition to your own experience, you will find some people say that the repeated stints hype up excitable horses beyond the point of control as they are constantly anticipating another gallop. Others say that such horses find the work boring and that it calms them down! Lazy horses prefer the system, some say, because it relieves them of the prolonged stress and effort of long, traditional canters for up to twenty minutes (depending on your sport), but yet other owners say that repeated requests for work annoy and sicken lazy horses. The best thing is to try interval training, if you want to, on your own horse or horses and just see what response you get. The idea is that frequent short stints allow *some* recovery during work and this helps the body clear out some of the toxins which can cause muscle damage and which build up in traditional long canters, but the repeated demands do stress the body slightly and cause it to respond with increased fitness, without overdoing the demands.

One thing is sure, however, and that is that with carefully devised fitness programmes horses in general can be made very much fitter than we have dreamed. Treadmill work and research studies, mostly in racehorses, admittedly, but in other categories of horse, too, have shown that heart output and blood supply can be increased enormously, far beyond what was thought possible, and with no adverse effects on the properly managed horse. The heart is quite capable of beating at 240 to 260 beats per minute and shifting 60 gallons of blood in that time – far in excess of what most of us ask of our horses in normal programmes or competition. And at present it seems the best way to condition a heart in the higher echelons of fitness is with interval training and anaerobic work, in which the use of oxygen in the body exceeds the rate of its possible supply by the bloodstream. This involves making the heart beat at more than 160 beats per minute – well within its capabilities once fitness has been brought to the right stage and only achievable by means of fast work.

There are some excellent books on attaining fitness in horses these days, and this one is not intended as a technical manual. As an initial guide, though, your horse's pulse (heart) rate is an excellent guide and crucial in interval training, to tell you how fit the heart (and the horse) is. After strenuous work, take the pulse and then take it again ten minutes later. You should notice that it has significantly slowed down. For general fitness, a fit horse's heart should have returned to his warmed-up, pre-work rate (say sixty to eighty beats per minute, depending on the work and the individual) within half an hour.

Natural Inclinations

In general, horses are best suited to work which simulates their natural activities – roaming, sometimes at speed if conditions dictate, in company over longish distances. The equestrian disciplines which best fit this description are hunting, hacking, racing, endurance riding and team chasing. Polo is performed in company but constant stops and starts at speed are not what the horse does naturally. The most artificial activities are obviously showjumping and dressage. Work indoors or in an enclosed outdoor manege is not only not natural, although horses adapt well enough to it, it is not so enjoyable and does not tax the horse's mind and common sense. If you can hack horses out in the open they become more responsive, alert yet sensible and better balanced due to changing terrain. Very often, too, riders used only to riding in enclosed conditions become timid of outdoor riding, less versatile and less quick-thinking. One of the disadvantages of horses used only to working in file in enclosed arenas is that they become very unwilling to vary their work or work alone. Following the leader in single file is a natural mode of progression for the horse as they move very like this when changing grazing grounds, only normally galloping bunched up when being pursued, which is why horses take to following each other round a manege so well. It gives them a false sense of security, like our following the lights of the car in front in fog! Then when they are faced with work requiring individual initiative they can't or won't cope.

When the only exercise you can give your horse is ridden, try to arrange that you go for long hacks with at least one other horse, as horses enjoy this type of activity. It is perfectly possible to school on a hack, of course – a manege of any kind is not necessary, although it can be an advantage when teaching new movements or when schooling youngsters.

Different Types of Fitness

Different disciplines require different types and stages of fitness, but the one thing all types of fitness, however achieved, have in common is the first few weeks of walking work. The highest standards of fitness are required by racehorses, eventers and endurance horses; polo ponies, too, need to be very fit for the fast, tough and strenuous work they do. Show jumpers and, depending on the frequency of days and type of their country, hunters come next, and gymkhana ponies are frequently overlooked when thinking of fitness programmes. It is a commom and very sad sight to see them fat, filthy and heaving on the gymkhana field because their connections don't think of them as athletes in their own right requiring feeding, grooming and graduated exercise if they are to work without undue risk of damage to themselves and maybe, through fatigue, to their riders due to unnecessary falls.

Dressage horses require fitness of a different kind – their work *can* be strenuous, for reasons explained in the next section – and show horses could do well to be made fitter (and leaner) than many of them are, although it's true they don't need to be as fit as more active horses.

'Built-in' Advantages of Gait

There are several reasons why the horse is a superb long-distance speed animal. Apart from natural 'transfusions' of oxygen-carrying red blood cells from the spleen during hard work and the tremendous capacities of the heart already discussed in Chapters 3 and 4, the horse's natural gaits are very economical of energy, yet highly efficient. He has no muscles below knee or hock. Muscle tissue tires the harder it has to work, of course, and the horse economises on this by having the muscles which move his limbs near the tops of the limbs, in forearm, breast and shoulder, so they do not have to move the legs very far, relatively speaking. The tendons, which are modified muscle tissue, run from the bottoms of their individual muscles and attach to various parts of the legs and feet (which are also lashed together and supported by ligaments and other connective tissue). The parts of the limbs which move the furthest, the feet, are light in relation to the body and legs, so taking less energy to move.

Tendons have an important and helpful quality in that they are slightly elastic: when weight is put on the limb they 'give' and store energy from the force of impact, then when the leg is due to leave the ground they recoil and give the limb an elastic push-off which costs the horse no energy at all. The higher the speed the more energy is saved as the tendons are stretched further, although, of course, there comes a point when the horse could overdo things, or be over-driven, and this is when tendon injuries occur. The gaits are not energy-free, of course, and fatigue causing inefficient movement and uncoordination is a common cause of tendon injury.

The horse also has natural 'gears' in which he travels most comfortably and most efficiently from the point of view of energy and oxygen consumption. In other words, each gait has an optimum cruising speed at which it is most efficient and comfortable for the horse to travel. Research in America and Scandinavia, and other countries, mainly using trained riderless animals on treadmills, has shown that horses will change gait naturally of their own accord when they are asked to speed up so that they are travelling at minimal energy-usage speed in the next gait up. If required to continue in the previous gait at the new speed energy consumption leaps dramatically, up to one and a half times more energy being used than if the horse were allowed to move up a gait. Interestingly, this also applies to horses asked to go slower in a given gait. It is just as tiring to go too slowly within a gait as too fast! Interestingly, too, and perhaps surprisingly, the amount of oxygen/energy used at the optimal speed for each of the three gaits walk, trot and canter was found to be the same. This means that it 'costs' the horse in energy only the same to walk, trot or canter/gallop a mile *provided* he is allowed to choose his own speed within that gait. Dressage horses who are constantly made to work at the 'wrong' speeds within gaits, using as they do collected, working, medium and extended variations of their three gaits, are probably using as much or more energy as if they were competing across country! Other horses, obviously, have their gaits interfered with by their riders, but probably not so unremittingly as dressage horses. It should be remembered, however, that all schooling on the flat is dressage and is correspondingly tiring.

The horses used in the studies were allowed to run free wearing measuring instruments on their hooves and legs, so that the researchers could check that, given free will, the horses did, indeed, change gait according to speed, choosing naturally to travel at the most energy- and oxygen-efficient gait for a given speed, which naturally varied between individuals. Each horse has his own preferred cruising speed in each gait.

If someone invents a treadmill on which horses can jump, presumably similar work will be able to be done for energy expenditure during jumping. However, as heart monitors, pedometers and other instrumentation have now been brought to a fine art, perhaps this will not be so far away as equipment will be developed which can measure oxygen consumption while a horse is jumping a course – if it hasn't been already.

And That's Not All

Another feature of the horse's gait is the way it is tied in to respiration at canter and gallop. In walk and trot the horse can breathe at any rate and in any rhythm he wishes, but at canter and gallop he has to breathe in time with his stride. Very generally, he breathes out when his forelegs hit the ground and in during the suspension ('in-the-air') phase. This is at least partly brought about by the construction of the horse's thoracic cage, comprising the ribs, the breastbone, shoulder blades and front part of the backbone. The horse's forelegs are not joined to the ribs or spine by a bony joint and the horse has no collarbone: the only attachment is by means of powerful muscles, ligaments and connective tissue. This is an excellent concussion-absorber, greatly reducing jar on the forelegs which carry two-thirds of the horse's weight, compounded during motion.

The chest cavity is separated from the abdominal cavity by a strong, dome-shaped sheet of muscle, the diaphragm. As the forelegs flex after the weight-bearing part of a stride, the shoulder blade is rotated slightly and the ribs pulled slightly up, out and forwards, assisting the enlargement of the ribcage necessary to suck air into the lungs. To breathe out, the muscles involved in expiration just relax and the ribcage returns passively, without energy use, to its previous position, forcing air out again. Some researchers also feel that the viscera (the contents of the abdominal cavity) move slightly backwards and forwards during movement, particularly at the faster gaits, and as weight falls on the forelegs they lurch slightly forwards, push against the diaphragm and assist in pushing air out: as they move back when the front half of the body lifts off the ground again, they slide backwards a little, helping increase the size of the thoracic cage, and so, the inspiration of air – all with no energy usage.

The horse's 'balancing pole', his head and neck, also play some part in this process. During canter and gallop, the head and neck move out and down as the forelegs hit the ground and up and back as they lift. The head and neck are suspended from the trunk by the powerful, elastic ligamentum nuchae (which extends roughly from the poll to the withers) and the neck muscles also play a part in the pendulum action of head and neck. During the suspension phase of canter and gallop, the elastic recoil function of the ligamentum nuchae brings the head and neck up and back. There is some action by muscles, too, which also draws the ribs and breastbone slightly forward, helping increase the expansion of the chest cavity as inspiration begins. The hind legs are, at this time, thrusting the horse forwards, which causes the abdominal contents to lurch slightly backwards (like being pressed back in the seat of a rapidly accelerating car) which, as previously mentioned, helps increase the chest cavity, too. The ribcage continues to be expanded by the lower neck muscles pulling on it as they start to bring the head and neck downwards again ready for impact by the forelegs – and the stride and respiration process begins all over again. Other mechanisms are involved but this does explain, I hope, another energy-saving technique in the horse's action and shows how important coordinated head and neck movements are during canter and gallop.

When a horse is tired, his head and neck movements are more exaggerated; also, as he breathes faster so the inspiration phase of his breathing becomes relatively shortened. However, researchers have also noted that tired horses have a longer suspension phase to their stride than when not tired, and this could be a natural effort to lengthen the inspiration phase for the horse.

Good instructors stress that the hands should let the horse's head and neck move backwards and forwards in canter and gallop, 'going with the horse's movements' and, having regard to the fact that gait and respiration are tied into each other at these gaits, I hope more emphasis can be given to this and to allowing more freedom of head and neck than is often seen in non-racing and endurance disciplines. The horse not only needs free use of his head and neck to balance himself and to see where he is going but also to breathe properly.

12 A Roof Over His Head – Or Something

Probably one of the most artificial things we do to our horses is to stable them. Perhaps it could be said that, whatever else we do, the horse could stand most of it if only he were allowed the recuperative effects of liberty and open space, not to mention grazing, on a daily basis.

Early civilisations used the horse as a prey animal, following the herds much as predators do now. When horses were first significantly domesticated the herds were guarded by herdsmen, as some eastern peoples still do. Later, various sorts of fenced enclosures were invented and from these developed probably the worst mental torture man has yet, in general terms, inflicted upon the horse – The Stable. I don't mean to sound melodramatic but this is really what it amounts to. The loose box, or box stall, is a little softer on the horse than the standing or tie stall, because he does have some liberty to turn around and move about whereas in the latter he is tied up, almost always facing a blank wall, and I cannot think of anything more calculated to send an animal like a horse mad than this. Of course, we don't often see mad horses but we can see all around us in the horse world badly distressed and neurotic horses made so by confinement, either in a loose box or, less commonly these days, a stall.

Stables do, of course, have their place, and with well exercised horses (and I don't just mean a couple of hours a day) their occupants can feel content, settled and secure. The problems arise when they are kept short of exercise and when their owners and managers fail to accept and act upon the fact that *many* horses are slightly claustrophobic – hardly surprising when you consider their evolution. As in most other aspects of management, individuals react differently to their surroundings. Some take well to being stabled, even seeming to like it, particularly once they have learned to recognise their stables as havens from outside problems such as harsh weather at any time of year, bullying companions, respite from stressful work and so on, and associate them with somewhere comfortable to lie and rest. If horses are fed correctly with virtually *ad lib* supplies of roughage and water, this is even better, because food is the one thing that occupies a horse's mind almost constantly! If they associate their stables with the security of a constant food supply, such as would occur in nature and particularly if, as are most horses, they have been deprived of ample roughage in a previous ownership by being fed hay only twice a day or three times if they were lucky, they can be genuinely happy to be there – provided they receive sufficient time out and moving around, preferably much of it at liberty, for movement is the other thing which is fundamental to horses, as discussed in the last chapter and indeed throughout this book.

Management Systems

Apart from keeping horses in open country in herds, supervised or otherwise, there are four main ways of keeping them: stabled; on the combined system, part stabled and part out; yarded in surfaced enclosures, preferably partially covered; or completely out at grass.

There is nothing new about stabling horses all the time. Stalls for tying up horses have been excavated on archaeological digs dating from some of the earliest civilisations known. King Solomon's stables were world-famous in his day and Caligula is said to have housed his favourite horse (whom he made a member of the Roman senate) in a marble stable with golden fittings.

Many of us do not like to recognise the fact, but a stabled horse is a prisoner – a poor reward for all he does for us. He is a hostage to our whims and is there for our benefit only, not normally his own. It's true we may well be doing a horse a favour by bringing him in at night in winter or during the day in summer. This is not the same thing as keeping him in an individual cell virtually all the time, only letting him out when we see fit, feeding and watering him when we see fit, exercising him when we see fit and, on top of all that, controlling his every movement under saddle or between the shafts when we do exercise him.

Most stables do not offer a horse anything like as much space as he needs to be content. We are generally advised that a stable should be roughly 12ft square as a minimum for a 16 hands high horse, yet this does not even cater for the invisible boundary of the horse's personal space, which seems to be roughly 14ft around him, probably in an oval shape to accord with his body shape. If horses are given 14ft-square loose boxes we consider that they are living in a kind of luxury normally only afforded to Thoroughbred stallions of the bluest bloodlines.

Height, too, is normally inadequate. A horse standing on his hind legs, as some occasionally do indoors, will reach a height of about 10ft 6in with the top of his head but most commercially prefabricated loose boxes on the market only offer a height of about 9ft at the ridge of a double-planed roof, and many not even that. Single-planed roofs are often so low at their lowest point that even a horse standing normally can touch the roof with his head.

Ventilation, that is to say, the lack of it, is a major bugbear in almost any stabling, as discussed in Chapter 4. The physical disadvantages of an impure, even toxic, atmosphere are things the horse would never experience in wild and feral conditions. But probably the most under-rated disadvantage of stabling is the lack of freedom and the feeling of being closed in which puts a great burden of over-stress on so many horses.

The lack of natural company is also quite inappropriate and stressful to horses. Simply being able to see other horses in the yard is by no means enough to keep them mentally content and secure as they are in a herd situation. Many stables don't even offer the basic facility of a grille in the wall so that horses can at least 'chat' to neighbours. Such isolation, often with walls up to the roof, may be advised to help prevent the spread of disease but is ineffective in this regard.

Keeping horses on the combined system is much better for their mental and physical health, and easier on their attendants, too. The actual length of time and precise periods during which the horse is either stabled or out can vary to suit the requirements of both, but generally it works well if the horse is in at night in winter and out during the day, and vice versa in summer. The facility to exercise at will and, it is hoped, in company is a great boost to the morale and well-being of a horse and makes life less restricting for the owner or manager.

Yarding horses in surfaced enclosures, wholly or partly covered in, is a great improvement on both stabling and the combined system, and with due attention to the horse's needs and human convenience can be made into the ideal method of housing horses. It is sometimes called the 'open stable' system, and seems to be much more popular on the continent of Europe than in Britain and many other countries.

The ideal facility would offer the horses the option of being under cover or out in the open in an enclosure, and for the enclosure itself to open out into a grass paddock as large as possible. The horses then will have complete freedom to be where they want, space, liberty and company. The area can be supplied with long communal racks for hay and other roughage (probably best at horse's head height down the walls of the covered area) and even long troughs for feeding concentrates, provided an expert eye is kept on the horses to see that special requirements are catered for – some horses may over-eat and others not get enough, so these need special attention accordingly. Even so, the system is far less expensive of human labour than stabling, while still giving the horses everything they need. Obviously, only compatible horses must be mixed together and any trouble-makers removed from the main group.

The covered area can be bedded down conventionally, perhaps with straw or shavings, and the outdoor surfaced area can be surfaced with earth, sand, fine shale or wood chips, all of which have proved successful.

Keeping a horse outdoors all the time is fine for the horses, provided they have access to truly effective shelter, that there is adequate grass keep or they are fed supplementary feed and that the area is large enough and well maintained with, finally, congenial company. From the human point of view, it is more difficult to keep horses clean and fit on this system, but it is certainly not impossible if the type of grass is carefully selected and judicious use of turnout rugs is made in muddy conditions. Good rugs are a help to outdoor horses in winter, anyway.

Natural Environments

The horse is usually thought of as a creature of wide open spaces, of grassy plains with little in the form of natural shelter, and perhaps this is why some people seem to think it is all right to keep a horse in a bleak, windswept field exposed to everything the weather and the local insect population can throw at them. This is far from the case. Horses and their relatives throughout the world are found in quite a wide variety of environments among which, it's true, there is a predominance of grassy plains, along with bleak, bitter tundras and slightly more hospitable steppe country. *Equidae* (zebras and wild asses) live in deserts where they have to, although within reach of food and water, feral horses are to be found in areas of good to apparently nil food supply (stressing once again the need for generally poorish keep for horses rather than rich pickings), in hilly, even mountainous areas, in forests (such as the home of the reconstituted Tarpan of Poland and in the albeit rather open New Forest of Britain), in highlands and in wet lowlands: in fact, within reason there are few environments horses cannot adapt to.

Far back in their evolution, horses were forest creatures and a propensity for forest living and arboreal behaviour patterns remains obvious in some individuals. Forests do provide excellent natural shelter. Horses also find shelter in hilly areas, soon seeking out the sheltered spots behind cliffs and high ground, even a hollow in the ground providing some respite from the wind most of them hate so much. Although not cave creatures, they have been seen sheltering around the mouths of caves (and around the openings to field shelters in domesticity). But wherever they are, they usually show their dislike of being closed in too much unless very mentally secure in their habitat.

Rethinking Domestic Housing

Basically, the sort of housing we offer horses caters for *our* idea of what is good for them rather than theirs – rather like our giving a child the sort of Christmas present we think it ought to want rather than what it actually does want. Yet with a little knowledge, imagination and little if any expense, we could keep horses handy, clean and on a controlled diet, if any of these things are considered essential, but at the same time mentally secure, settled and content.

It has been noticed by researchers and observant horsepeople alike that horses often seem to prefer the highest ground with the clearest, widest view they can get. Given a field of varied terrain, they usually seem to spend most of their time on the highest part, and not only when the ground is wet to get away from the mud. They like to gather in small, friendly groups where they can be together and keep a herd lookout, all around them, on the surrounding area.

One study done in America showed that horses are happier and more settled when they can see all around them, whether indoors or out. It seems obvious, then, that one of the most important improvements we can make to horse housing is to provide windows or other see-through facilities in *all four sides* of a conventional stable or field shelter. As far as stables are concerned, at least half of the dividing wall between them could be lowered to a height of about 5ft and the space to the roof filled with bars or mesh, if desired, so the horses are still separated (if this is really what is wanted by the human side of the operation) yet can see and smell neighbours. If the other half is higher, this means that a horse can have privacy if he really wants it, most probably when eating. It is obvious that horses who make frequent faces at their neighbours and are obviously unhappy about their being near should be stabled next to more congenial companions. The fact that a horse cannot see an unpleasant neighbour will not make him any happier, as he will know very well that he is next door, within his personal space even if out of reach from a practical point of view.

Field shelters should, anyway, be sited on the highest part of a field, but the addition of windows in all the walls (perhaps of wire-reinforced PVC or some other safe, see-through material) will add greatly to the occupants' contentment and encourage timid ones who don't like going in to use the facility.

Much more use could and, I feel, should be made of yarding or the open stable system where horses are kept in congenial groups. They are happier, just as healthy and fit and the workload of their human attendants is drastically cut. Such horses even feed right next to each other out of a communal trough without any hassle, as they graze in the wild. This sort of accommodation is suitable for all types of horses, including fit competition horses, not just breeding and youngstock.

Ventilation is one of the worst problems in artificial housing, but can be provided simply, logically and cheaply by just having the upper parts of the walls above the horses' heads made of Yorkshire boarding, as it is sometimes called – vertical boarding with alternate boards missed out. This allows a free flow of air and removal of waste air and excess water vapour while providing a very effective windbreak, lessening the force of the strongest winds. Even during storm force winds, the horses are sheltered in such housing and there is no significant disturbing air movement inside.

This type of boarding is also suitable for conventional individual stabling, although as most prefabricated stabling is very low it may not be possible to fit it to existing boxes.

With such an arrangement, which can be fitted to American barn-type complexes as well as covered yards, materials are saved, ventilation is provided and there is no need for expensive and complicated mechanical or electrical ventilation systems.

Bedding Systems

In individual stables, by far the most hygienic method of managing the bedding is to muck out fully every day, with skipping out and general maintenance at other times of the day. Deep litter systems can certainly be used where ventilation is good and semi-deep litter, so popular with working owners who only muck out fully at weekends, is also a good compromise, provided, again, that ventilation is good. Drainage is a moot point, because most urine is soaked up by bedding of any type, even so-called non-absorbent bedding such as straw, since modern straw is so crushed up during harvesting that it has lost its former drainage qualities.

Flooring in stables may be controlled by the local authorities' health and drainage requirements and some are remarkably obtuse when it comes to explaining the advantages of such things as free-draining floors such as loose-weave asphalt or bricks laid on gravel. Others are helpful and intelligent but what you might install may be out of your hands.

In the UK, at least, the commonest flooring is concrete and anything less suitable would be hard to imagine. It is hard, cold and absorbs and holds urine, none of which qualities is good for the horse. Old-fashioned floors such as stable bricks are now very hard to get and although hard-wearing, particularly the blue-brick, are largely superseded by the fact that most horses today are, thankfully, kept on full beds all the time, the old practices of keeping no beds, or only thin 'day beds', down during the daytime having largely gone out of fashion: therefore, the drainage qualities of the bricks are no longer needed.

It is still a good idea to have a stable floor sloping slightly, if only to prevent pooling of urine in one soon-soggy spot in the box. To test the drainage, simply pour a bucket of water in the middle of the floor when there is no bed down and watch what happens to the water. It is interesting to note that the old practice of putting an internal central drain in each box is creeping back. Instead of the grilles, today's seem to have finer mesh covers which will stop a lot of the old problem of their getting clogged by bedding, but they still need very regularly disinfecting and the mesh covers need to be extremely strong to withstand a horse standing on them – and, of course, firmly fixed to avoid dislodging, too.

My favourite floorings are naturally free-draining ones such as the loose-weave asphalt mentioned and bricks. In loose-weave asphalt, the coarse asphalt is laid but only lightly smoothed to level it over its foundation of stones and, further below, rubble on earth. This means the asphalt retains air spaces through which urine drains away naturally. If you tamp it down with a plank, as is done with ordinary asphalt, the air spaces are obviously destroyed, along with the drainage qualities of the floor.

Hard-wearing building bricks laid on their sides on gravel over clinker, with the spaces between them filled in with gravel, make excellent flooring, and the urine drains away in the same way as with the asphalt.

In practice, I have never found any problems of smell with such floors, but as a precaution, and especially in conventionally floored stables, you can now obtain special granules (currently marketed in Britain as 'Stable Boy') which you spread on the floor before bedding down, and which are claimed to absorb smells and toxic gases, keeping down flies, disease organisms and excess wetness. It has to be said that an economy-size sack of cat litter would do the job more cheaply and more or less as well.

Of course, the use of such a product is no excuse for not managing a bed properly or using hygienic bedding. A clean-air regime is an excellent modern system for any horse. Dust-extracted bedding (cleaned by means of vacuuming before sale, although machines are available for purchase) should be *de rigueur*, I think, in well run yards, and cleaned straw and shavings are marketed widely now. Peat is a dusty, cold, absorbent bedding not suitable for vacuuming and not suitable for bedding down horses, either, contrary to popular opinion. It holds the urine like nothing else and is so cold it even freezes in cold weather – and you can actually see the dust in the coat of a horse kept on it. When you leave a box you've just bedded down on peat you can smell it in the air and detect it in your clothes, nostrils and hair. Sawdust has similar qualities but is easier to manage than peat and, if scrupulously kept, is a suitable bedding material, although not for a clean-air regime as it is dusty. Shredded paper is widely marketed as a hygienic, dust-free bedding, recommended to be used on a semi-deep-litter basis. It *is* excellent provided you muck it out fully or keep it on semi-deep litter. Otherwise it has been found to start harbouring disease organisms. Like anything else, if you abuse it you get trouble.

Bedding-free systems, such as 'drainage' mats or semi-soft synthetic materials made into mats, are appalling in my view. Perhaps in this respect I am old-fashioned, but horses, I am sure, do like a cushioning, resilient material to roll in and lie on, not to mention to dig and root about in! They have precious little else to do with their time in the stable, so I feel we should not deny them these activities which they find mentally and physically comforting. Some floorings are more sympathetic than others, however, and are worth investigating.

There is a system of synthetic perforated interlocking tiles currently on the market in Britain which can be laid over a conventional (or any) floor, enabling urine to drain straight through to the floor below and have minimal contact with the bedding, so making great savings. It works best with long-shredded paper and in practice is really effective, so well worth looking into. Called the 'Ridry Stable Flooring System', it is also useful for horse owners who have to rent accommodation as it will improve their horse's environment and they can lift it and take it with them should they move stables.

As housing is one of the biggest causes of distress in horses, I do hope the suggestions given in this chapter will receive acceptance and should like to finish by mentioning one last research project which took place in the USA concerning the horse's preference, or otherwise, for light.

Horses were kept in a windowless barn and, by passing through the beam of a photoelectric cell, could turn a light on in the barn for one minute. The researchers, Katherine Houpt and

Richard Houpt of Cornell University, found that the horses turned on the light at all hours of the day and night, most often between six and ten in the morning. They soon learned the trick and kept the light on more often than not. These researchers also found, apparently, that the horses kept eye contact with other horses for about half their time.

To me, one of the most salutary findings of this same study is that, when free to move about at will in the barn (not being confined to individual stables), *the horses spent between 88 and 95 per cent of the time OUT of their stables*. They couldn't tell us any more plainly just what they think of conventional stabling!

The Equine Behaviour Study Circle

The EBSC was founded in 1978 by Susan McBane and the late Moyra Williams, a clinical psychologist by profession and also an intrepid horsewoman and breeder of competition horses, also an author of several books on horses.

The Circle aims to study on both a scientific and amateur basis all aspects of equine behaviour in an effort to improve our understanding of it. It produces a six-monthly newsletter, *Equine Behaviour*, organises informal discussion groups, visits to places of interest in the horse world and projects for members to carry out at home with their own horses. However, horse ownership, or even access to horses, is not necessary to be a member.

For full details, send a s.a.e. to The Secretary, EBSC, Grove Cottage, Brinkley, Newmarket, Suffolk, CB8 0SF, England.

Index

Other Equestrian titles from Methuen

David Broome and Steve Hadley	*Ride*
John Hislop	*Breeding for Racing*
Susan McBane	*The Horse in Winter* (hardback and paperback)
Janet MacDonald	*The Right Horse* (hardback and paperback)
Wilhelm Müseler	*Riding Logic*
John Oaksey	*Oaksey on Racing*
Sally Swift	*Centred Riding* (hardback and paperback)
Jane Thelwall	*The Less-Than-Perfect Horse*
Mary Wanless	*Ride With Your Mind*
	Ride With Your Mind Masterclass